AF560237

ALTAR OF POWER

The Temple and the State in the Land of Jagannatha

STUDIES IN ORISSAN SOCIETY, CULTURE AND HISTORY

Editors: HERMANN KULKE and BURKHARD SCHNEPEL

Vol. 1: Jagannath Revisited: Studying Society, Religion and the State in Orissa, edited by Hermann Kulke and Burkhard Schnepel

Vol. 2: The Jungle Kings: Ethnohistorical Aspects of Politics and Ritual in Orissa, by Burkhard Schnepel

Vol. 3: Text and Context in the History, Literature and Religion of Orissa, edited by Angelika Malinar, Johannes Beltz and Heiko Frese

Vol. 4: Altar of Power: The Temple and the State in the Land of Jagannatha, by Yaaminey Mubayi

ALTAR OF POWER

The Temple and the State in the Land of Jagannatha Sixteenth to Nineteenth Centuries

YAAMINEY MUBAYI

MANOHAR
2005

First published 2005

ISBN 81-7304-586-0

Published by
Ajay Kumar Jain for
Manohar Publishers & Distributors
4753/23 Ansari Road, Daryaganj
New Delhi 110 002

Printed at
Lordson Publishers Pvt. Ltd.
Delhi 110 007

Contents

Foreword

In the beginning of the nineteenth century, 'Juggernaut' figured as the major target of Evangelicals in British Parliament against 'British connections with idolatry', whereas at the end of the twentieth century, Puri, with its famous Jagannath cult emerged as India's best-researched 'sacred complex', superseded temporarily perhaps only by Ayodhya. The impact of the colonial regime, however, on the temple realm and the ritual position of Puri's Gajapatis has only recently become a focus of research.

Dr Mubayi's study consists of two distinct but strongly interconnected major parts, viz., the precolonial development of Gajapati kingship and its penetration by and modification under the impact of the colonial regime. Both are connected by an intermediate third part on early European travel accounts and their images of 'Juggernaut'. The first chapter begins with a short description of the different historical stages of the Gajapati kingship which is followed by a systematic analysis of the temple-kingship nexus under the local Khurda dynasty during Mughal and Maratha rule in Orissa. The 'politics of patronage' of the Khurda Rajas was characterized by a system of political subordination and ritual dominance which allowed them not only to survive under non-Oriya rule but also to uphold their ritually dominant status among the feudatory chiefs of Orissa. The second chapter 'Access, Status and Redistribution in the Temple Realm' explores the temple as an arena of constant contestation of hierarchy, power and authority between king and priests. It analyses the various nuclei of power and the specific spheres and means of contestation, e.g. access to the diety, redistributive networks of *bhoga/prasada*, and illustrates them paradigmatically by Puri's famous *ratha jatra*. The third chapter depicts the early European travel books of Thomas Bowrey and François Bernier and their influential accounts of Puri as

'Precursors to Colonial Policy'. The epistemology of their descriptions of the car festival is interpreted by Dr Mubayi as a juxtaposition of 'western norm and eastern deviants' and 'western rationality *v.* eastern credulity' and as an attempt to 'feminise' Indian society. The fourth chapter 'The Temple, the Raja and the Colonial State' analyses the stepwise destruction of the old Gajapati regime and the colonization of the sacred kingship of the Khurda Rajas through their reinstallation as bureaucratically supervised 'Superintendents' of the Puri temple. The colonial appropriation of the temple realm through extensive documentation is exemplified by an analysis of three key documents of the early colonial period. The final chapter on 'Power and Property: The 'Profanization' of Temple Networks' is an elaboration of further changes under the colonial regime. Its major focus is the struggle for control over landed property and the process of its profanization through colonial settlement policies and litigation. The attitude of objectification and circumscription of property was largely instrumental in the delinking of resources from their sacred context.

Dr Yaaminey Mubayi succeeded in demonstrating the unbroken continuity of Puri's temple realm as a 'fulcrum of the balance of power in Orissa' even during the colonial period. Whereas previous studies on the 'Jagannath/Gajapati complex' were overlaid with a sense of the dominance of royal authority as an integrative agency, she seeks to redefine relationships of power as possessing a certain ambiguity, of portraying a great deal of ambivalence. In this context her interpretation and portrayal of *vamsavali* chronicles, certain rituals and festivals of Puri as an arena of contesting interests and of negotiation of status and power are particularly revealing. Her story of early colonial penetration of Puri's temple realm as Orissa's most important focus of political power, its subversion and final appropriation through bureaucratic means is equally fascinating. Dr Mubayi therefore is certainly right to conclude her study with a reference to C. Geertz's well known dictum that ritual is not merely the illustration of power, but power itself.

Kiel
2003

HERMANN KULKE

Acknowledgements

My earliest memory of Orissa is as a four year old, peeping out from my vantage point between two gigantic (or so they seemed then!) pillars at the door of the Collector's office, at the streams of visitors that passed through, *tehsildars*, sanitation inspectors, the Superintendent of Police, village officials in their unbleached *dhotis*, local contractors in their silk *kurtas* and oiled hair. I almost never saw my father, the Collector, who sat within and evaluated their concerns that ranged from famines to floods, communal riots to the inauguration of local schools. Twenty years later, I stood in the same office, reading a list of former Collectors of Cuttack district that stretched back into the early years of the nineteenth century, and tried to imagine the extent of power and responsibility inherent in that position. It was a realization of this continuum between colonial and contemporary realities, embodied in the office wherein I stood, that prompted me to embark on this exploration of the roots of current political and cultural institutions in Orissa.

The nurturing and supportive atmosphere at the Centre for Historical Studies, Jawaharlal Nehru University provided ideal conditions for the development of this book. My Ph.D. supervisors, Dr Neeladri Bhattacharya and Dr Kunal Chakrabarti, were unstinting in their academic generosity and emotional support, coaxing, exhorting and even bullying me to draw from reserves within me that I did not know existed. They were with me all the way. Other members of the faculty, Dr Muzaffar Alam, Professor Romila Thapar, Dr Shereen Ratnagar, Professor R. Champakalakshmi and Professor B.D. Chattopadhyay in particular, were always there for a chat, advice, a pep talk, ticking me off or pulling me out of a crucial impasse. Mrs Kapoor at the CHS office was frequently an angel of mercy, rescuing me from some administrative disaster or the other.

Professor Hermann Kulke, one of the pioneers of the Orissa Research Project of the University of Heidelberg, has guided my work since my first tentative attempts at formulating a research question in 1992. He has been a constant source of ideas, information and encouragement, a true 'Doctor Father' and I acknowledge him as such. Georg Berkemer and Martin Brandtner have been true friends and compatriots. Dr Bishnu Mohapatra has provided valuable inputs. I also wish to acknowledge the help and support of friends in Orissa, Sri and Smt. K.P. Singh Deo of Dhenkanal, Sri Dibyasinghdev, Gajapati Moharaja of Puri, Professor S.N. Rajaguru, Sri Nilamani Misra, Sri S.R. Pal, Sri R.K. Bhujabal, Sri Vivek Pattanayak, Sri M.Y. Rao, Sri M.P. Das and the staff at the Orissa State Archives, the staff at the Temple Administrator's office, Puri, the people of Jakeda village in Nayagarh with whom I spent a very pleasant day, but doubtless wasted quite a lot of their time, the *Pandas*, *Suaras* and *Mathadharis* of the Jagannatha Temple who gave me the most important input of all—a 'feel for the game'. There are many others, and I apologize for not being able to include them all in this list, however, that does not in any way detract from their contribution to this book.

In the summer of 1995, I was awarded a scholarship by DAAD (German Academic Exchange Service) that enabled me to work on the extensive archive of manuscripts at the South Asia Institute, University of Heidelberg collected under the former Orissa Research Project. I was also able to work closely with Professor Kulke at the University of Kiel and refine my ideas. In 1999, an archival grant from the Charles Wallace Trust made it possible for me to work at the India Office Record Room of the British Library, London. I would like to gratefully acknowledge the cheerful cooperation and help that I received from the administrative and support staff at each of these institutions.

My parents unhesitatingly gave me their emotional, logistical and financial support, my mother even accompanying me on field trips to Orissa in order to look after my infant daughter. My husband has suffered and rejoiced with me through the years of research and writing, typing and formatting for me late into the night after I had fallen asleep. In moments of stress, he claims that he has changed large sections without my realizing it! Finally, my daughter Kaatyaayani has grown with this book—

she travelled all over Germany while still in the womb, and all over Orissa ever since—some of her earliest scribbles were on the Jagannatha Temple Correspondence! This book is for her—for her belief in her mother.

YAAMINEY MUBAYI

Abbreviations

JTC	Jagannath Temple Correspondence
ORP	Orissa Research Project, University of Heidelberg, Germany
GOMLM	Government Oriental Manuscript Library, Madras
OHRJ	*Orissa Historical Research Journal*
JBORS	*Journal of the Bihar and Orissa Research Society*
JAHRS	*Journal of the Andhra Historical Research Society*

Introduction

In 1803, the troops of the British East India Company entered Puri and took over the administration of the province of Orissa. This led to far-reaching changes in relationships of status, rights and access to land and structures of authority in the region. The penetration of local institutions, particularly the temple of Jagannatha at Puri, by colonial apparatuses of control led to the creation of a separate discourse of power that re-contextualized the prevailing ritual and political structures. Prior to the advent of the British, the long-established link between the temple at Puri and the Gajapati kingship of Orissa (after evolving over a period of seven centuries), was an important factor underlying political and cultural institutions and relationships. This link played a major role in the reformulation of these institutions in the colonial environment. The following chapters discuss the manner in which the temple–state relationship formed a backdrop for the shifts and changes in the balance of power in the region, both prior to colonial incursion and subsequently.

My study deals primarily with perceptions of order within the social realm surrounding the temple in the pre-colonial and early colonial periods. This order was re-expressed in the period of the freedom movement, when issues of identity and the politics of nationality caused a reformulation of the past with a sense of cultural nostalgia. One such reconstruction is an Oriya play written in the 1940s, recalling the martyrdom of Bakshi Jagabandhu, the commander-in-chief of the Khurda raja, who led a rebellion in 1817, against the large-scale dispossession of the Khurda *paiks* (royal militia) by the new agrarian policies of the Company government. The retelling of the 'story' of British entry into Orissa is replete with contemporary rejection of colonial rule and the nationalist view of the British as a defeated culture. I will now present a section from 'Bakshi Jagabandhu' by Manoranjan Das, as I believe that it will communicate a sense of the ritual and political linkages and hierarchies of privilege and status which were disrupted by colonial incursion. The centrality of the raja to these linkages and his essential connection to the maintenance of order in society, is significantly expressed in this account.

In the jail, there are two adjacent cells. Evening has fallen. In one of the cells, holding the iron railings, stands Jayikrushna Rajaguru, *Diwan* of Khurda. In the next cell, Kasturi (a dancing girl) stands in a similar position. Jayikrushna's mind was far away in the past. Kasturi's melodious voice rises in song.

'What is the good of relating the past,
  again and again the mind awakens,
and drifts far away along with the clouds, . . . '

KASTURI. Master! (A deep sigh may be heard from the adjacent cell) How did all this happen, Master? (Another sigh) Master. . . . .

JAYIKRUSHNA. (starts violently) Eh . . . ?

KASTURI. Were you asleep? Did you call out?

JAYIKRUSHNA. Not sleep . . . but the dreams. . . . .

KASTURI. Dreams? Ah! . . . Surely, Master, there is happiness only in dreams. What dreams?

JAYIKRUSHNA. The *phirangis* (British) had besieged Barunei (the site of Khurda fort) . . . days went by . . . twenty-one days went by . . . food and arms were finished . . . the only thing that remained was the courage and enthusiasm in the hearts of the *paiks*. The situation was dangerous. *Chhamu* (the Gajapati raja) was undecided . . . could not perform his duty (*kartavya*) . . . then there was an argument between the minister (himself) and the Bakshi. The capable Bakshi, whose ancestral right was rebellion (*Biplab jara banshasiddha adhikara*) . . . who had earlier made the mistake of agreeing to a settlement with the British . . . the minister tried to make him realize his mistake, and a single mistake had a lasting effect. The Bakshi's skill could not prevent the minister and the raja from being taken prisoner. . . . [1]

The dream context reinforces the fluidity of the situation, when the entire structure of social and political order was subverted on account of a single mistake by the Bakshi. This itself indicates the interconnectedness of the land with the raja and the aristocracy. The raja's obligation to his people and his land was pressing upon him, yet he did not fulfil it. The imprisoned Jayikrushna is still 'master' to the dancer, Kasturi. Thus, a glimpse from the play illustrates the dynamism that linked and energized the structures of order and authority in the region, as well as displays the layering of rights and status. This amalgam of status, privilege and reciprocity forms the cultural context for my study.

Situated on the north-eastern coast of the Bay of Bengal, Orissa has stood at the confluence of northern and southern cultural and political influences. Patterns of kingship and ideology and networks of resource distribution established since early medieval times led to the creation of an integrative dynamism that energized the region. Within Orissa, its fertile coastal belt and the surrounding semi-circular tracts of forest bound in the west by the Eastern Ghats, comprise geographically distinct cultural and political zones. The social milieu depicts this diversity through the existence of a dynamic interaction between diverse groups, including tribals. Orissa has been regarded as one of the finest examples of synthesis between tribal and Brahmanical cultures, reflected in the crystallization of the cult of Jagannatha.[2]

The temple of Jagannatha at Puri has been viewed as forming a nucleus of political and cultural integration in Orissa. There are a number of references to Puri as a place of pilgrimage in the Puranas. The *Anargharaghava Nataka*,[3] a ninth century play by Murari Mishra, mentions the god Purusottama (later identified with Jagannatha) on the eastern sea-shore. An inscription at the Saradadevi temple at Maihar in Madhya Pradesh (tenth century) also identifies the deity Purusottama with the '*Odra*' (Orissa) country, i.e. the area around Puri. Sankaracarya is believed to have visited Puri and founded the Gobardhana *matha* there in the eighth century. Caitanya lived in the temple for a number of years in the sixteenth century and is believed to have died in Puri. The thirteenth century poet Jayadeva, author of the *Geeta Govinda*, is believed to have composed his magnum opus in the precincts of the temple.[4] Thus, Puri had long been a centre of sacred activity, even before the construction of the present temple of Jagannatha by Anantavarman Codagangadeva in AD 1147.

The first millennium witnessed the evolution of a unique cultural and political dynamism in Orissa. The rise of the great northern empires such as those of the Guptas and the subsequent struggle for supremacy between powerful rulers like Harsa, Sasanka of Gauda and Pulakesin II of the Calukyas, is believed to have affected Orissa only marginally.[5] The formation of what Hermann Kulke terms 'nuclear areas of sub-regional power', politico-ritual core areas that assimilated surrounding tribal areas into the Brahmanical fold, was the key to the unique political development of the region at a later date, when the Gangas imposed their authority over the land.

Anantavarman Codagangadeva belonged to the dynasty of the eastern Gangas who had their capital at Kalinganagara, near modern Visakhapatnam. He initiated the construction of the great temple at Puri to commemorate his conquest of the Orissan territory and to consolidate his authority over the region by honouring a popular local cult. An inscription recording a land grant made by the ruler, eulogizes his achievement. 'What king can be named that could erect a temple to such a god as Purusottama, Whose feet are the three worlds, whose navel is the entire sky, whose ears the Cardinal points, whose eyes the sun and moon and whose head the heaven (above)? This task which had hitherto been neglected by previous kings was fulfilled by Gangesvara.'[6]

Large-scale settlement of Brahmanas as well as the construction of new, massive temples has been viewed as a policy to create a centralized politico-ritual structure of authority by rulers. Although the cult of Purusottama–Jagannatha evolved in Puri, which was removed from the earlier political centres such as Cuttack, Jajpur and Bhubaneswar, it was absorbed into the political mainstream through the impetus provided by the Ganga kings. This trend reached its peak during the reign of Ganga Anangabhima, the grandson of Codaganga, who declared his territory to be the 'empire of Jagannatha' (*Jagannatha Samarajya*).[7] Henceforth, the temple and the cult became inextricably linked to the political process and state formation in the region, a link that was reinforced during the reign of the Suryavamsi Gajapatis who succeeded the Gangas in the fourteenth century.

In AD 1565, the Mughal Emperor Akbar signed a treaty with Gajapati Mukundadeva in an effort to check the growing power of the Afghan Sultans of Bengal and Bihar. In 1568, an Afghan general, popularly referred to as *Kalapahar* (the Black Mountain) in the *Madala Panji* (the temple chronicle), sacked the temple and burned the images of the deities, posing a major threat to the Gajapati kingship. For the next three decades, Orissa became the arena for a power struggle between the Mughals and the Afghans with the former finally succeeding. In 1590, Raja Mansingh defeated the Afghans and declared Puri and its hinterland as being *Mughalbandi*, or 'crown land' of the Mughal empire.[8]

The political turbulence saw the rise of a new dynasty, the Bhois of Khurda, as successors to the Gajapatis. Ramacandradeva of Khurda ceremonially reinstalled the images of the deities on the *ratnasimhasana* at Puri in 1589 and was hailed by the priests, thus continuing the tradition of the temple–state linkage and validating his own authority through it. The Khurda dynasty continued to occupy the seat of power in Orissa throughout the period of domination by the Mughals and the Bengal Nawabs in the seventeenth and early eighteenth centuries and, from mid-eighteenth century, the Marathas. In this period, there was a proliferation of independent and semi-independent feudatory (*Gadajata*, or 'fortress-born') states, particularly in central and western Orissa, which caused a shift in the balance of political and ritual authority. The Gajapati's sovereignty was further threatened by the Marathas, who confiscated a significant portion of the Khurda territory. This initiated the disintegration of the ritual kingship of Orissa, a process that was accelerated following the advent of the British into the region in 1803.

The entry of the East India Company administration into Orissa was followed by their removal of the Khurda raja and the resumption of his lands in 1804. Simultaneously, the British followed a policy of 'conciliation' of local traditions that also influenced their take-over of the direct administration of the Jagannatha temple. In 1809, after numerous complaints of 'mismanagement' within temple functioning and attempts to 'systematize' its accounts and personnel, the Company administration decided to recall the raja into the temple realm and appointed him temple superintendent. This initiated the reformulation of the ritual link between the raja and the temple and a modification of traditional networks of dominance and material and ideological reciprocity in the region.

BODY, SPACE AND TEXT: EXPRESSIONS OF STATUS, POWER AND CONFLICT

The temple realm constitutes a particular socio-political environment, with its own norms of belief and behaviour that are expressed in the body language of the personnel. During my fieldwork at Puri in the winter of 1996, I was struck by the peculiar gestures, stance and voice modulation of a head *suara* (cook) of the temple kitchen, with whom I spent a whole morning discussing recipes for various dishes of the *mahaprasada*. Seated on a cold and well-worn stone floor in one of the alcoves adjoining the *Jagamohana*, we were strangely secluded from the milling crowds of pilgrims that thronged the main audience hall of the temple. Frequent gusts of wind off the cold stone flags made me shiver, but appeared to have no effect on him as he sat there, wearing only a calf-length muslin *dhoti* and the reddish-orange *angavastram* that is characteristic of the temple servitor. The confidence of his speech, almost an arrogance, echoed in the tilt of his head and rapid and multiple gesticulations, indicated his acquisition of a ritual persona that was palpable to me as I sat across. It was interesting to discover that he ran a milk distribution scheme outside of his temple duties. It made the separation between his mundane life and his sacred role more acute and reinforced the popular perception of the temple as infusing the servitors with the ritual significance of their characters as soon as they entered its precincts and put on their *angavastram*.

The manner in which systems of belief resonate in the language and functions of the body has been elaborated by Pierre Bourdieu.[9] According to this view, body functions reflect the 'natural manifestations' of 'order' in a society—a 'feeling for the game'. The expression of power and confidence in the body and gestures of the *suara* was amalgamated with values of service and obligation with respect to his status in the temple. This complex oriented him within the spatial and temporal continuums that characterized the temple's diaspora in the region.

Prior to the advent of colonial domination, order in society was embodied in the person of the raja, the Gajapati, with his temporal authority and special ritual bond with the deity.

Foucault has argued that in the pre-modern Europe of the seventeenth century, the king's body was not simply a metaphor for kingship but a political reality whose physical presence was necessary for the functioning of the state.[10] One may recall a ubiquitous image of the *ratha jatra*, the annual chariot festival at Puri, wherein at one point a certain tension of expectancy descends upon the milling crowds. The sea of humanity finally parts to reveal the red turban and white *shervani* of the raja, surmounted by an ornate silk umbrella, as he makes his way to the chariots to perform his sacred duty, the *chhera pahara* (ritual sweeping). A glimpse of the red turban symbolizes the perpetuation of the ordered state for the crowds, the raja's presence reaffirming prevailing social structures through the annual regenerative ritual of the festival.

The notion of the king as a 'concrete embodiment' of political power was officially subverted following the establishment of colonial domination in the region. The diffusion of power over a many-limbed bureaucratic structure that focused on revenue exaction while simultaneously creating a discourse of 'conciliation' and 'distanciation' with respect to the temple and related institutions, caused the erosion of the links of authority and obligation that connected the raja to the temple and the land. Colonial subversion of the raja's ritual link with the temple also involved the British authorities' appropriation of his person, initially through his imprisonment in 1804, and later through the reformulation of his temple role by his appointment as temple superintendent.

The Jagannatha temple as a physical and ideological space where hierarchies of status, links of dominance and networks of privilege and obligation were articulated, was a well-developed entity since medieval times. As an important place of pilgrimage, it was constantly energized by the inflow and outflow of people, resources, intellectual trends and opinions. As an area of influence, it was trans-regional and the parameters of its authority were determined not by spatial boundaries, but through the far-flung networks of pilgrims who came to it each year. In his analysis of the pre-modern state in Bali, Geertz describes the 'delicate' balance between 'scattered' nucleii of power which build up towards an 'exemplary centre' through a combination of 'ethos', symbolized by myth, and 'worldview', characterized by civil ritual.[11] In the case of the Jagannatha temple, we see a nucleation of power and resources that deemed it an 'exemplary centre', a microcosm of the universe in which were reflected prevailing patterns of material and ideological reciprocity and redistribution. Through its link with the raja, the temple formed an area where the nature and extent of political authority was negotiated and the status and sovereignty of the raja was infused with a ritual validity.

The penetration of this space by colonial legal and bureaucratic processes caused a reformulation of the status hierarchy and the de-contextualization of the raja, from sovereign status to official position. Colonial appropriation of the temple sphere through large-scale documentation of its functions also circumscribed its domain, reducing it to a limited spatial and temporal entity and disengaging it from its redistributive networks that had earlier extended its influence beyond the region. The temple's appropriation resulted in the formulation of a separate discourse through plethoric representation in official correspondence. Textual representation of this sort disempowered the raja as well as temple personnel and institutions, reducing them to sites for the formation and perpetuation of colonial policy.

The colonial administrators' preoccupation with textual evidence in order to affirm the institutions that they encountered, led them to avidly explore indigenous literature and contextualize it within their perspective of 'truth' and 'evidence'. The role of the text in representing relations of power between different interest groups depends primarily on the relationship between the author and his audience. Henrietta Moore in a discussion on Paul Ricoeur's analysis of the meaning underlying the formulation of a text, argues that in order for interpretation of a text to occur, the reader must 'appropriate' its context, situating himself within the world of the text. Thus, the 'sense' depicted in a text must find a 'reference' in the minds of the readers.[12] Thus, textual representation of Indian conditions by Western authors created 'knowledge' and 'insight' into those conditions, as well as images that were points of reference for the Western appropriation of Indian society.

The dominant position accorded to the written text was a fundamental part of the development of modernity in the West, according to Foucault. Writing was viewed as the supreme representation of the natural order, and thus was alone believed to be the expression of Truth.[13] An image of 'Truth' as being in consonance with an essentially male-oriented, Euro-centered perspective has been analysed by Loomba as underlying the representation of Indian society by European travelers and colonial administrators. According to this view, racist and patriarchal images underlay the 'construction' of Indian institutions as Europe's cultural 'other', and text-writing and imperialist coercion were closely interlinked.[14]

Colonial officials thus sought textual validation of indigenous institutions and practices and read local literature from that perspective. One such 'source' of information on the state and society (both categories that derived their validity from Western perceptions) was the *rajavamsavali*, the royal chronicle for the different states. Romila Thapar has argued that *vamsavalis*, which were usually a part of a bardic tradition, recorded the transference of political power from those who claimed it on the basis of birth or kinship to those whose claim was established through administrative and economic control. Such *vamsavalis* were thus an arena for the assertion of a higher status for dominant groups, as well as provided linkages with a 'greater' Brahmanical/Sanskritic cultural complex.[15] The underlying logic of the *vamsavalis* was thus quite different from the 'evidence' sought by colonial administrators: they were a means for the acquisition and legitimization of an exalted status by dominant social groups.

Status was not a given reality in the temple realm—it was mediated between the various groups through resistance and validated through links of dominance. Milner describes status as being 'relatively insulated' from other types of power, particularly 'economic' and 'political' power and largely confined to a ritual realm.[16] However, Raheja argues that power is inherent in links of status and operates both through the *dominance* of the landowners over the service castes as well as the *right* of the subordinate groups to their share of material and ideological resources.[17] In such a framework, the distinctions between 'economic', 'political' and 'ritual' power are diffused and authority and obligation, dominance and rights are negotiated in accompaniment with expressions of power. Such a complex of ritual and political factors finds a physical representation in the body language of the servitors and in the manner in which they relate to the temple environment.

AUTHORITY, ORGANIZATION AND RECIPROCITY IN THE TEMPLE REALM

The temple provides a space for the convergence of networks of status and privilege and channels of material and ideological reciprocity in the realm. Its unique role in the political and cultural environment of Orissa has been explored in detail by different scholars resulting in multidimensional debates and varying perspectives. Prabhat Mukherjee's chronological account of the relationship between the temple and the colonial government in the nineteenth century is a richly documented exposition of the issues surrounding key events of the time, particularly the manner in which the Khurda raja lost his sovereign status and became an appointee of the Company regime, the debates surrounding the imposition of the pilgrim tax and so on. The sheer volume of correspondence and textual sources that he presents gives an idea of the complexity of interests that underlay the events.[18]

B.C. Ray's analysis[19] focuses on the conquest and control over Orissa by the Company since the end of the eighteenth century. The conflict between the Marathas and the Company troops forms an important part of Ray's argument. He views the initial four decades of diplomacy with the Marathas and finally the military conquest by the Company army in 1803 within the framework of a strategy with political dominance as its goal. In fact, his entire discussion portrays the notion of a calculated, premeditated plan of action by the British administration. Following a methodology that was common to certain kinds of conventional historiography, Ray divides the colonial acquisition of power into separate topics centred on the notion of 'policy', such as 'Economic Policy', 'Religious Policy', etc. This infused the entire gamut of bureaucratic decision-making from the initial entry of Company troops in 1803 through the next four decades, with a teleological continuity. This perspective homogenizes all the interest groups other than the Company administration and polarizes them without tracing the nuances of their interrelationships. The Khurda raja in particular is marginalized in this exposition as the theocratic suzerain of the region.

An integrative perspective of the state and the temple that draws together political and ritual factors and delineates their interaction, is provided by Hermann Kulke. He recognizes the role of the Jagannatha temple as being the crux of the conflict between the colonial government and the Gajapati kingship in Orissa.[20] He examines the temple as the focus of a process of political legitimization that began with its inception in the twelfth century. The link between the conquest of Puri by the Company forces and the ideological influence of Jagannatha in the region is strongly made by Kulke. The Compact ideal, the policy of conciliation towards local traditions and the removal of the Khurda raja by the British government are all viewed as a part of the primary connection between Jagannatha and the state in Orissa.

The evolution of the Compact ideal in the area of colonial policy-formation is further elaborated by Nancy Cassels in her exposition on the pilgrim tax.[21] She regards the imposition of the tax as a representation of the 'Cornwallis Code', and through its renewal and transformation as a colonial bureaucratic instrument of control over temple affairs, she traces the formulation of British policy in the region. Her analysis of the pilgrim tax brings out the tension between the paternalistic domination of the 'conservative' members of the administration and the rising tide of Utilitarian–Evangelical 'reform' that influenced colonial management of temple affairs.

These are some of the major arguments wherein the role of the Jagannatha temple and its related institutions in the articulation of political and economic shifts occurring as a result of colonial penetration of the region, are presented. The broader issues of temple–state interaction and colonial subversion of ritual and political institutions occupies a historiographical corpus on its own. My study has been greatly enriched by the view of Nicholas Dirks[22] who, in his delineation of the colonial transformation of state and society in a 'little kingdom' in south India, presents an argument skillfully wrought regarding the 'deconstruction' and 'reconstruction' of prevailing institutions by colonial processes. Dirks has focused on the essential link between ritual and political power, a combination that underlay the authority and legitimacy of traditional institutions of state in the pre-colonial regimes. The de-linking of such institutions from networks of power, obligation, rights and reciprocity through bureaucratic mechanisms of control, led to the creation of separate domains for the 'religious', the 'political', the 'economic' and other aspects of the state.[23]

The interaction between a temple economy and colonial bureaucratic and legal processes has been closely examined by Arjun Appadurai. His study of the penetration of the ritual and administrative functions of a temple in the Triplicane district of Tamil Nadu by colonial bureaucratic and legal structures, highlights the clash between divergent forms of authority.[24] Driven by the objective of revenue maximization, the colonial administration introduced fundamental tenurial changes and set in place legal structures to endorse them. This resulted, in the case of the temple, in peculiar discrepancies between the traditional perception of the role of the state in the temple realm, the ritual authority embodied in the notion of '*prajanam paripalanam*', and the attempt by the colonial bureaucracy to control the day-to-day management of the temple. Appadurai focuses on the numerous legal disputes related to the temple as portraying alternative and conflicting views of notions of 'right' and 'property'.

The revenue policies instituted by the colonial regime were chiefly instrumental in reformulating the existing relationships and rights in land. An analysis of the multiple motivations underlying the crystallization of the most well-known of colonial revenue policies which formed the backdrop for the economic, social and cultural penetration of India, the Permanent Settlement of Bengal, has been provided by Ranajit Guha.[25] He elucidates the diverse ideologies that fed into the construction of an apparatus of control over the production and distribution of resources, from the mercantilist Oriental Despotism of Alexander Dow, the physiocratic agrarianism of Philip Francis and Henry Patullo, to the 'Free Trade' utilitarianism of John Law and Cornwallis. The imposition of a new perception of property upon existing Indian revenue and tenurial hierarchies had far-reaching ramifications in terms of the reorganization of rural and landed structures.

The appropriation of ritual networks and institutions by

colonial apparatuses of coercion and control may also be viewed from the perspective of the multiple trends and tensions underlying European imperialist expansion. Foucault's model of the changed perceptions of order and knowledge in European thought with the onset of the Enlightenment in the eighteenth century, is particularly relevant in this respect.[26] The episteme of modernity was symbolized by the dominance of the sciences as knowledge par excellence, wherein an exhaustive agenda of ordering the world reduced cultural systems to simple formulae which were decipherable to the Western spectator through analogy. The position of the West as a 'spectator culture' accorded it a position of power while simultaneously disempowering the societies that were being 'explored' and 'observed'.

The emergence of a 'planetary consciousness' in Europe that was oriented towards the construction of 'global-scale meanings' through the 'descriptive apparatus' of the natural sciences, has been analysed by Mary Louise Pratt.[27] She postulates that travel writings by Europeans constructed the East as the 'domestic subject' of 'Euroimperialism' and engaged the European reading public with the expansionist enterprises of colonialism. The theme of India's representation in European writings as being linked to the imperialist exercise of power, has also been developed by Kate Teltscher.[28] The motifs of the submissiveness of the Indian populace, the decadence and theatricality of the Mughal state and the 'superstition' and 'backwardness' inherent in Indian society, reinforced the image of India as a deviant from European normative values. 'India' was constructed, according to Teltscher, as Europe's cultural 'other'.

The argument that colonial textuality and processes of documentation was a masked use of force, has been strongly made by Loomba.[29] According to her, economic plunder, the production of knowledge and strategies of representation were symbiotically linked in the colonial context. The construction of specific categories articulating racial and cultural differences underlay the setting up of colonial mechanisms of control with respect to Indian institutions.

The temple constituted a social, material and cosmic microcosm for its community. Patterns of reciprocity and hierarchies of status in the realm of the Jagannatha temple were thus linked with economic and ritual processes throughout the region. Issues of order and authority and the shifts in these domains brought about by colonial incursion depicted the particular discourse that arose as a result of the imposition of imperialist coercion on one hand, and resistance to it by the local institutions. Such interaction must be viewed in the context of the intellectual climate of the Enlightenment in modern Europe, that was fed by and simultaneously reinforced knowledge-making apparatuses, such as exploration and documentation of other cultures. I have viewed the advent of the colonial regime into Orissa from such a perspective. I endeavour to examine the shifts and changes in redistributive patterns brought about through colonial penetration in the context of relationships rather than structures. Thus, shifts at one level echo at others. Such a perspective also enables one to mediate between the pre-colonial milieu and the colonial environment, since the relational structure highlights the changing conditions and the context for their reformulation.

THE THEMES

In my study on the relationship between the Jagannatha temple and the state in Orissa, I have problematized the issues of status and privilege that underlay the articulation of royal authority vis-à-vis the temple in the pre-colonial period. This was a time of shifts and changes in the balance of power in the region, particularly following the fall of the Suryavamsi Gajapatis and the assumption of power by the Bhois of Khurda. I go on to analyse the manner in which European perceptions of state and society impacted upon the cultural complex of Jagannatha and coastal Orissa, beginning with accounts by travelers and culminating in the colonial takeover of the region in the early nineteenth century.

In the first chapter I have explored the multiplexity of relationships which linked the Khurda raja to the temple sphere, consequently validating his dominance amongst the networks of feudatory, or *Gadajata* chiefs in the sixteenth, seventeenth and eighteenth centuries. The shifts and changes in the nature of the Gajapati kingship that occurred following the assumption of the title by the Bhoi raja, Ramacandradeva of Khurda, led to a large-scale reorientation in the balance of power in the region.

The role played by the Mughals in the reorganization of landed structures through their demarcation of the coastal belt as *Mughalbandi*, land that was under the direct administration of a Mughal *subahdar*, led to an increased competitiveness for territory as well as ritual dominance in the region amongst the various feudatories. The territorial sovereignty of the Gajapati being diminished, the raja negotiated his position of authority amongst the *Gadajata* chiefs through his manipulation of the temple's ritual networks of reciprocity. An examination of the royal genealogies, *rajavamsavalis*, of the Gajapati dynasty as well as those of the *Gadajata* kingdoms offer valuable insight into the forms of legitimacy and the links with the land that the rajas called upon to validate their authority.

The second chapter focuses on the temple realm as a pluralistic community wherein the integrative mode of the ritual kingship was countered by various nucleii of power. In particular, the *sasana* Brahmanas, the landed ritual élite of the region, the *Savaras*, 'tribal' priests believed to be the kinsmen of Jagannatha and the *mathas* as focal nodes on the networks of material and ideological reciprocity were alternative structures of authority. Through myths and legends, these institutions expressed their notions of order and *sebas*, or temple services, and were media for the negotiation of status and ritual authority between the different centres of authority in the temple sphere. In the second section of this chapter, I have explored the annual *ratha jatra* as a time for the reaffirmation as well as the re-negotiation of the ordered state, wherein established structures of authority and status were open to questioning and refiguring. Accounts of this event in writings by foreign travellers elucidate their diverse perceptions of the fervency and zeal surrounding this event, also bringing to light varying notions of 'normative' behaviour and its 'transgression' during the celebrations.

This theme is further developed in the third chapter, wherein the writings of two European travelers, Thomas Bowrey and Francois Bernier are explored as expressing popular views in Europe regarding Indian society in the seventeenth century. The objectification of the land and the people, the compartmentalization and ordering of the society that facilitated European appropriation of it, is reflected in the accounts. The writers' view of property, kingship and the 'credulity' and 'passiveness' of the populace, measured Indian conditions against Euro-centred norms of order, and negated their validity. I go on to illustrate the manner in which the Indian milieu was 'feminized' in the writings and thus lay open to penetration and domination through its appropriation by the accounts. This form of feminization/subordination later found expression in colonial subjugation.

In the fourth chapter I have concentrated on the interaction between the raja and the colonial regime as they both attempted to assert their claim over the temple sphere in the first decade of the nineteenth century. The advent of the Company administration into Orissa in 1803 led to the destruction of the raja's sovereignty and an undermining of his ritual status vis-à-vis the temple. Through a reinstallation of the raja within the temple as temple superintendent, the appropriation and re-formulation of the old state through the mechanisms of colonial bureaucracy was effected. The second section of the chapter deals with the initiation of a particular discourse through the official documentation and 'systematization' of the temple sphere. Through a rhetoric of 'discipline' inherent in such documentation, the administration sought to control the ritual institutions while emphasizing their 'otherness' and separation from the European ideal. The administration's perceptions were also characterized by a peculiar ambivalence towards local institutions, which was prominently expressed in the policy of 'conciliation'.

The fifth chapter analyses the colonization of the networks of rights and status surrounding temple property. This was effected through interaction between prevailing ritual and material institutions and the Company administration which attempted to introduce large-scale revenue and legal changes, a process I have termed 'profanization', as it involved the destruction of ritual linkages between the institutions and the land. The colonial government's rhetoric of 'withdrawal' from temple affairs masked the setting up of structures of control over property, embodied in the transfer of the *Sataishazari* land to the raja for the purpose of temple maintenance. Conflict between alternate domains of power, represented by the raja's ritual authority and the administrative dominance of the Company government, were articulated in disputes within the sphere of temple functions.

The de-sacralization of temple services, particularly those dealing with access to and control over property, occurred as a result of increased litigation and disputes over ownership in courts of European law. A longstanding dispute over a particular endowment for the provision of *bhoga* (food) for the deity, illustrates the reformulation of property entitlements through the classificatory mechanisms of colonial bureaucracy.

A point which deserves explication is the pertinence of Kulke's argument regarding what he terms 'osmotic penetration' between the Jagannatha cult and the state, to my analysis. His model of the vertical and horizontal integration of ritual and political institutions in Orissa is fundamental to any study of the temple and the state in Orissa. However, his view is overlaid with a sense of the dominance of royal authority as an integrative agency. His examination of the royal genealogies as validating the state structure is imbued with a certain instrumentality. My account of the temple-state relationship, while acknowledging many aspects of Kulke's integrative model, seeks to redefine relationships of power as possessing a certain ambiguity and portraying a great deal of ambivalence. I have viewed the negotiation of power between different groups not merely in terms of dominance and subordination, but have explored the tensions that challenged and restructured them. While acknowledging the structures underlying the ordered state of the temple-state framework, I have sought to portray their fragility and the danger of their collapse.

In a study of this type, where perceptions and belief systems relating to order, authority and status are extended across both time and space and contemporary reflections on a living cult and its tradition are strong and vibrant, it is difficult to confine sources to archival or textual material, or even to formal questionnaires during fieldwork. Such material has contributed significantly to my analysis. I have examined archival records at the Orissa State Archives, Bhubaneswar, at the Board of Revenue, Cuttack, the Record Rooms of the Office of the Temple Administrator, Puri, the Puri and Cuttack Collectorates and the National Archives, New Delhi. In Heidelberg I worked intensively on the Orissa archive collected under the former Orissa Research Project. The Cuttack Board of Revenue records have been exhaustively collected and amalgamated through this project into a series called Jagannatha Temple Correspondence, which I have referred to often. The reports of Maddox, Ewer and Stirling and the settlement reports of the various states are important sources on land settlement that also reflect trends and motivations underlying colonial policy. Legal records, Board of Revenue cases as well as those recorded in the Sadr Diwani Adalat Records, illustrate a complex amalgamation of conflict over access to resources as well as the exigencies of colonial legal rhetoric. Travel accounts of the sixteenth and seventeenth centuries throw light on the manner in which Indian society and its traditions were appropriated through textual representation and classification.

I have examined the *rajavamsavalis*, the royal genealogies of the different states as reflecting structures of legitimation and access to authority and affirming royal status as linked to other rulers. Ritual texts of the temple, primarily the *Niti* of Jagannatha and the *Jagannatha Sthalavrttantam* illustrate the complex role played by the notions of *seba*, obligations and privileges within the elaborate hierarchy of *sebayets* and the detailed performance of daily pujas. The *Chhamu Chitau*, the (unpublished) royal letters issued by the Khurda raja commanding the performance of temple duties and proclaiming temple privileges and punishments, are an important source on the raja's role as chief arbitrator as well as the dispenser of temple honours. The (unpublished) daily accounts of the temple also illustrate the manner in which material and ideological resources, *sebas*, honours and land and food, were exchangeable. Aside from these, myths and legends focusing on the temple and the deity depict popular perceptions of order and authority, as well as the ways in which these were challenged and subverted.

I still believe that my understanding of the situation that I go on to discuss, comes from experiences that are beyond these sources. A 'feel for the game', I feel, has emerged from the hours I spent discussing recipes with the temple cook, the times that I sat in the courtyard of a *sasana* Brahmana's house while his widowed mother, with shaved head and draped in a tattered saree, sat in the far, fly-infested corner with the buffaloes. The trip that I made to a *Kondh* tribal village brought home the realization that Jagannatha was not the prime deity there, a fact that threw my Puri-centred perspective into disarray. The initial years of my life that were spent in provincial towns in Orissa, the subsequent twenty-five years spent in training in the Odissi dance style, have all played a role in my particular insight of my subject.

NOTES

1. Manoranjan Das, *Bakshi Jagabandhu* (7th edn), Nalanda: Binodbehari, 1989. Translation mine.
2. Anncharlott Eschmann, Hermann Kulke and G.C. Tripathi, *The Cult of Jagannatha and the Regional Tradition of Orissa*, New Delhi: Manohar, 1981, Introduction.
3. *Puri District Gazetteer*, 1977, p. 796.
4. This is according to one tradition. Another viewpoint consigns Jayadeva to the twelfth century and situates him in Bengal.
5. Hermann Kulke, 'Royal Temple Policy and the Structure of Hindu Kingdoms', in Eschmann et al., 1986, pp. 120-30, hereafter 'Royal Temple Policy'.
6. Korni Plates of Codagangadeva, *Orissa Historical Research Journal* (*OHRJ*), 17, pp. 211-12.
7. Hermann Kulke, *Kings and Cults: State Formation and Legitimation in India and Southeast Asia*, New Delhi: Manohar, 1993, pp. 17–33 (hereafter 'Rathas and Ragas').
8. Kulke, 'Royal Temple Policy'.
9. Pierre Bourdieu, *The Logic of Practice*, tr. Richard Nice, Cambridge: Policy Press, 1990.
10. Michel Foucault, *Power/Knowledge: Selected Interviews and Other Writings*, ed. Colin Gordon, Sussex: The Harvester Press, 1980, pp. 55-62.
11. Clifford Geertz, *The Interpretation of Cultures*, New York: Basic Books Inc., 1973.
12. Henrietta Moore, 'Paul Ricoeur: Action, Meaning and Text', in *Reading Material Culture*, ed. Christopher Tilley, Oxford and Cambridge, Ma.: Basil Blackwell Ltd., 1990, pp. 85-118.
13. Michel Foucault, *The Order of Things*, London: Tavistock Publications, 1970, pp. 35-40 (hereafter *Order of Things*).
14. Ania Loomba, *Gender, Race, Renaissance Drama*, Manchester: Manchester University Press, 1989, pp. 1-20.
15. Romila Thapar, *Clan, Caste and Origin Myths in Early India,* New Delhi: Manohar, 1992, pp. 3-15.
16. Murray Milner Jr, *Status and Sacredness: A General Theory of Status Relations and an Analysis of Indian Culture*, New York: Oxford University Press, 1994 (hereafter *Status and Sacredness*).

17. Gloria G. Raheja, *The Poison in the Gift: Ritual Presentation and the Dominant Caste in a North Indian Village*, Chicago and London: University of Chicago Press, 1988, pp. 1-20.
18. Prabhat Mukherjee, *History of the Jagannath Temple during the 19th Century*, Calcutta, Firma KLM, 1977.
19. B.C. Ray, *Foundations of British Orissa*, Cuttack, 1959.
20. Hermann Kulke, 'Juggernaut under British Supremacy and the Resurgence of the Khurda Raja as Raja of Puri', in Eschmann et al., 1986 (hereafter 'Juggernaut').
21. Nancy G. Cassels, *Religion and Pilgrim Tax under the British Raj*, New Delhi: Manohar, 1987.
22. N.B. Dirks, *The Hollow Crown*, Cambridge University Press, Cambridge, 1987.
23. I have viewed Dirks' argument from an integrative perspective, as depicting the interaction of ritual and political domains of power. It is possible to argue that such a view is not entirely in consonance with the Subaltern perspective of Ranajit Guha, from whose analysis of the complex ideologies that influenced a seminal colonial revenue policy that had far-reaching repercussions for the hierarchy of land rights in India my study has benefited. However, I do not view them as mutually exclusive.
24. Arjun Appadurai, *Worship and Conflict under Colonial Rule*, Cambridge: Cambridge University Press, 1981.
25. Ranajit Guha, *A Rule of Properly for Bengal*, Paris: Mouton and Co La Haye, 1963 (hereafter *A Rule of Property*).
26. Foucault, *Order of Things*, 1970. Also Foucault, *Power/Knowledge*, 1980 and Herbert L. Dreyfus and Paul Rabinow, eds., *Michel Foucault: Beyond Structuralism and Hermenuties*, Sussex: The Harvester Press, 1982.
27. Mary Louise Pratt, *Imperial Eyes: Travel Writing and Transculturation*, London and New York: Routledge and Kegan Paul, 1992 (hereafter *Imperial Eyes*).
28. Kate Teltscher, *India Inscribed*, New Delhi: Oxford University Press, 1995.
29. Ania Loomba, *Colonialism/Postcolonialism*, London: Routledge, 1998.

CHAPTER 1

The Context of Royal Authority

INTRODUCTION

A study of the interaction between temple and state presumes the compartmentalization of the cultural matrix of the region. Indeed, the very terms, 'temple', 'state' and 'society' imply the existence of exclusive domains, which may interact but not enmesh. Our study, too, is a victim of the limitations of terminology and the enforced selectivity of available sources. It is necessary, therefore, to be vigilant about the complex interrelationships surrounding symbols and institutions so that culture is not simply reduced to 'an extra genetic program'.[1] Forms of cultural expression, relationships of status, privileges and obligations, links of reciprocity and dominance, are not superficial reflections of the core of institutions—they are institutions in themselves.

In the following chapter, I have explored the shifts and changes that altered the context of the Gajapati kingship in Orissa in the period following the Afghan invasions of the sixteenth century. In order to appreciate the nature of these changes, it is important to examine the structures of political authority and networks of economic relationships in the early medieval period, and observe their influence on the establishment of a pan-regional politico-ritual framework in the sixteenth century.

Prior to the Ganga expansion into Orissa in the eleventh century, there were a number of small kingdoms and principalities scattered over the region, which Kulke has termed 'nuclear areas of sub-regional power'.[2] The Matharas, Vasishthas and Pitribhaktas of the southern Kalinga region, (Srikakulam and northern Visakhapatnam districts) donated numerous rent-free lands for the establishment of Brahmanical settlements in the fifth and sixth centuries AD. Similar grants are also recorded for the Nalas of the Jeypore–Bastar region in the sixth century and the Sailodbhavas of the Banpur–Parikud region in the seventh and eighth centuries, among others.[3] A political dynamism involving the chieftains' authority over the cultivating hierarchy, particularly through the deployment of Brahmanical influence over the populace, had already been initiated at a local level. By the sixth century, rulers of Sonepur, the Tustikaras had strengthened their legitimacy by patronizing autochthonous deities like Maninageśwari of Ranapur, and Stambheswari.[4] In many cases, like that of the Pulindas and the Sailas, the tribal origin of the dynasties illustrates the ethnic as well as social and political involvement of tribal groups into a predominantly Hindu cultural mainstream. Later, these *Samantarajas*, or feudatories, further consolidated their control over local traditions and cultures under the overarching authority of the Gangas and the Gajapatis. Thus, core areas of political and ritual authority projected a particular image of kingship over their hinterlands, which later contributed to the formation of a pan-regional state with a syncretistic cult at its core.

The notion of ritual kingship—those linkages of dominance and reciprocity that accorded the raja divine legitimacy through a pan-regional deity, as well as projected his authority over the landed hierarchy, has been extensively explored in studies on the Pallava and Chola regimes in South India. Burton Stein views large temples as an integrative link between centres of royal authority and powerful corporate rural bodies. Dirks argues that the royal gift, *dana*, particularly to the temple, validated and strengthened the structure of the raja's authority.[5] In coastal Orissa, the period from the tenth to the fifteenth centuries saw a rapid agrarian expansion, illustrated by the flood of copper plate inscriptions recording land grants.[6] The opening of forested areas to agriculture and the increased settlement of Brahmanas in designated *sasana* villages involved the rulers, the temples and the cultivating hierarchy in a dynamic interaction. The ritual authority of the temples, particularly the Puri temple from the time of the Gangas, was reciprocally linked with the temporal dominance of the kings, and flowed outwards onto the relationships in land, which, in turn, upheld the rulers' supremacy. Thus, status relationships, access to resources and structures of legitimacy were extensively reorganized, a process in which the temple played a pivotal role. The Jagannatha temple increasingly became the focus of royal patronage under the Gangas, along with a growing significance as an important centre of pilgrimage. The temple–state nexus became a nuclear zone of political and ideological influence, both within the region and beyond its frontiers.

In 1590, when the commander-in-chief of the Mughal armies, Raja Mansingh signed a treaty with the Afghans and assumed control over Orissa, a large section of the coastal belt was classified as *Mughalbandi*, under the direct supervision of a Mughal *subahdar*, while the feudatory chiefdoms were recognized as *Gadajata* (fortress-born) states. This distinction persists till today, particularly in the subtle sub-regional ethnic identities within Orissa. It must be emphasized that these categories are not culturally or even territorially circumscribed. The *Bhoi* dynasty of Khurda which succeeded the Suryavamsi Gajapatis were also referred to as 'Gurhjat Rajah . . . of Khoordah',[7] in British records, although it was their link with the Puri temple, the core of the *Mughalbandi*, that gave them their special status.

UNFOLDING THE WEB OF EVENTS SINCE 1568

The middle of the sixteenth century was a period of intense turmoil and political realignment in the Deccan and eastern India. The Vijaynagara empire fell in 1565 to the combined armies of Golkonda, Bijapur and Ahmadnagar. In 1568, the Gajapati state in Orissa was plundered by the Afghan Sultan, Sulaiman Karrani, and the Jagannatha temple was also looted and the images of the deities were apparently burnt by his general, *Kalapahar*.[8] The southern fringes of the Gajapati empire had been increasingly threatened by Krishnadeva Raya of Vijayanagara and Quli Qutb Shah of Golkonda since the early years of the sixteenth century. By the close of the reign of Gajapati Prataparudradeva in 1540, Orissa had lost the Godavari delta and its southern boundary was once again reduced to the Rsikulya river, as it was prior to the territorial expansion carried out by Kapilendradeva.

The two sons of Prataparudradeva were killed and the Gajapati throne usurped in 1541 by Govinda Vidyadhara, a former minister of Prataparudra. An inscription issued by him on the door of the temple introduces the *Gadajata* rajas for the first time as political entities in the region, indicating their growing impact on the central kingship.[9] The fact that the Gajapati was required to call on the authority of Jagannatha to enforce his injunctions, illustrates the growing insecurity and loss of influence of the central kingship at Puri. The successor of Govinda Vidyadhara, Mukundadeva (1557-68) signed a treaty with the Mughal Emperor Akbar in order to check the growing influence of the Afghan Sultan Sulaiman of Bengal. In 1568 the Afghans led a campaign against the Gajapati, whose defenses were weakened owing to revolts and instability in his own territory. Finally, the Gajapati was killed and the temple desecrated by *Kalapahar*. The two events complemented each other in striking at the root of the ritual kingship in Orissa. However, this very act of destruction lay at the core of the reconstruction and reorganization of the politico-religious structure in Orissa, as it led to the rise of the Bhoi dynasty.

From 1568 to 1590 Orissa, especially the central areas and Puri, remained largely under the influence of the Afghans. All this time, however, they were engaged in conflict with the Mughals. Yet they did not loosen their grip on Orissa, rather, it increasingly became a refuge for them as they were subdued by the Mughals elsewhere. The circumstances changed dramatically in 1590, when Raja Mansingh defeated the Afghans decisively and signed a historic treaty with them, according to which Puri and its environs were declared *Mughalbandi*, or crownland.[10]

This move was extremely significant, since not only did it circumscribe the influence of the Afghans, it also created a barrier to the northward expansion of the Golkonda ruler, who had advanced up to Athagada in Ganjam (southern Orissa) by 1571-2. However, this development was relatively peripheral to the temple and its redistributive system which required the position of Gajapati to be filled for the continuation of its ritual legacy. This position was still a powerful one, and various contenders wished to occupy it. Among them was Narasimhadeva, who was related to Mukundadeva, the previous Gajapati. He advanced northwards from his kingdom in Rajahmundry and announced his claim to the position of Gajapati by way of an inscription, in which he instituted his own regnal year, symbolizing his declaration of authority over the area.[11]

The person who eventually acquired the Gajapati status was Ramacandradeva of the Bhoi dynasty of Khurda, who had no direct links of blood or status with the previous Gajapati dynasty.

Ramacandradeva is believed to have been the son of Danai Vidyadhara, a minister in the court of the last Gajapati, Mukundadeva. Following the upheaval caused by the Afghan invasions of 1568, he had fled to the south. According to one version of the royal genealogy of Puri, the *Chakoda Pothi*, Ramacandra was imprisoned at Rajahmundry by Gajapati Mukundadeva.[12] This fact hints at a tension between the two families, with Ramacandra posing a possible threat to the Gajapati raja's authority, even during his lifetime. After Mukundadeva's death in 1568, he returned to Puri and established the fort of Khurda at the foot of the Barunei hill, about 80 km from the temple town, after ritually killing the *Savara* chief who had ruled there.[13] A legendary account of the retrieval of the images states that Ramacandradeva rediscovered the *brahma padartha*, the divine essence of the Puri deities, in Kujang, a neighbouring principality where it had been hidden by one Bisar Mohanty, a loyal devotee, following the desecration of the images by *Kalapahar*.[14] The images were reconstituted through the ritual of *navakalevara* and ceremonially reinstalled in the temple around 1589 under orders of Ramacandra.[15] Ramacandradeva was honoured highly and the title of *Dvitiya Indradyumna*, 'Second Indradyumna' (alluding to the legendary king who is believed to have had the temple constructed and the original images installed),[16] conferred on him by the priests.

It is interesting to note that Ramacandra first installed the restored images in his own capital at Khurda in 1587, before transferring them to Puri two years later.[17] Significantly, the political climate had also changed, the Afghans having been decisively defeated by the Mughals in 1590. Possibly, Ramacandradeva kept the images in his possession for two years in order to strengthen his own link with the deities in the eyes of the temple management and the people. Hence, by the time they were installed in the temple, he was already closely associated with their re-establishment, having been hailed as the incarnation of the mythic king Indradyumna.

Ramacandra consolidated his influence in the region in the next two years and was a significant figure in the renewed conflict between the Mughals and the Afghans in 1591-2. According to Mughal sources, he had provided shelter to some Afghan troops in his fort at Sarangagarh against the advancing Mughal forces. He was referred to as 'Raja Ram Chand . . . a great landholder in that country (coastal Orissa)' in the *Akbar Nama*.[18] When Mansingh besieged Khurda and prepared to crush Ramacandradeva, he was apparently censured by Akbar himself, who ordered him to recall his troops and apologize to the raja.[19] Mansingh eventually made his peace with Ramacandra and signed an agreement with him, through which he was awarded a *mansab* of 500 and recognized as a powerful and sovereign chief.

Mughal intervention into Orissan affairs caused considerable political and territorial reorganization in the region. Broadly, the coastal plains came under direct Mughal administration while the surrounding hilly tracts were recognized as separate zamindaris, the principal independent ones being Mayurbhanj and Keonjhar. Thirty-one zamindaris were assigned to Khurda as hereditary fief, covering all the feudatory states of central Orissa between the Brahmani and the Rsikulya rivers, a territory of about 1,300 square miles. Thus Khurda became a state of considerable consequence that lay like a buffer between the *Mughalbandi* and the kingdom of Golkonda.

Ramacandradeva concentrated on consolidating, rather than expanding his territory. He donated five *sasana* villages to Brahmanas, all of which were situated near Puri on the Khurda–Puri road.[20] This was simply one instance of his efforts to strengthen the ideological link between Khurda and Puri. Supported by the temple priests, Ramacandra successfully acquired the status of Gajapati for himself and his descendants in the eyes of the people.

Akbar's policy of benevolence towards the Khurda raja was not sustained after his death. In 1607, Orissa became a separate *subahdari* with its capital at Cuttack, where a Mughal *subahdar* was posted. Emperor Jahangir began a campaign to capture the southern state of Rajahmundry, which was under the Sultan of Golkonda. Mughal forces defeated the Sultan in 1636 and 1656, by which time the latter sued for peace and signed a treaty with Jahangir. Consequently, the significance of Khurda as a buffer state between Golkonda and the Mughal territories, was greatly diminished by then.[21]

Under Hashim Khan, the first Mughal *subahdar*, a Rajput *jagirdar* of Orissa called Keso Dasa Maru, took advantage of the changed political climate, attacked the temple and plundered its treasure. When Purusottamadeva, the Khurda raja tried to defend the temple, he was crushed by the Mughal *subahdar* and forced to sign a humiliating treaty. In 1611, Raja Kalyana Singh, the Mughal *subahdar*, attacked Khurda and pillaged it. Owing to the established link between the raja and the temple and anticipating its desecration following the raja's defeat, the priests hid the images on an island in Chilika lake.[22] Under Makarram Khan (1617-20), the third *subahdar*, Khurda was attacked again and even occupied for a period.[23] Thus the political primacy of the Gajapatis in the region, already diminished, was now severely under threat.

The reign of Shahjahan ushered in a relatively peaceful re-continuation of temple worship, and the return of pilgrims to Puri. Loss of pilgrim revenue may itself have prompted the administration to ensure the maintenance of regular temple functions. In this period, Gajapati Narasimhadeva attempted to consolidate his position vis-à-vis the temple management by introducing certain reforms in the ritual, which was met with much opposition from the priests.[24] The raja also introduced a light rent on the *sasana* villages, and carried out some reforms in the temple management hierarchy, including the designation of certain élite Brahmana groups. These changes may have been resented by certain groups in the temple hierarchy, and there was an uprising against the raja in 1647, following a conspiracy between the Mughal *subahdar* and a temple priest. The raja was killed and his palace looted. This indicated that the Mughal officials were, by now, closely involved in the shifting political trends within the region.[25]

The period of Shahjahan's illness and subsequent supercession by Aurangzeb, saw a considerable reorganization among the Mughal officials in Orissa. The *subahdar* Ihtisham Khan was replaced by Khan-i-Dauran in 1660. At this time, a number of *Gadajata* rajas also attempted to assert their authority and resist Mughal domination. Krishna Bhanja of Hariharpur (Mayurbhanj) had 'spread his power' over the country from Midnapur to Bhadrak, while the raja of Keonjhar had seized the fort of 'Macchara' from the Mughal forces stationed there. Within the next three years, Khan-i-Dauran 're-conquered' Orissa for the

Mughals, marching through the region and acquiring the feudatories' allegiance, either voluntarily or by force. It is significant that despite his diminished authority over the feudatories, the Khurda raja still appeared to the Mughal general to command the obedience of the other rajas.[26] The Mughals had initially established an ideological link with the region through their validation of the Gajapati's kingship. This link with a politico-ritual structure enhanced the Mughals' dominance over the region, and was thus defended by Khan-i-Dauran. Moreover, the *subahdar* increasingly began to participate in local politics, particularly those involving the temple and the Gajapati.

The raja also collaborated with the Mughal *subahdar* on occasion. In 1692, when Aurangzeb ordered the destruction of the Jagannatha temple, the raja arranged with the *subahdar* to send some stones and a fake image of the deity to the Emperor, to delude him that the temple was indeed destroyed. Later, when the Emperor learned of the deception, he replaced his *subahdar*. But the raja managed to bribe the new officer as well, and the performance of the daily *seba* went on, albeit secretly.[27] After Aurangzeb's death in 1707, the temple doors were forcibly opened by a minister of Khurda and the chiefs of eighteen *Gadajata* states and the worship was formally re-established, despite the *subahdar* at Cuttack. In this way, by diplomatically manipulating the balance of power between the Mughal overlords and the ritual networks of the temple, the raja managed to preserve his unique status among the rajas of the region.

In the early eighteenth century, Orissa gradually passed into the hands of the powerful Bengal Nawabs who took over the function of appointing their *subahdar* at Cuttack. During the tenure of Taqi Khan, regarded as one of the most cruel and avaricious of the *subahdars*, the conflict with the Khurda raja intensified. In 1729, Gajapati Ramacandradeva undertook a campaign of expansion into *Mughalbandi* territory and central Orissa. This was partly to compensate for the loss of all the territory south of the Chilika lake to the powerful state of Hyderabad. In 1730, after the initial success of the campaign, there were internal dissensions in the ranks of the military structure of Khurda. During the turmoil that followed, Taqi Khan captured the Gajapati and imprisoned him. It is believed that Ramacandradeva was forcibly converted to Islam by Taqi Khan.[28]

His sons freed Khurda from the *subahdar*'s troops, but were eventually subdued and Taqi Khan installed a puppet on the Khurda throne, and even posted his own police in Khurda and Puri. In 1731, Taqi Khan supervised the annual festival of *ratha jatra* and in 1732, he caused the appointment of Ramacandra's son, Virakesarideva, as the new Gajapati. This indicates the increased influence of the *subahdar* in the politics of the region, as well as the susceptibility of the weakened Gajapati kingship to manipulation by the powerful Bengal Nawabs.

Ramacandra continued to fight for his throne, even after Taqi Khan's death in 1734, but the Nawab, Murshid Quli Khan, did not favour him. The Nawab placed a minor raja, Padmanabha of Patia on the throne in an effort to manipulate the position of Gajapati through a puppet ruler. The protracted conflict between Ramacandradeva and Taqi Khan had resulted in the images being once again removed from Puri by the priests. Thus, no pilgrims had arrived and the loss in revenue was to the tune of nine lakh rupees. This explains the increased interference by the Nawab in local and temple affairs. Padmanabha was not able to generate the adequate amount of pilgrim tax, however, and in 1739, Virakesari was reinstated as Gajapati after he had promised to pay back the debts incurred by Padmanabha and ensure the regular collection of pilgrim tax, the customary cess on all pilgrims to Puri, particularly during the annual chariot festival.[29]

Orissa was ceded to the Marathas by Nawab Alivardi Khan in 1751. The first two governors were Muslim and appointed by mutual consent of the Nawab and the Marathas. However, once the Marathas began to expand their influence in the region, the new *subahdar*, Seo Bhatta Sathe began to devise ways to assert his own authority over the Gajapati. When Jagannatha Narayanadeva of Parlakhemundi attacked Khurda in order to claim the Gajapati throne, the Marathas agreed to help Virakesari drive him out only on payment of Rs. 100,000. The raja was unable to repay his debt, and consequently, the Marathas confiscated from him the four key *parganas* of Limbai, Rahang, Serain and Chabiskud, which included the Jagannatha temple, and removed fourteen *Gadajata* zamindaris from the control of Khurda. Thus, a financially crippled raja was now reduced to being a nominal chief of a local estate.

His link with the temple, however, still accorded him

enormous symbolic influence over the land. In the reign of Virakesari, we see a proliferation of royal letters, or *Chhamu Chitau*, through which the raja mobilized financial and political resources from other states through the link of the temple. Thus, the eighteenth century saw a fall in the raja's territorial and financial status, but a prominent strengthening of his relationship with the temple.

POLITICS OF PATRONAGE

Much has been written on the temple–state nexus at Puri and on Jagannatha as a legitimizing factor for the Gajapati kingship in Orissa. Now, we need to pause a little and reflect on the mechanisms of material and ideological exchange that underlay social and political formations in the region in the late medieval period. Cultural idioms, including temples, royal eulogies and *rajavamsavalis* (royal genealogies), had at their source a reciprocal relationship between their creators and their sponsors. This relationship, or an exchange, often of tangible assets like gold, cattle, land, etc., with intangible forms of creativity, was fundamental to the process of patronage.[30]

It has been argued that ceremonial centres, particularly temples, have provided a focus for the concentration of political power and the means for its legitimation since the early medieval period.[31] The *Madala Panji*, the chronicle of the Jagannatha temple, is seminal to our exploration of the temple–state relationship. Broadly, it includes genealogical material, myths, social commentaries, enumerations of daily transactions of the temple and its financial and legal records. Popular perceptions of this corpus relate all documentary material connected with the temple to this nebulous chronicle, which is, at one level, a conceptual construct. The dimensions of this corpus were circumscribed in 1940, when the genealogical section was published as '*Madala Panji*', indicating thereafter that it was primarily a royal chronicle.[32] This perception has been debated by Kulke, who postulates a broader framework for examining the material comprising the *Madala Panji* than genealogical records. He has also examined the numerous versions of the royal genealogy of the Gajapatis that were collectively subsumed by the version published by A.B. Mohanty.[33]

Romila Thapar in her analysis of the *rajavamsavali*, describes it as an 'official' account of the royal family, compiled by a court poet.[34] The genealogies follow a pattern of continuity with the Puranas, drawing upon popular mythic heroes and deities. The '*Rajabhoga Itihasa*', or the royal genealogy of the kings of Puri, traces their origin to the Mahabharata and the mythic king Pariksita. Then, several thousand years later, the list of kings arrives at the Gangas, Gajapatis and finally the Bhoi dynasty of Khurda. As a legitimizing device, the chronicle provides an undiluted link between the current family of kings and the greatest of mythic monarchs whose reign was extolled in all Puranic literature. It is interesting to note that the version of the *Madala Panji* that is available to us was compiled around AD 1600, possibly from older records. This was a period of political restructuring, when the Bhois were attempting to gain legitimacy as the true Gajapatis. It was a time when their territorial strength was challenged and their link with the temple redefined. Thus, the chronicle was vital to the new rulers as they claimed the status of an older, illustrious dynasty. Kulke has viewed 'the reconstruction of Orissa's holy tradition of Jagannatha', the compilation of the chronicle in the seventeenth and eighteenth centuries, as being intertwined with the establishment of the new Gajapati dynasty.[35] The reconfirmation of the cult tied in with the legitimization of the Bhoi kingship—a symbiotic process that strengthened the link between the two institutions.

The Bhoi raja's attempts to negotiate his temple status as Gajapati between the *subahdar* on one hand and the powerful feudatories on the other, are reflected in the accounts of temple conflict in the *Madala Panji* and the *Chhamu Chitau*. In these descriptions the temple priests come across as the most powerful legitimizing factor in upholding the king's sovereignty, causing it to prevail in the face of challenges and hostility. Representing the voice of the deity, as it were, the priests were extremely influential players in the dynamics of state in the region.

It is also worthy of note that the chronicle, specifically the genealogy, was not one single centrally composed entity. Different versions were maintained by the *Deula Karana* (the temple scribe), the *Tadhau Karana*, and by the Khurda Raja.[36] Apart from the records maintained in the temple complex, a

Telugu text, known as *Odradesarajavamsavali*, was collected by British administrators as part of the famous Mackenzie Collection. Another text, the *Katakarajavamsavali*, is believed to have formed the basis of Andrew Stirling's account of the temple chronicle.[37] Stirling's derisive comment on the '. . . less certain and trustworthy guides than the above (the three main genealogies that he had examined during his research)' which were 'possessed by nearly every Panjia or almanac-maker in the province . . .',[38] indicates that numerous versions of the *Rajabhoga* tradition existed at various levels.

Royal patronage by the Gajapatis was not the only motivation behind the proliferation of the genealogies, nor were they the only patrons. Different *vamsavalis* often presented alternative perspectives to the same issue. The existence of various Telugu versions such as *Odradesarajavamsavali*[39] and *Barabati Virakrsnadeva*[40] indicates that the southern dynasty of Parlakhimedi also claimed the genealogical tradition of the Gajapatis, a fact that is corroborated by the ongoing rivalry between the Puri and Parlakhimedi rajas (discussed later in this chapter). In *Barabati Virakrsnadeva*, the genealogical tradition of the Gangas and Suryavamsi Gajapatis is enumerated upto the reign of 'Sri Virakrsnadeva Gajapati', who ruled from 'Barabati Kataka and Khurda–Rathipur'.[41] Thereafter, the scene of activity shifts to 'Kalinganagara' in northern Andhra Pradesh, the seat of the southern Gajapatis. In *Languleswara Itihasa*, the genealogy of the southern principality of Sanakhemundi,[42] the first and most famous Ganga ruler, Codagangadeva, is described as having originated from this region. The issue central to the diverse versions of the Gajapati genealogy appears to be one of access to a ritual status, and, by inference, to Jagannatha. The different accounts contradict as well as corroborate each other, thereby indicating an ongoing debate and a certain amount of tension between the various dynasties over access to the ritual link. This is particularly relevant since the territorial supremacy of the Khurda dynasty had diminished by the eighteenth century, while their primary rivals, the southern Gajapatis of Parlakhimedi were powerful rulers of a large chiefdom. The genealogies of feudatory principalities indicate their affiliation with one or another centre of power by corroborating their genealogies as well as linking their own dynasties with them and, through this, establishing their own channel of access to the Puri tradition. Thus genealogies were complex and colourful expressions of the interplay of political trends in the region.

Thapar has explored the notion that a bard or a poet who composed a *prasasti* or royal eulogy was accorded an immense amount of power as he had the authority to pass judgement on the king. We see this to be so in the case of the *Madala Panji*, which is full of eulogies of the various rulers and lengthy descriptions of their heroic exploits, as in the case of the *Kanci–Kaberi* legend.[43] Interestingly, it also recounts myths which are often critiques of the ruling powers, i.e. the myth of Nihsankabhanudeva and the hair on the garland of Jagannatha. This story projects the superiority of the personal bond between the deity and a temple servitor, owing to the intimate interaction between them, over the temporal authority of the raja. It projects a voice of dissent against the established structure of status hierarchy, social relations and rules of purity/pollution (see Chapter 2). This ability of the priestly literati to judge the actions of a raja, may not actually make them an alternative power centre but certainly does indicate their ability to voice dissent against political authority. The temple was a politically active entity playing a significant role in local conflicts, as is obvious by the manner in which the priests brought about the downfall of Raja Narasimha in 1647 in connivance with the Mughal *subahdar*.[44]

At another level, the *vamsavali* created a space for the expression of alternative forms of political authority. Thapar has argued that the depiction of society in the royal genealogies is marked by a lack of homogeneity, with respect to the cultural environment depicted. There is a consciousness of an earlier, frequently pre-monarchical society, which has been taken over by the monarchical state. This is particularly true in the case of Orissa, as we shall see, where tribal chiefdoms were frequently conquered by landowning royal officials. This occurrence is recounted in detail in order to illustrate the superior power and status of the conquering chief. However, it also acknowledges the continuation of tribal elements in the new state.

The context for recording the genealogies changed with the advent of the British. The period following the occupation of Puri by the Company's troops in 1803, and the codification of temple records by the British administration appears to have made the raja and the priests aware of the significance of their traditions to the new rulers.[45] Around 1820, following the drive to collect local genealogies in the Madras Presidency by Col. Colin Mackenzie, a number of Sanskrit and Oriya chronicles and *Mahatmyas* were collected and translated into Telugu, and possibly even created, for the rising local dynasties of central and southern Orissa. This may be the reason that Stirling, who was also in Orissa at that period, found a proliferation of genealogies, and questioned their veracity.

The notion of patronage operates at two different levels here. The older royal chronicles involved only the rajas as their sponsors, and the priests. The later ones depict a third element, the Company government, as the new focus of political authority to whom the account was addressed. The older state, then, became a passive subject of a literary performance. However, it retained the power to represent a certain structure of authority, represented, for instance, by forms of relating with subordinate chieftains. In an account of the dynasty of Khallikota, a principality to the south of Puri, the original founder was believed to have been a *Bhuiyan*, a lower level of landowner, whose descendant was honoured with the title of '*Mardaraja*', a royal epithet, by the Khurda raja, Divyasimhadeva (1781-97).[46] In 'History of the Rulers of Kimidi',[47] the Parlakhimedi dynasty was referred to as the 'original Gajapatis', who were forced to move southwards in the sixteenth century due to political exigencies. The importance of a title, along with the accompanying status, either conferred by a higher authority or contested, is brought out through these examples. The older state, in this case, the Gajapati kingship, represented an idealized order that served to validate the feudatory states' contemporary claim to their royal status.[48]

The *vamsavali* also challenges this structure by recounting conflicts of power between different states. The genealogies of smaller states presented alternatives to the overarching hegemonistic view of the Gajapati state represented in the *Madala Panji* and its various versions. For instance, the account of the Khallikota dynasty describes the manner in which one of the rulers, who enjoyed the patronage of the Khurda raja, succeeded to the title after murdering his father, while the younger son left to take refuge with the raja of Parlakhimedi. The elder son was not liked, while the younger son was popular. This incident depicts a tension between the ruling family of Khallikota and the Puri Gajapatis, their original patrons. There appears to be a shift in allegiance towards the southern 'Gajapati', an alternative power centre in the region. In this manner, the *vamsavali* was a judgement on the current political authority and a powerful channel for its legitimation as well as its critique. In the next section, we observe the different elements that coalesced to form the complex of royal authority, the persona of a raja, and the ways in which this authority was challenged as well as negotiated.

THE RAJA IN RELATIONSHIPS OF SUBORDINATION AND DOMINANCE

The disintegration of the Gajapati kingship had set in even during the reign of Prataparudradeva (1497-1540), when most of the territory annexed by his predecessors was lost to the expansion campaigns of Vijayanagara and Golkonda. In the north, the growing threat of the Afghans of Bihar and Bengal also put the Orissan state under considerable stress. Even so, in 1565, Gajapati Mukundadeva was a raja of considerable consequence, so that Akbar entered into an alliance with him against the Afghan Sultan, Sulaiman Karrani. Three years later, the Afghan armies defeated the Gajapati and desecrated the temple, thus seriously threatening the politico–ritual structure of the state in Orissa.

When Raja Mansingh signed an uneasy treaty with the Afghans in 1590, the future of Orissa's ritual kingship lay in a balance.[49] Telinga Ramacandradeva and Chakoda Bhramarabara, both sons of Mukundadeva, and Ramacandradeva of Khurda, were rivals claiming the throne of the Gajapatis. Raja Mansingh was doubtless aware of the significance of the temple in the region as well as its link with the Gajapati kingship. Hence, his acquisition of Puri as *Mughalbandi* gave him an overarching authority over the ritual kingship through the privilege of conferring the coveted title of Gajapati. Two types of power were interacting here, the military authority of the Mughals by virtue of their conquest over the region, and the status of the Gajapati, linked with the temple and wielding a tremendous influence over the people. Raja Mansingh outwardly held the privilege of deciding the Gajapati, but his choice was determined by multiple factors, particularly the opinions of temple personnel and of the people. Ultimately, his choice of Gajapati had to be in consonance with dominant ideological trends in the region, which would then uphold Mughal suzerainty.

When the Afghans broke the treaty in November 1590 and captured Puri, Mansingh advanced into Orissa from Bihar while Said Khan, the Mughal 'viceroy' in Bengal, attacked the Afghans from the north.[50] The victorious Mughal army advanced into the region on the heels of the fleeing Afghans and captured Cuttack, their capital and stronghold. At this point, unexpectedly, Said Khan, allegedly jealous of Mansingh's growing influence among the local zamindars, withdrew his troops. Simultaneously, Ramacandradeva of Khurda, chafing under the Mughal treaty and suspicious of Mansingh's intentions, supported the Afghans and gave them refuge at his fort in Sarangagarh. Thus, Mansingh came under pressure both from within his own team of allies, as well as from the combination of two political rivals in the field.

Raja Mansingh, a seasoned warrior and diplomat, then decided to go on a pilgrimage to Puri. Perhaps he saw the difficulty in capturing Sarangagarh without the Bengal troops, and wished instead to permeate Ramacandra's stronghold, Khurda, while controlling Puri, over which the Bhoi raja was strengthening his influence. Realizing that his military supremacy gave him substantial authority to nominate the Mughal ally, who would then be Gajapati, he may also have desired a closer contact with the hub of ritual authority in the region. At this juncture, Mansingh was constantly being waited upon by Ramacandradeva, who, for all purposes, would be a loyal and subservient Mughal ally.

As the Mughal army advanced towards Khurda, Ramacandradeva quailed, and even sent his son, Birabar, to Mansingh with gifts. Yet he did not come personally, nor did the fort of Sarangagarh capitulate. Moreover, the Afghans rose again in Jaleswar, and attacked the Mughals from the rear. Mansingh launched an offensive against Khurda, and a number of *killadars*, or chiefs of local forts like Kaluapada, Kharagarh, Sahajapal, and others who were loyal to Ramacandradeva resisted the Mughals, but were eventually defeated.[51] However, the conflict was far from over. Khurda, at the foot of the Barunei hill, was well fortified, and Ramacandradeva, although militarily far inferior to the Mughals, could successfully evade them by taking refuge with his allies, thus continuing local resistance against the Mughals. On the eve of a difficult showdown, however, there was a message from Emperor Akbar, ordering the withdrawal of troops and an end to hostilities with the Khurda raja.[52] A treaty was signed between Mansingh and Ramacandradeva in which the latter was conferred with the title of 'Maharaja' and designated as the commander of three thousand five hundred horses. He was allowed to retain the principality of Khurda, which comprised seventy-one forts, and Puri and the four *parganas* of Limbai, Rahang, Serain and Chabiskud were assigned to him 'in zamindari'.[53] Moreover, he was given authority over the estates of twenty-nine other chiefdoms consisting of one hundred and twenty-nine *killas*, or forts. Ramacandradeva, in his turn, agreed to pay revenue to the Mughal treasury and even gave his daughter in marriage to Mansingh, appearing personally to wait on the Mughal general. This agreement sealed the Bhoi raja's claim to the title of Gajapati, supplementing his ideological influence in the temple with territorial authority.

A number of reasons lay behind the Emperor's recall of his armies at this point. Perhaps it was politic to appease Ramacandra who had demonstrated his military superiority over all other chiefs by defying Mughal strength. It is possible that any more hostility would have pushed him into allying with the Golkonda ruler, and, given the recent rebellion by the Afghans, would have added strength to the local resistance against the Mughals in the region. Finally, Ramacandra possessed a vital advantage—he had reinstalled the deities in the temple after *Kalapahar's* desecration and was hailed as the 'Second Indradyumna' by the priests. Their loyalty lay with him.[54]

From the account recorded in the *Madala Panji*, there does not appear to have been any doubt about Ramacandra's accession to the throne of the Gajapatis. He was credited with having traced the '*brahma padartha*' (divine essence of the deity) and restored the images to the *ratnasimhasana* in the temple. Ramacandra kept the images in his own palace at Khurda and reinstated the regular worship there for two years, while the Afghans were active in Puri. After their defeat by the Mughals, he brought back the images to Puri amidst great fanfare.[55]

An astute politician, Ramacandra shrewdly established his claim on the deities and won the favour of the priests, thus proving himself a worthy successor to the Gajapatis in the eyes of the people. The finely-tuned political situation also fell in his favour, to which his confidence in defying the Mughals contributed in a big way. According to one account, Ramacandradeva of Khurda was offered the *Khadi Prasada*, the Gajapati's share of *prasada* in the temple, by Mansingh himself, as a sign of acceptance of his royal status.[56] In a sense, the title of Gajapati was not simply conferred upon him by the superior military authority of the Mughals: he claimed it by virtue of his suitability.

The amicable settlement with the Mughals which involved the other contenders—Telinga Ramacandra and Chakoda Bhramarabara received the principalities of Ali and Patia respectively—established a longstanding relationship between Orissa and the Mughal empire.[57] Through this link, the Mughal pattern of administration and revenue exaction was also introduced into the region. Land revenue collection necessitated certain arrangements, economic processes and official designations that had far-reaching political consequences. Mughal official terminology, such as *mansabdar*, *zamindar*, *chaudhuri* and *qanungo* became common.

Under the *subahdari* of Makarram Khan, Emperor Jahangir recorded the 'conquest' of Khurda, and the flight of the raja to Rajahmundry in his memoirs.[58] In 1629-30, *subahdar* Baqar Khan asserted his authority over the region; it is said that he imprisoned and massacred seven hundred chiefs, of which only one escaped to inform the emperor of their plight. In 1657, there was anarchy at the Mughal court following Shah Jahan's illness, and the troops were withdrawn from the province to assist in the wars of succession. According to an account by the Mughal general Khan-i-Dauran, in this period, most of the *Gadajata* rajas are believed to have withheld revenue payments to the Mughal government, fortified their capitals and added to their treasuries by looting the countryside.[59]

There appears to have been an increased interaction between the temple, the Gajapati and the Mughal administration following Akbar's demise. During the reign of Jahangir, this took the form of hostile raids on the temple and the raja by the *subahdars*, leading to the removal of the deities and the suspension of regular ritual.[60] Between 1628 and 1657, cordial relations between Emperor Shahjahan and Gajapati Narasimha resulted in a continuation of regular temple functions. In fact, an account by the British traveler, Bruton, gives an image of the *ratha jatra* in 1633, wherein the festivities were being supervised by '. . . one of the Moghuls . . . ', presumably the *subahdar*.[61] The involvement of the Mughal *subahdar* in temple affairs increased to such an extent that in 1647, he was part of an open revolt against the raja Narasimha along with a faction of the priests, which resulted in the murder of the raja. Thus we see that Mughal administration was gradually becoming more involved in the interplay of local political trends, as well as structures of status and authority. Whether or not by conscious policy, Mughal intervention in local politics was a fact.

This intervention happened at two levels. The *subahdar's* involvement in the local political and economic scenario was an immediate pressure on the fragile Gajapati kingship, and was a closer response to prevailing trends than the far away Emperor. Imperial policies were often a faded echo by the time they reached the far-flung pockets of the empire. However, they intrinsically had the power to subvert all moves made by the local representatives, as one had observed in the manner in which Akbar turned the tense situation surrounding the Gajapati throne around in his favour. The power of the Emperor was still awesome, and could not be openly flouted until the end of the reign of Aurangzeb, and even afterwards.

This is obvious by the manner in which the Gajapati colluded with the *subahdar* in order to protect the temple. After Aurangzeb's decree of 1692, ordering the destruction of the temple at Puri, the *subahdar*, in return for a sum of money from the raja, agreed to arrange a false demolition and sent a fake image of the deity to the emperor as proof of the destruction.[62] This indicates that the Mughal administration, too, far from being a monolithic presence, was a complex conglomerate of varying, often opposing trends, that played their own role in the political and cultural processes. The temple and the Gajapati kingship apparently related with the Mughal authorities at multiple levels; namely, those of the local administrative personnel and the higher imperial government, which was further away.

The term of the Marathas in Orissa was far too short to evolve a comprehensive policy towards the existing politico–ritual institutions. Stirling's account of their reign epitomizes the British attitude towards their immediate predecessors in the region, one of righteous indignation at their tyranny and rapacity.[63] However, the *Odradesarajavamsavali* records that most of the Maratha leaders of Nagpur, including Januji Bhonsle and Chimna Bapu had been to Puri and paid their respects to the deity. Januji issued a *sanad* to a *Gaudiya mahant* at Puri, on the top of which was respectfully stamped the name of Lord Jagannatha, with whose favour the order was issued. The *sanad* orders the restoration of certain revenues that were previously collected by the *Gaudiya Gosvamis*, and is addressed to all administrative officers of the entire *subah* of Orissa. It may be worth mentioning that the *mahant*, Basudeb Gosvami, was the 'mantra guru' (spiritual preceptor) of Virakesarideva, the Gajapati.[64] The Marathas, being Hindus, had access to the temple and its ritual framework, a status that was intrinsically denied to the British. This may explain the Company officials' antipathy to the Marathas' links with the temple, and their desire to denigrate their predecessors' motives in dealing with the politico–ritual networks in Orissa.

It would appear that the Marathas were, in some ways, reaffirming the networks of rights and obligations that also involved the Gajapatis. Certain events indicate, however, that the Marathas also wished to acquire the ritual status of the Gajapati. During the *subahdari* of Seo Bhatta, (1760-64), the ruler of Parlakhimedi visited the temple and was given the *sirapa* (royal turban) by the Maratha *subahdar*, in the absence of the Gajapati.[65] The gift of such a symbolic honour was specifically a function performed by the Gajapati, and it would appear that the *subahdar* was attempting to exclude the raja from the networks of his own status. The Marathas also played upon the traditional rivalry between the Parlakhimedi raja and the Gajapati,[66] demanding a large sum of money from the latter in return for help in repulsing an attack by the former. When Virakesari was unable to repay the sum, the Marathas confiscated the key *parganas* of Limbai, Rahang, Serain and Chabiskud, which included the temple sphere, the *Sriksetra*. In this way, they struck at the ritual base of the Gajapati's authority, reducing him to an insignificant local zamindar.

In order to uphold his ritual dominance among the *Gadajata* chiefs, the raja had to mediate the shifting relations of power as three successive governments dominated the political scenario in the region, following the decline of Mughal authority. The Marathas were obviously interested in dismantling the raja's ritual status, and may perhaps have attempted to replace him, had they remained in the region. As it is, the four *parganas* that they had confiscated from the raja, which were vital in the maintenance of his ritual authority, became the key issue of conflict between the raja and the Company administration when they advanced into Orissa in 1803.

THE GAJAPATI AND THE FEUDATORIES: STATUS UPHELD

In the last section, we observed the manner in which the position of Gajapati was claimed and maintained by the Bhoi dynasty of Khurda. Their relationship with the Mughal administration was doubtless militarily a subordinate one, yet the emperor could not replace the Gajapatis, nor could he interfere in their functioning. This was true primarily owing to the raja's link with the temple which accorded him a special status among all the feudatory chiefs, 'whom all the other zamindars in the country worship like a god . . . and disobedience of whose order they regard as a sin . . . '.[67]

This image of the raja as being ritually linked with Jagannatha, so palpably clear even to a Mughal general who may not have been familiar with the intricacies of temple cosmology, was acknowledged and upheld by the feudatories, the *Gadajata* rajas. Thus, the raja's authority rested on certain ritual and economic relationships with the other chiefs that were alive and dynamic, and not simply a memory of a glorious past. It was this dynamism that legitimized and upheld the claim of the Bhois as they stepped into the position of the Suryavamsi Gajapatis. The Khurda raja occupied a particular status vis-à-vis the other rajas, a status that he had to constantly negotiate and which evolved with changing political exigencies.

In the sixteenth and seventeenth centuries, there was a marked expansion in the number of feudatory states in Orissa. In 1592, only a handful of states were recognized as independent principalities by Akbar. These included, apart from Khurda, Keonjhar,

Haripur (Mayurbhanj), Aul and Sarangagarh.[68] However, we do know that there were a number of feudatory chiefs at the time of Kapilendradeva who had voiced their resentment against his authority, and were accordingly chastised.[69] These states, such as Ranpur, Kujang, Kanika, Dompara, Khallikota, etc., were linked to the temple and the Gajapati both territorially and ideologically.[70] The military account of Khan-i-Dauran (1660-3) lists a number of *zamindars* and *killadars* who fought the Mughal armies on behalf of the Khurda raja, such as Ranpur, Kaluapada, Banki and others.[71] This indicates that certain surrounding principalities were under the dominant influence of Khurda, both through the temple–Gajapati link as well as independently, as military vassals.

The disintegration of the territorial cohesion of the Gajapati state in the fifteenth and sixteenth centuries, coupled with the increased influx of personnel and offices of the Mughal administration, may have contributed to the increase in the number of independent landowners in this period. The presence of the Afghans, Mughals, Rajputs in the region would doubtless have caused considerable social and political changes, not to mention territorial reorganization. For instance, the state of Dhenkanal, previously ruled by the Bhanjas, was apparently conquered by a Rajput clan, approximately in the period following Mansingh's incursion into the region.[72] This re-organization also involved a restructuring of the status of Gajapati vis-à-vis the other ruling powers in the region.

The intricate web of the links of obligation that connected the Gajapati with the *Gadajata* rajas, were expressed through a combination of military, ritual and economic terms. Indeed, it is difficult to separate and define the diverse motivations that underlay this interaction. A statement from the Ranapur *raja-vamsavali* recording the resolution of military conflict in ritual terms illustrates these linkages: 'The Maharaja (of Puri) had a battle with the Nawab and Jagannatha Patnaik (of Ranapur) helped the Maharaja of Tapanga Gada. So Maharaja ordered to honour the Raja Narendra Mahapatra of Ranapur with the presentation of white umbrella and bugle.'[73] The ritual gift of the umbrella and bugle, both symbols of royal sovereignty by the Gajapati, marked an acknowledgement of the Ranapur raja's support and of his status as independent ruler.

The state of Ranapur was within the sphere of influence of the Khurda–Puri complex, both by virtue of territorial proximity as well as ideological and military linkages. The Ranapur rajas were offered a large number of special privileges in the temple during their annual pilgrimage; these were conferred by the Gajapati as a mark of favour. The enhanced status of the feudatory raja, in this case, his ritual status in the temple, reflected the greatness of his overlord, hence it was in the interest of the Gajapati, as well as that of the Ranapur raja, to mutually honour each other. In another instance, the *rajavamsavali* of Khallikota recounts the appointment of its founder, a *Bhuiyan-Khandait* (landowner) by origin, to being appointed feudatory chief by Gajapati Purusottamadeva during the *Kanci-Kaberi* campaign.[74] The state of Keonjhar is described as having been a gift from the Gajapati to his son-in-law, a Rajput prince.[75] Once again, the adoption of the Rajput persona by the ruling family is explained, while simultaneously being legitimized through its association with the Gajapati. Thus, it is evident that the Gajapati stood for a particular state of order, which legitimized the status of the feudatory rajas, and was itself revalidated in the process by being acknowledged as authoritative.

The dynamism of the feudatory–Gajapati relationship was kept alive through ritualized economic relationships in the seventeenth and eighteenth centuries, especially through the redistributive system of the temple. The socio-economic and revenue networks of the feudatory states were mobilized within the temple sphere, and these links were sanctioned by, and channelized through the Khurda Raja. The *Chhamu Chitau*, or the royal proclamations of the Gajapati, issued primarily in the seventeenth and eighteenth centuries, are vibrantly illustrative of this ritual mobilization of goods and services. For instance, a letter issued by Virakesarideva in 1741 to the temple *Paricchas*, pertaining to the privileges of the Ranapur rajas, runs as follows: 'On the 22nd day of (the month of) *Mesa* in the 7th *anka* of this king written order of the king was issued. "You should give sadi and mahaprasad from the Temple to the king [Narendra] of Ranapur in the traditional manner for supplying ropes (simuli)."'

Another letter issued by the same ruler in 1750 requests the Dhenkanal raja to supply iron for building the *rathas* and bestows the usual honour of *sadi* and *candana* in return. Owing to a more tenuous political status of the Gajapati and greater independence of the feudatory states in the eighteenth century, what was previously simply requisitioned, even for temple functions, now had to be requested. These links of supply and demand were restructured within a changed political milieu, wherein the Khurda raja was negotiating his status as Gajapati while attempting to achieve a balance with the pressures exerted by higher military authorities—the Mughals and the Nawabs. The Gajapati's ritual link with the temple, however, was a powerful one, and his ability to legitimize the feudatory rajas within the temple's network of privileges, accorded him a unique authority.

This is not to say that the Khurda raja had completely lost the ability to confront the *Gadajata* rajas in battle. Stirling's account records a campaign by Ramacandradeva (1727-37) against the chief of Banki who had been 'treacherous' and created 'anarchy'.[76] This raja was effectively quelled and imprisoned. Thus the raja maintained his authority as 'the leading zamindar of this country'[77] through a combination of ritual mobilization of resources and military strength.

The seventeenth and eighteenth centuries saw a curious interplay of political trends in the region, wherein cultural factors played as significant a role in state formation as military strategy. The Khurda raja achieved the status of Gajapati through shrewd foresight and military superiority as much as it was conferred upon him by the Mughal emperor. Thus, while he was militarily subordinate to Delhi, he was ideologically superior, even dominant in the region. On the other hand, his status of supremacy depended largely on his relationships with the feudatory rajas. While they upheld his ritual dominance, as the status of their own lineages was linked to the superior position of the Gajapati, the increased circumscription of his temporal power limited his authority to the temple sphere. These elements have been explored in detail in subsequent sections.

These conflicting trends were set against the backdrop of great social and economic upheaval, political turmoil, and the wresting of power by new groups, and the eclipsing of old elites. The influx of the Afghans and Rajputs into the region's societal networks, the opening up of tribal communities to pan-regional socio-political processes, and the creation of a whole new hierarchy of revenue collection and military bureaucracy, served to make this period a chaotic one in the history of Orissa.

'*PRAJANAM PARIPALANAM* . . . ': THE RAJA'S PERSONA AND TEMPLE NETWORKS

Earlier in this chapter, we had observed that the succession to the title of Gajapati by the Bhois of Khurda was followed by considerable reorganization of political relations in the region. The territorial and military supremacy of the Gajapati had diminished, and by the time the Marathas assumed authority over the *subahdari* of Orissa in the mid-eighteenth century, Khurda was a fairly small, localized principality. In this context, what was the popular perception of the raja's status? What was the nature and extent of his authority over the temple, its functionaries, over the feudatories and the people at large? What were the forms taken by the projection of royal authority at the different levels, and how did events at one level reverberate throughout the ritual and material networks of the region? I have explored these questions in the following section in an effort to unfold the various dimensions of the raja's ritual status in the region.

The notion of '*prajanam paripalanam*', or the protection and support of his people and of the economic and moral order in his realm by the raja, is a pervasive one in classical Hindu political theory.[78] This ideal underlay the functioning of the most minor of landed chieftains as well as powerful kings. I have focused on the different levels of the raja's interaction with temple processes and functionaries in the context of the values subsumed by this royal ideal, primarily his authority to arbitrate in disputes, to make donations and to accord temple privileges. My concentration on his temple role stems from the fact that the raja's authority was increasingly concentrated within this realm by the seventeenth and eighteenth centuries. Moreover, the temple being at the centre of landed and pilgrim networks, the interplay between the raja and temple functions was often channelized through these networks and projected outwards over the region. The manner in which the raja negotiated his status in the temple and in the region, forms the dominant theme in my argument.

Arbitration

Arjun Appadurai has discussed the 'administrative' nature of royal judgements or *vyavasthas* as opposed to the legislative decisions of modern European law. The latter is distinguished by the universality of its application and permanence of its character, while the royal pronouncements are markedly context specific.[79] In the Jagannatha temple, the arbitration of disputes and according of punishment by the raja was frequently done to render authoritative public and communal decisions via his participation. The raja, while pronouncing judgement, acted as part of a system, which included other elements such as temple functionaries and local assemblies. Far from being arbitrary, the raja's judgements were influenced by established usage and other forms of legitimation.[80] Thus, the judgement was not a random one for a particular situation, but was based on custom and usage.

The following two incidents illustrate the manner in which the raja's judgement indicated his authority over the temple's material networks as well as over the functionaries. A letter from Raja Virakesarideva [1737-53] to the *Pariccha* (high-ranking official) of the temple describes a quarrel between two functionaries during which one of them, the holder of the deity's umbrella, beat the other man with it and broke it. The offending servitor was fined for his 'crime'. The fact that he used the sacred object as a weapon was considered reprehensible in the raja's judgment, rather than the quarrel itself being a breach of discipline. The judgement reflects a desire to protect the 'purity' of the sacred objects and prevent them from being defiled.

Another such letter records an incident of negligence on the part of two *suaras*, Krupasindhu Panda and Madhab Panda, belonging to the temple kitchens of one Rama Mishra's *matha*. These kitchens supplied *bhoga* to the temple for worship and in this case, all the supplied material for its preparation had been 'stolen'. Moreover, the ovens too had not been cleaned. Hence, a steep fine of forty *kahanas* was extracted from the two functionaries in charge.

It is interesting to observe that the two offences described here, theft of the *bhoga* as well as negligence, were considered to be equally reprehensible, meriting the same punishment. This may be explained by the fact that both the functionaries in their official capacities were participants in a system of redistribution of both resources and services. By stealing the material, Krupasindhu deprived the system of resources and by not cleaning the oven, Madhab deprived it of his service. Both offences merited a similar punishment, the offenders having to forego their own resources (in terms of a fine) to make up the loss to the system.[81]

In the next incident, we see the manner in which the raja's authority was challenged by the temple functionaries, through their projection of an alternative vision of a moral and physical order. The temple astrologer reported the theft of the deity's head ornament and blamed one Krusna *Pasupalaka* for the crime. The raja asked the *Pasupalaka* to undergo an ordeal by holding a 'hot ball', which he did, without letting it drop. Consequently, he was restored to his position and also presented with a *sadi* and sandal paste, symbols of honour.

Theft was once again the offence here, but a theft of a much more serious nature than the offences discussed earlier. This was not merely the withholding of a service or the 'negligence' in the supply of resources. This was a crime against the deity himself, which reverberated throughout the system. The ordeal of punishment, too, was a unique public event, a reaffirmation of the system's authority in the presence of all its elements. However, the accused survived the ordeal, indicating his loyalty and indispensability to the temple's ritual and material networks.

The incident highlights the primacy of the *Pasupalaka's* bond with the deity, which stemmed from his intimate access to Jagannatha. This bond presumably overrode the raja's temporal authority over the temple realm, indicating the limit of that authority and an alternative perspective to the established moral order, which was preserved by the raja. The *Pasupalaka* was redeemed by divine grace and his offence was pardoned through the deity's intervention. This was, at one level, a challenge to the structure of order and authority represented by the raja. The latter, however, acknowledged the primacy of the servitor's bond with the deity by honouring him.[82]

Authority to Accord Honour and Privilege: The Power of Seba

In the twelfth *anka* year of Sri Virakesari Maharaja and in the fourteenth day of *Mithuna*, a letter of privilege was written by the Maharaja as follows:

> Let this be known to the *Pariksa* and all the concerned officers of the Bada Deula from this letter that Shakira Sricandana of Banki will accomplish darsana of the Gods. So, on our behalf, he should be given all due honours due to convention. . . . In the former days the Sri-candanas of Banki were appointed *Pariksa*. So he should be supplied with a silk fan for his fanning service . . . . The bhoga prasada should be supplied to him in a similar way as the Pariksa of the Temple enjoys the honours. . . .[83]

This *Chhamu Chitau* issued by Virakesarideva in the mid-eighteenth century illustrates the manner in which feudatory chiefs were accorded a privileged status in the temple realm, through the performance of a *seba*, a ritual service. The fact that this event was announced and validated by the Gajapati, indicates his status of primacy in the temple sphere and the predominance of his right over temple functions. A closer analysis of these processes will clarify the situation.

The reign of Virakesarideva, who succeeded his father Ramacandradeva after a struggle (discussed earlier in the chapter), was characterized by a proliferation of *Chhamu Chitau*. Kulke views this as a consequence of Virakesari's efforts to mobilize material resources as well as re-establish his diminished authority over the *Gadajata* rajas, which he did through his link with the temple.[84]

Temple *sebas* were a privileged share in the process of worship—they were honours that constituted authority in the temple realm. In a broad sense, the status inherent in the notion of *seba* lay in the degree of access to the deity that it afforded. Moreover, temple honours publicly affirmed the receiver's involvement in the temple's redistributive system, access to which was its own kind of ritual authority in society.

The raja had been intimately connected to the temple since Ganga Anangabhima declared himself the *rautta* (deputy) of Jagannatha in the thirteenth century.[85] The raja's links with the temple had been further strengthened by the Gajapatis, particularly by Purusottamadeva, who established the tradition of *Chhera Pahara* (ritual sweeping), the raja's exclusive *seba*, as an essential part of temple ritual.[86] In the eighteenth century, the Bhoi rajas of Khurda were struggling to retain their position of primacy among the *Gadajata* rajas of the region. In this context, the raja's ritual status as Gajapati, the *adya sebaka*, recipient of the first *bhoga* in any ceremony, symbolizing his predominance in the temple's material and status networks, was central to the maintenance of his position.

By conferring temple privileges upon the *Gadajata* chiefs, the raja mobilized material resources via the temple's ritual networks. For instance, the raja of Daspalla was given the privilege of providing wood for the *rathas* during the annual car festival, while iron and ropes came from Dhenkanal, Talcher and Ranapur. What had possibly been requisitioned earlier, was now concretized into a ritual exchange, sealed with the *sadi* and sandalwood, symbols of privileged status in the temple. Thus, at a time when the Gajapati's temporal status was increasingly diminished and the feudatory chiefs became more powerful in their respective realms, such linkages of privileged exchange served to project the former's authority over the latter. Such authority was apparently not accepted unquestioningly and the feudatories negotiated the offering of their allegiance to the Gajapati through larger shares in temple privileges.

The raja of Banki was allowed *darsana* at night, an exclusive privilege of the Gajapati. He was also appointed *Pariksa* (*Pariccha*), being accorded honours due to the highest temple official. He was allowed to perform *camara seba* or fanning service and was provided with a silk fan with a golden handle as symbol of that honour. Service was considered to be a great privilege, as it implied a direct participation in the daily routine activity of the deity and thus a greater proximity to the deity. The Gajapati himself performed *chhera pahara* at each *ratha jatra*, a privilege that reaffirmed his direct link with the deity before thousands of devotees. By formally honouring their service, the Gajapati was allowing the feudatories a share in his own niche in the redistributive system. It also reinforced his own position of primacy in that system.

This point is beautifully illustrated in a manuscript of the former Rajaguru of Keonjhar. It describes the manner in which the raja of Keonjhar mobilized the tribal hinterlands of his own capital in exactly the same way as the Khurda raja engaged the feudatory chiefs in the service of Jagannatha. Keonjhar had its own Jagannatha temple along with the annual *ratha jatra* celebration. The raja placed on the *Bhuiyans* and *Juangs*, semi-tribal landed groups belonging to that area, the responsibility of preparing the ropes for pulling the *ratha*. On the day itself they came with their ropes shouting 'Hari Gola' before tying them to the chariot wheels. For this service, they were awarded a *sadi* and an honourarium from the temple. They were also asked to pay a tax in kind called *paluka* on lands that were previously rent-free, as a part of their status. The imposition of a material obligation affirmed their involvement in the dominant re-distributive network. The ritual nature of their mobilization subsumed the material obligation that they were placed under.

As I had mentioned earlier, there was an inherent power in the symbol of service, a status arising from the share in the ceremonial system, that was conferred on the tribals and other landed groups by the chiefs. This special status, that was their link in the redistributive chain, was publicly affirmed at the great annual festival. Their obligation to pay tax reconfirmed that status and rendered permanent their special position in the service of Jagannatha. The tax was paid in oilseeds, again stating its ritual significance, as food was the primary symbol of reciprocity with the deity. It is not coincidental that temple lands are referred to as '*amrita manohi*', or those providing ambrosial food for the lord.

In summation, the notion of temple *seba* indicated privileged access to the deity. Yet, underlying the ritualized distribution of these services by the Khurda raja in the eighteenth century was a sense of insecurity, material and territorial, owing to his diminished temporal status. The imposition of ritual obligations on marginal groups may also have served to limit and re-channelize their resistance to being assimilated into the dominant material networks. The status accompanying the ritual obligation softened the pressure of taxation.

The Raja as Donor–Relationships with the Land

In the previous section, I had observed that temple privileges such as *sebas* and titles were granted by the Gajapati as an acknowledgement of his being the highest repository of such honour in the region. It was also a share in the hierarchy of privileges, of which he was at the head. In the case of land and material wealth, also, the raja was the highest donor, his gift doubly significant as it constituted a share in his own sovereignty. The Gajapati had held this position of honour for the region since early medieval times, but each feudatory chief also had this privilege within his own domain. The Puri–Gajapati nexus thus formed a blueprint for patterns of material and ideological reciprocity within the region.

Ganga Anangabhima's declaration that his kingdom was the 'empire of Jagannatha' (*Jagannatha Samarajya*) confirmed the raja's absolute control over his land. As the *rautta* of the predominant deity of the region, the raja had assumed a level of authority that had the sanction of divine power, its ritual nature being more effective in the case of a rebellion than mere military supremacy. In the Pataleswar inscription, the regnal year of Anangabhima was mentioned first, followed by the *anka* (regnal) year of 'Sri Purusottama', or Jagannatha.[87] The earlier practice was simply to honour the king by recording the inscription in his *anka* year. By equating his own *anka* year with that of the deity, Anangabhima acknowledged his dominance over the region while simultaneously linking his own sovereignty with divine authority. Appadurai has discussed that *dana*, the royal donation, usually land, became central to the notion of sovereignty in early medieval times. This development coincided with a period of intense temple-building activity in south India, and royal donations became a means for the articulation of their sovereignty and authority by rulers.

A unique kind of reciprocity underlay the process of donating wealth and material resources. Jens Lerche, in his study of the *jajmani* system in contemporary coastal Orissa, describes *dana* as a ritual prestation where the act of receiving the gift constitutes a service, indeed, an obligation. In the context of the temple, the functionaries obliged the raja by accepting the royal gift and thus gained a moral ascendancy over him. This was at one level. From another perspective, Kulke's view of *ksatra*, the ideology of kingship, being intertwined with *ksetra*, territory, explains the development of the regional cultures of medieval India in a more holistic manner. Whether he was a local chief or a pan-regional ruler, the raja's relationship with the land was acknowledged in ritual terms, as part of a complex of royal status and privileges.[88]

This status was negotiated at many levels. Such negotiations of power were articulated in terms of myths, legends and miracles, events that provided triggers for mass memory. In the origin myths of many of the *rajavamsavalis*, for instance, we see that a state was founded at a spot where a miracle had occurred. In 'An Account of the Gangavamsa of Odradesa', a genealogy of the Khurda royal family, the fort of Khurda was believed to have been established at a spot where a pigeon attacked a hawk. The *Bhuiyan* chief of Khallikota built his capital at a spot where a dog was chased by a deer during a hunting expedition.[89] The place where the miracle is believed to have occurred is of primary significance, as it is believed to possess an inherent power, the ability to challenge and overturn the mundane natural order. Such a space is made sacred through the revelation of its power, and is believed to be suitable for the establishment of a new state. In this way the miracle, centred in the particular territory, is revealed to the chosen chieftain, thus involving the raja with the land in a unique dynamic act of creation.

While a chief may be linked with his land through a miraculous epiphany, he was also linked to his overlord, the higher raja, to whom he offered his allegiance. It is interesting that in the origin miracles, the hunted turned and attacked the hunter. The formation of a new state within the purview of a higher monarch's authority was, at one level, an act of defiance. It involved the acquisition of a share in the raja's sovereignty by the subordinate chief, an act of aggression that could be mitigated by acknowledging that sovereignty. Thus, the relationship between a higher monarch and a newly appointed chief involved the negotiating of royal privileges, a process that was fraught with tension.

Thapar has described the *rajavamsavalis* as frequently recording a movement of political power from tribal/kinship-based structures to those whose claim was based on administrative and economic control. This also involved a change in religious manifestations from aniconic to Puranic deities. In this context, the *vamsavali* mediated the transition to caste society and monarchical kingship through 'acculturation'.[90] During the course of establishing his authority over a people, the chieftain frequently acknowledged the worship of autochthonous local deities, particularly so in the light of the large tribal population in much of Orissa. For instance, the raja of Sanakhemundi accepted the tribal goddess Khilamunda as his *istadevata* (tutelary deity).[91] The continuum of linkages between local autochthonous deities and pan-regional, mainly Sanskritic gods, was often maintained by viewing the local deity as an incarnation of the Sanskritic deity. For instance, the 'Nisada' ancestor of the Ranapur rajas is believed to be none other than the tribal chief Visvavasu, who worshiped the wooden image of Nilamadhava-Jagannatha in the Indradyumna legend, popularized in the *Utkala Khanda* of the Skanda Purana.[92] In 'The Account of Ganjam', the Puranic sage Agastya is said to have installed the *linga* of Siva-Akhandesvara at the mouth of the Rsikulya river. The *linga* fell into disuse over time. A low-caste officer of Gajapati Purusottamadeva (here again there is a link with the *Kanci-Kaberi* campaign) was requested by the sage in a dream to restore the glory of the place, and thus, the state of Ganjam was established.[93]

The presence of a 'low-caste' officer (the category is specifically mentioned) involved in performing the auspicious act of resurrecting the ruined shrine and founding the kingdom, is significant. At one level, it indicates the magical nature of this act which is believed to be beyond the mundane categories of purity/pollution, so much a part of the natural order. It was a momentous occasion—a cosmogony in itself. At another level, the 'low-caste' officer may be seen as representing the tribals of the region, who were thus linked with the reorganization of their own political structure. The dream, which is believed to have guided the course of events, is an expression of divine sanction for the chief, and further legitimized his assertion of dominance over the area.

The motif of the conquering chief adopting the persona of the conquered chief and the people is a popular one in the origin myths. For instance, 'The Account of the Gangas' relates that one Gopinathadeva became king of the *kiratas* (tribals) and adopted their emblem, the rope, as his royal insignia.[94] The state of Dhenkanal was supposedly named after its tribal chief, Dhenka, who was defeated by a raja of the Sulki dynasty in the eighth century.[95] A raja who killed and conquered a chieftain, honoured him by worshiping his tutelary deity or his totemic emblem. In order to be accepted as a ruler, the conqueror had to assume the symbolic form of the previous ruler's persona. He had to reassure the people in ritual terms, that their order of existence would not be disrupted. Thus we see that myths, miracles and ritual symbols played an important role in relating the ruler to the land. They were key motifs that influenced popular perception through familiar symbolism, yet gave a unique and miraculous quality to the raja's reign over his land and his people.

The Raja's Ritual Link with the Temple

We have analyzed the Gajapati's persona from different perspectives in an effort to explore the various dimensions of his unique ritual status in the region. The most specific and obvious expression of this status is to be found in the raja's role in temple ritual, wherein symbols of royal authority and privilege were interwoven with temple cosmology in a dynamic and complex relationship. It is pertinent to observe that the Gajapati's link with the Puri temple was frequently echoed in the relationships between local chieftains and their tutelary deities. However, the pan-regional nature of Jagannatha as well as the position of Puri as an important pilgrim centre gave the temple–Gajapati link an extra-regional significance.

The Gajapati's involvement in temple ritual may be traced to the reign of Purusottamadeva (1467-97) who gave credence to the practice of *chhera pahara,* the sweeping ceremony performed at the time of the *ratha jatra.* At this time, the raja sweeps the ground before the three chariots with a golden handled broom, thereby imbuing a conventionally menial service with a sacred quality. This event is celebrated in the *Kanci–Kaberi* legend, a well-known narrative represented in various poems and plays. (The public nature of this ceremony is discussed in Chapter 2). This ceremony is exclusively performed by the Gajapati, symbolizing his indispensability to temple functions and affirming his ritual status in the largest public spectacle in the region.

Ritual texts such as the *Jagannatha Sthalavrttantam* and *Rajaguruniti* record the raja's role in the deity's routine. The raja's personal ritual, the *Raja Niti,* was and still is, performed in the temple at different festivals, particularly *Bamana Janma*, *Shola Puja*, *Laksminarayana bheta* and *Campaka Dvadasi*. He enjoys unique privileges for himself and his family members, viz., the first share in the *Mahaprasada* called *Rajabhoga*, as well as special *prasada* on festivals. He has first claim to the daily *arati*, the morning *abakasa* (teeth brushing ceremony) water from the deity and morning *prasada*. He is virtually worshiped as *Calanti Visnu* (the moving deity) by the devotees and is entitled to go into the temple on a *palaki* (palanquin) along with his royal emblems.

The raja's daily ritual is a private affair, usually performed in the innermost sanctum of the temple. An account is presented thus in the *Rajaguruniti*:

> Like that of the deities, the sleep of the Raja is called *Pahuda*. Early in the morning, the Raja listens to the servants call . . . '*manima*' (majesty) and breaks his sleep . . . after morning ablutions and prayers . . . The *Prasada* . . . of the time of *Mailum* (morning dress ceremony of the deities) which had been brought to the palace are touched on the head of the Raja by the Rajaguru . . . at that time the Raja does not sit, but remains standing. . . . Then the Raja proceeds to the Temple. These palace servants carrying umbrella, camara bugle, Trailanga drums, other servants and the Rajaguru go in this procession. While the Raja enters the Temple, Behera Khuntia goes ahead, striking a cane on the floor. The Raja enters the Temple through the Lions Gate. The umbrellas, *camaras*, drums, etc., of the Raja can be taken upto the inner compound of the Temple.
>
> First, the Raja pays his respects to *Patitapabana* (followed by a routine darsana of many other deities). When he enters the Jagamohana, the royal emblems are kept aside. The Raja . . . bends . . . and touches his head at the Garuda pillar. . . . The *Akhanda Mekapa* conducts the Raja up to the *pokharia* (throne). Then the *Abakasa* of the deities begins. . . . One *oli* (measure) of the bath water and one tooth brush of the Deity is sent to the palace of the Raja . . . then the Rajaguru touches the water and brush to the head of the Raja . . . (who) . . . drinks a little of the water. Then the Raja comes to the *Mukti Mandapa* and salutes the Brahmins by touching his head to the floor and taking their blessings . . . some pilgrims might be waiting to pay their respects to the Raja as representing the moving Visnu, at his palace when the Raja returns there. When the Raja sits on the throne with umbrella and camara, the pilgrims pay him respect and give him presentations.

The raja's day began with that of the deity, their awakening ceremonies being parallel to each other. This indicated that the raja's daily routine was in synchrony with the divine cosmology of the temple. It also equated the raja with the deity, whose 'moving image' (*Calanti Pratima*) he was believed to have been. The raja entered the temple bearing his royal insignia, a special privilege accorded primarily to the Gajapati. However, when the procession crossed the *Jagamohana* (outer audience hall) and entered the sanctum, the symbols of temporal power were discarded and the raja faced the deity shorn of his royal status. The raja had authority over the temple functionaries, yet during his *darsana*, his status, an amalgam of his temporal authority and his ritual link with the deity as his *adya sebaka*, was deliberately discarded while theirs was enhanced. This contradiction was at the core of the raja's link with the temple and the *sebayets*, and distinguished the raja's *seba* from that performed by other functionaries. The process reflected the raja being honoured with the highest privilege, yet showed that honour to be limited before divine authority.

The ceremony of *abakasa*, the teeth brushing ritual, is particularly significant in this respect. The bath water and toothbrush 'used' by the deity was sent to the raja each day as a mark of the highest honour. The intimacy of this contact was affirmed when the raja drank some of the water that had been sanctified by the deity. The raja was thus infused by the divine essence, a unique privilege that was reinforced through daily repetition.

The priests had an ascendancy over the raja in ritual matters—they dictated his mode and form of worship, however privileged it was. His temporal authority was limited within the sphere of his ritual obligations, a fact that he was reminded of each day. This brings us to the two dimensions of the raja's ritual identity, the public and the private. His public image was dominated by his unique service, *chhera pahara*, which he performed accompanied by his royal insignia. The contrast of values between the menial nature of the service accompanied by the symbols of the highest privilege, is almost bizarre. His daily ritual began with fanfare, as he proceeded towards the sanctum attended by the symbols of his royal status. However, he performed the actual *darsana* and *abakasa* ceremonies privately, in the presence of only the relevant priest. Thus, opposing trends, menial service and privileged status contested each other in forming the unique ritual persona of the Gajapati.

The raja's status as central to the networks of territorial and ritual relationships within the region was thus mediated between his position of authority over the populace and his obligation to uphold the material and moral order. To return to the dramatic representation of the raja's position vis-à-vis the land and the people in the play, 'Bakshi Jagabandhu', such a state of order is frequently illustrated through notions like '*kartavya*', the 'duty'/ obligation/ service of a king towards his people, of a subordinate towards his overlord.[96] '*Kartavya*' is cited by the raja's *Diwan,* Jayikrushna Rajaguru as a blanket statement of his loyalty towards his king that is inherent in their bond that does not require overt expression. Later, when the British forces had crushed the Khurda troops following the siege of the Khurda fort on Barunei hill, the imprisoned *Diwan* blames their defeat on the breakdown of the links of right and obligation between the raja and his commander, Bakshi Jagabandhu.[97] The raja was 'indecisive' (*anyamanaska*)—his defense of his land primarily lacked the force of conviction of his own moral authority, according to this account. The Bakshi let his people down because he did not exercise his 'ancestral right' (*bansagata adhikara*) to rebel against the undermining of the prevailing ordered state. The defeat of the raja, the Bakshi and the land was seen in terms of a disintegration of links of right and obligation that inextricably enmeshed the chiefs with the land.

This state of 'order' was a fluid zone, which was constantly negotiated between the different foci of authority, as we have seen. The Bhoi rajas of Khurda increasingly asserted their ritual status in order to consolidate their position of authority in the face of the growing power and independence of the feudatories. This simultaneously led to an increased interplay between the raja and temple personnel, with a greater overlap between the different domains of authority that each represented, which were also in a state of redefinition. Thus, power and authority, obligation and privilege were important elements in the maintenance as well as the reconfiguration of the balance of power in the region at this time.

NOTES

1. Geertz, 1973, pp. 1-30.
2. Kulke, 'Royal Temple Policy', pp. 127-54.
3. 'Andhavarman Plates of Anantasaktivarman'; 'Brihatproshtha Grant of Umavarman'; 'Rithapur Plates of Bhavadattavarman', in S.C. De, *A Guide to Orissan Records*, vols. 3 and 4, Bhubaneswar: Orissa Sahitya Akademi, 1961, pp. 1-30.
4. Kulke, 'Royal Temple Policy', pp. 129-30.
5. See Burton Stein, 'The Economic Functions of a Medieval South Indian Temple' and 'Temples in Tamil Country, 1300-1750 A.D.', in Burton Stein, *All the Kings Mana: Papers on Medieval South Asian History*, Madras: New Era Publications, 1984. Also D.N. Jha, 'Temples as Landed Magnates in Early Medieval South India (c. A.D. 700-1300)', in R.S. Sharma (ed.), 1974 and *Indian Society: Historical Probings in the Memory of D.D. Kosambi*, New Delhi: Peoples Publishing House, pp. 28-30.
6. 'Bhubaneswar Inscription of Anangabhima III'; and 'Puri Inscriptions of Anangabhima III, A.D. 1211-38', *Epigaphia Indica* 30; 'Nagari Plates of Anangabhima III, A.D. 1231', *Epigraphia Indica* 28, pp. 235-58; 'Asanakhali Plates of Narasimhadeva II, A.D. 1302', *Epigraphia Indica* 21, pp. 109-28, and others.
7. 'T. Fortescue to C. Groeme, Collector, Juggernath', in Prabhat Mukherjee (ed.), all the Important Temple Records During British Rule (A Collection of Papers), Bhubaneswar: Orissa State Archieves, 1984, p. 29 (hereafter 'Temple Records').
8. A.B. Mohanty, *Madala Panji*, Bhubaneswar: Utkal University, 1969, pp. 60-1.
9. In the inscription, the king is reported to have prayed to Lord Jagannatha, and issued a warning to the *Gadajata* kings with respect to the incoming pilgrims, saying that '. . . whoever violates this . . . rebels against Jagannatha'. The exact nature of the statement is obscured owing to the damage to the inscription. See Kulke, 'Jagannatha as State Deity under the Gajapatis of Orissa', in Eschmann et al., 1986, p. 208.
10. Ibid., p. 324.
11. The use of the regnal year as a means of recording events in the temple and the region, was a particular privilege accorded to the Gajapati, ibid., p. 325.
12. *Chakoda Pothi o Chakoda Bhasana*, ed. S. Pattanayak, Cuttack, 1959; Kulke, 'The Struggle between the Rajas of Khurda and the Muslim Subahdars of Cuttack for Dominance of the Jagannatha Cult', in Eschmann et al., 1986, pp. 321-45 (hereafter 'The Struggle').
13. Kulke, 'The Struggle'.

14. Ibid., p. 328.
15. Mohanty, 1969, pp. 61 ff.
16. See Krsnadasa, *Puri Deula Tola* (construction of the Puri Temple), translated by M. Sarma, ORP. Mss. 663 .
17. Kulke, 'The Struggle', p. 326.
18. Ibid., pp. 326-7.
19. *Akbar Nama*, in Kulke, 'The Struggle', p. 327.
20. Ibid., p. 328.
21. Jadunath Sarkar, 'The History of Orissa in the Seventeenth Century Reconstructed from Persian Sources', *Journal of the Bihar and Orissa Research Society*, vol. II, 1916, pp. 152-65, 308-19 (hereafter 'The History of Orissa').
22. Kulke, 'The Struggle', pp. 330-1.
23. Emperor Jahangir, in his memoirs, recorded that Makarram Khan had 'conquered' the country of Khurda, which was one of the two important 'zamindars' in the region, the other being the 'Rajah of Rajmahendra' (Rajahmundry). See Sarkar, 'The History of Orissa', p. 156.
24. See Mohanty, 1969, pp. 66-8 and Kulke, 'The Struggle', p. 333.
25. Kulke, 'The Struggle', pp. 333-4.
26. The raja was referred to as the 'leading zamindar of this country, whom all the other zamindars . . . worship like a god,' in Sarkar, 'The History of Orissa', p. 161.
27. Kulke, 'The Struggle', p. 334.
28. There is an account of his having fallen in love with the *subahdar's* daughter, and having consequently been excluded from his caste, ibid., p. 335.
29. Ibid., p. 336.
30. Romila Thapar, *Cultural Transactions and Early India*, New Delhi: Oxford University Press, 1994, pp. 25-6.
31. Thapar, 1992, p. 4.
32. Mohanty, 1969.
33. Kulke, 'The Chronicles and the Temple Records of the Madala Panji of Puri–A Reassessment of the Evidence', *The Indian Archives*, 36, 1, 1987, pp. 1-24 (hereafter 'The Chronicles').
34. Thapar, 1992, pp. 15-17.
35. Kulke, 'The Chronicles', p. 4.
36. Ibid.
37. Ibid., pp. 5-6.
38. Andrew Stirling, *Orissa: Its Geography, Statistics, History, Religion and Antiquities*, London: John Snow, 1846, p. 87.
39. *Odradesarajavamsavali* Local Records, vol. 60, pp. 303-7, GOMLM.
40. Local Records, vol. 6, pp. 1-41, GOMLM.
41. *Barabati Virakrsnadeva*, Local Records, vol. 6, pp. 1-5.

42. *Languleswara Itihasa*, Local Records, vol. 37, GOMLM, pp. 6-9.
43. This is one version of the tradition of *Kanci–Kaberi*. Others are also to be found, for instance, in *Kanci–Kaberi*, a narrative poem in Oriya by Purusottama Dasa, edited by S. Sen and Sen and *Kanci–Kaberi,* a play by Ramashankar Das, 1881. See Eschmann et al., 1986, 'Bibliography', p. 493. The account was adapted to represent different situations and ideologies, and is one of the most popular legends of Orissa today. The southern campaign of Gajapati Purusottamadeva was often used to explain the founding of different principalities in their genealogical accounts.
44. Kulke, 'The Struggle', p. 333.
45. Kulke, 'The Chronicles'.
46. 'Account of Ganjam', Local Records, vol. 9, pp. 372-458, GOMLM.
47. Local Records, vol. 4, pp. 141-64, GOMLM.
48. In this context, Dirks has pointed out that institutionalized honours, such as temple privileges, were often 'fetishized' by the chieftains, following the demise of the old regime. Colonialism redefined the temple and its political networks in its own terms. See Dirks, 1987, pp. 289-90. The *vamsavalis* in their current form were compiled in the post 1820s, following Mackenzie's impetus. Colonial documentation and categorization recorded the originally fluid bardic narrative, which was usually an oral account, into a fixed literary pattern. This must be kept in mind while reading the *vamsavali*.
49. The terms of the treaty between the Afghans and the Mughals were as follows: Nasir Khan, the Afghan governor of Orissa, personally submitted to Mansingh that he would read the *Khutba* and stamp coins in the name of the Mughal emperor. In return, he was confirmed in the government of northen Orissa as a faithful vassal. Mansingh, however, demanded the cession of Puri and the surrounding areas as *Mughalbandi*. Thus, there were undercurrents of conflict over the temple territory between the Mughals and the Afghans as well, and Mansingh may have wished to highlight his role as the saviour of the temple from the Afghans. See B.C. Ray, 'Raja Mansingh and the Final Conquest of Orissa by the Mughals', *Proceedings of the Indian History Congress*, Nagpur, 1950, pp. 243-53 (hereafter 'Raja Mansingh').
50. Ibid., pp. 244-5.
51. The names of the forts are listed in the *Akbar Nama*, and are believed to correspond with some villages in the area today; 'Kaluapada' being Kalupada on the west bank of the Chilika lake, 'Kharagarh' being Aragarh on the north of river Daya, and so on. See Ray, 'Raja Mansingh', p. 249.

52. Ibid., p. 250.
53. Stirling records that these areas, including the temple, were alienated from the '*khaliseh*', or *Mughalbandi*, and placed under the authority of the raja. These *parganas* later played a vital role in the determination of the raja's status, particularly with respect to the Marathas and the Company administration. See Stirling, 1846, p. 73.
54. 'All the gathered Brahmanas and Sannyasins hailed Maharaja Sri Ramacandradeva as the "Second Indradyumna" and honoured him with a *sadi* . . .', Mohanty, 1969, p. 63. (Translation mine.)
55. *Odradesarajavamsavali*, pp. 38-41, Mohanty, 1969, pp. 62-3.
56. Mohanty, 1969, p. 63.
57. Ray, 'Raja Mansingh', p. 252.
58. Sarkar, 'The History of Orissa', p. 158.
59. Ibid., p. 162.
60. Kulke, 'The Struggle', pp. 329-32.
61. Ibid., p. 331.
62. Ibid., p. 334.
63. Stirling, 1846, pp. 115-17.
64. 'Puri Sanad of Janȯji', *Journal of the Andhra Historical Research Society*, 16, 1945.
65. Stirling, 1846, p. 61.
66. The Parlakhimedi rajas regarded themselves as the rightful heirs to the Gajapati throne, as they were believed to have been directly descended from the Gangas of Kalinga. Parlakhimedi was a larger and more powerful state than Khurda, a fact that added to the Parlakhimedi raja's claim to the highest status vis-à-vis the temple. Indeed, the Parlakhimedi chief also called himself 'Gajapati'.
67. Sarkar, 'The History of Orissa', p.161.
68. Eschmann et al., 1986, Map no. 3, 'Feudal Ties in Late Medieval Orissa'.
69. 'Jagannatha Temple Inscription of Kapilesvaradeva of the year AD 1464', in S.K. Panda, *Medieval Orissa*, New Delhi: Mittal Publishers, 1991, p. 38.
70. These linkages were often expressed through myths and symbolic expressions of solidarity with the temple and the Gajapati. For instance, Kujang was associated with the popular legend regarding the retrieval of the deities by Ramacandradeva, for which he was hailed as the 'Second Indradyumna'.
71. Sarkar, 'The History of Orissa', p. 162.
72. The adoption of Rajput names, lineages and persona by many of the ruling families of Orissa has often been attributed to the advent of Raja Mansingh and a subsequent migration of Rajput families

into Orissa. During a personal interview with a member of the ruling family of Dhenkanal, I came across a legend regarding the original tribal ruler of the Dhenkanal area, called Dhenka. When he was defeated and killed by the Bhanja king, he requested that the territory be named after him, and the deity of his tribe worshiped by the subsequent rulers. In honour of this request, there is a tribal deity installed within the palace compound, and the new daughters-in-law are taken there for worship as a part of their initiation into the family. It is interesting that the tribal deity is worshiped within the house and by the family, while the *istadevi* of the family resides in a separate temple and is worshiped publicly.

73. 'Genealogy of the Royal Family of Ranapur', ORP Ms. 866, Sanad, p. 28.
74. *Khallikota Zamindar*, Local Records, vol. 59, ORP, GOMLM, Mss. 423, p.1. The *Kanci–Kaberi* legend forms an interesting device to explain the formation of many of the feudatory states that traced their origin to the southern campaign of Gajapati Purusottamadeva. Being a part of this popular legend sanctified and legitimized the establishment of these states.
75. K. Misra, *Kendujhar*, tr. P.C. Misra, ORP Ms. 552, p. 5.
76. Stirling, 1846, p. 58.
77. Sarkar, 'The History of Orissa', p. 161.
78. See J.D.M. Derrett, *Religion, Law and the State in India*, London: Faber and Faber, 1968, pp. 148-70.
79. Appadurai, 1981, pp. 68-71.
80. Derrett, 1968, p. 162.
81. It is pertinent to note that there was a closely-knit network between the various *mathas* and the temple, especially with regard to the production of *bhogas* for the various rituals. The *mathas* were obliged to provide the *bhogas*, following which they were entitled to receive *prasada*, as well as other privileges, viz., the performance of different *sebas* by the *mahantas* of the *mathas*. The *matha* was an independent though related organization *vis-à-vis* the temple, and the raja's authority was also channelized through those links and helped maintain the cohesiveness of the relationships.
82. This theme has been explored in detail in Chapter 2.
83. *Chhamu Chitau*, in *Jagannatha Sthalavrttantam*, ORP Ms. 441, p. 94.
84. Kulke, 'Ksetra and Ksatra: The Cult of Jagannatha of Puri and the "Royal Letters" (Chhamu Chitau) of the Rajas of Khurda', in Kulke, 1993, pp. 51-65 (hereafter 'Ksetra and Ksatra').
85. D.C. Sircar, 'Puri Inscription of Anangabhima III' *Epigraphia Indica* 30, (5), 1954, p. 202.

86. This ritual involved the interplay of royal authority which had infiltrated the realm of temple services, and the acceptance of this authority by the priests. See the case of Jagannatha Narayanadeva of Parlakhimedi, who attempted to perform this ritual and was refused the honour by the priests. Reign of Raja Virakesarideva, 31-7-1753, *Chhamu Chitau* collected by H. Kulke, un-catalogued and unpublished.
87. Satyanarayana Rajaguru, *Inscriptions of the Temple of Puri and the Origin of Sri Purusottama Jagannatha*, vol. I, Puri: Sri Jagannatha Sanskrit Visvavidyalaya, 1992.
88. Jens Lerche, 'Dominant Castes, Rajas, Brahmins and Inter-Caste Exchange Relations in Coastal Orissa: Beyond the Façade of the Jajmani System', *Contributions to Indian Sociology*, 27, 2, 1993 (hereafter 'Dominant Castes'); and Kulke, 1993.
89. *Khallikota Zamindar*, p. 2.
90. Thapar, 1992, pp. 15-17.
91. *Langulesvara Itihasa* (Account of the *taluka* of Sanakhemundi), Local Records, vol. 37, GOMLM, ORP Mss. 459, pp. 23-4.
92. 'Genealogy of the Royal family of Ranapur', p. 3.
93. 'Account of Ganjam', Local Records, vol. 9, p. 372-458.
94. 'An Account of the Gangavamsa of Odradesa', Local Records, vol. 6, GOMLM, pp. 154-71.
95. Personal interview with a member of the Dhenkanal royal family in 1995. Also see Kulke, 'Tribal Deities at Princely Courts: The Feudatory Rajas of Central Orissa and their Tutelary Deities', in S. Mahapatra (ed.), *Realm of the Sacred*, Calcutta, 1992, p. 65.
96. Das, 1951, p. 11.
97. Ibid., p. 36.

CHAPTER 2

Access, Status and Redistribution in the Temple Realm

In the previous chapter I had observed the diverse linkages that formed the unique bond between the Gajapati and the temple. This multifaceted relationship formed a point of reference for other social and cultural institutions to interact, particularly as the temple formed a contextual framework within which systems of landed relations, hierarchies of status and privilege and forms of political hegemony were represented. As a major centre for pilgrimage, Jagannatha Puri had a large economic and ideological hinterland, which was energized by the ritual and resource networks of the temple.

The dedication of his kingdom to Jagannatha by Anangabhima in AD 1230 and the forging of a unique territorial bond between the king and the deity also placed a large amount of power in the hands of the temple priests. As custodians of a powerful and richly endowed deity, the *sebayets* formed a counterpoint to the raja's authority. Incidents of conflict between the two are woven into the mythology of the temple and highlight the ways in which power was contested and negotiated in the temple realm.

In this chapter, I shall explore the temple community as a pluralistic entity, consisting of diverse groups with varying interests, many of which were involved in close interaction and often conflict as well. The prestigious *sasana* Brahmanas of Puri, who were endowed with rent-free lands by the Gajapatis, the various categories of temple personnel and the *Daitas*, another specialized group of *sebayets* with low-caste origins, all occupied different categories with varied status and interests. From one perspective, these groups were hierarchically ordered, yet we observe that this hierarchy was continuously challenged by the different forms of access to the deity that was claimed by the groups. Thus the notion of *seba*, the privilege of performing ritual service in the temple, was a focal space for the negotiation of status between the different stakeholders.

In the second part of the chapter, I have explored the *ratha jatra*, the annual chariot festival of Jagannatha as a complex cultural event with varying spatial and temporal dimensions. The celebrations were characterized by great devotional fervour and riotous abandonment of 'common' norms of behaviour by the devotees and *sebayets* alike. It was a time when established structures of power and authority were re-examined and regenerated, and could be threatened as well. I have examined the festival as a visual and experiential phenomenon, based on the impressions of numerous foreign travelers who recorded their versions of the event. The importance of the experience and the impression of that experience, then, are the focus of my analysis.

The primary source of power in the temple community was the deity, and status accrued from access to that fountainhead of power. However, there was another source of power as well, that which emerged through the numerous conflicts and negotiations that happened between the different groups in the temple realm. The establishment of dominance by one group over another was also a source of enhanced status for that group. I had earlier described the distinctive body language and manner of speech that I encountered in the *suara* (temple cook) with whom I had an interesting and colourful conversation, (see Introduction). The acquisition of a particular persona by temple personnel was, in itself, an expression of their status in the realm. Their dress, appearance and mannerisms distinguished them in their ritual capacities, also physically delineating the boundaries of their status. This was a physical and ideological space through which their role in the temple and in society was defined. The *sebayets* wore their *angavastrams* and their distinctive manner as emblems of honour, which were also highly contested amongst the various personnel. We shall explore these forms of negotiation of power between separate domains of authority in this chapter.

ACCESS TO THE DEITY: NEGOTIATION OF AUTHORITY BETWEEN THE RAJA AND THE PRIESTS

We have observed in the previous chapter that the raja was a focus of political authority in the region, whether it was the chief of a local principality or the Gajapati himself. Since early medieval times, the notion of kingship was imbued with certain qualities, values, status and obligations, all of which played an important role in the structuring of a state of order. This state was based on continuous interaction between authoritarian forces, political and social, and alternative expressions of power and identity, which contested these at a local level. Gloria Raheja in her analysis of the *jajmani* system describes the social hierarchy in a village as being layered around the politically dominant group, the *Gujars*. The various service castes had a right to certain material payments from the *Gujars*, as well as a status accruing from these rights.[1] This combination of authority/obligation on the part of the dominant group and rights/subordination of the service castes, lay at the foundation of the social order, according to Raheja. In this essay, we shall go beyond the perception of order as a structured state in order to discern the types of tensions that underlay expressions of dissent by subordinate groups, as well as the ways in which space was created for voicing such dissent. This form of reciprocal exchange, involving the negotiation of questions of power and identity, underlay the evolution of political and ritual structures in the region.

Kulke has discussed the processes of political and cultural development that had been taking place in Orissa since the second half of the first millenium AD. The evolution of sub-regional 'nuclear areas' or chiefdoms, created a politico-cultural dynamism that gave rise to the peculiar composite culture of greater Orissa.[2] The inscriptions of early medieval dynasties like the Matharas, the Pitribhaktas and Sailodbhavas indicate that widespread grants of land and wealth to Brahmanas were an integral process of state formation in the fifth and sixth centuries.[3] At the core of each such sub-regional unit stood the raja and his court, encircled by *sasana* villages representing honours and privileges granted to Brahmanas by the ruler. This resulted in the integration of hitherto peripheral areas into the mainstream of the raja's court through the influence of the Brahmanas as well as recognition of autochthonous deities in Brahmanical circles.[4]

The amalgamation of the various centres of sub-regional power into a composite regional entity required more than the political annexation of the numerous principalities by a dominant power.

It involved the establishment of a ritualized bond between them and the creation of institutions that ensured their continuous participation in a pan-regional process of territorial and ideological integration. Through the patronage of syncretistic cults such as Siva-Lingaraja and Jagannatha, the Somavamsi Kesaris and the Gangas became regional powers that provided an interface of ritual and social reciprocity between the different political centres at the dawn of the second millennium AD.[5] The maintenance of a multi-layered hierarchy of privilege and obligation was negotiated between the raja and other authoritative groups, particularly Brahmanas, who were a dominant presence in the region since the middle of the first millennium AD. According to Kulke, this was carried out through the following means:

1. Royal patronage was extended to popular places of pilgrimage. By the end of the first millenium, *tirthas* had come to play a significant role in the Bhakti movement and had also become sufficiently well-entrenched in Brahmanical ideology. In the case of Puri, an established *tirtha*,[6] the Gangas enforced their control over it through lavish patronage, building the great temple and settling Brahmana *sasanas* around it.
2. From the fifth century onwards, Brahmanas were patronized by chiefs of principalities in remote areas.[7] Later, ruling dynasties like the Somavamsi Kesaris and the Gangas placed them near their own political centres. By maintaining a symbiotic relationship with the state, their presence was significant in building up a political and administrative hierarchy, and the legitimization of royal authority.[8]
3. The temple became the symbol for the overarching structure of royal authority. It was a centralized nucleus where the diverse processes of legitimization converged, and through its height and grandeur, represented the hierarchy of political and social relationships at whose apex sat the raja. By constructing the temple of Jagannatha, the Gangas sought to depict the integration of diverse ideologies and project their own glory over the land, as protectors of the deity.

Kulke's model is of a 'vertical' integration of the region under the overarching influence of Jagannatha and the 'horizontal' legitimization of the Gangas and Gajapatis among the Hindu rajas of the area. This perspective highlights the notion of royal authority as a dominant agency in the articulation of structures of authority and status relationships. My interpretation of the situation is of extremely nuanced negotiations of power among different groups, relationships of dominance and subordination as being fraught with tension and ambiguities. Thus, while acknowledging Kulke's integrative perspective of royal authority, I closely examine the different groups that interacted with the ruler, their diverse motivations and interests and their mutual conflict. The temple priests were one such group that frequently questioned the supremacy of the raja at different levels. As a group, they were not socially and ritually homogenous, comprising at least thirty-six traditionally recorded categories, including the non-Brahmanical priests, such as the *Daitas*.[9] Together they constituted a body that supervised the inner management of the temple, and owing to their close proximity to the deity, had access to the full scope of his divine authority.

The priests possessed their own form of power that offset royal authority in a number of ways. At one level, they had a degree of authority over the raja as they were chiefly responsible for upholding his sovereignty in the region, through the temple and pilgrim networks. At another, they were involved in intimate interaction with the deity through regular ritual: their status in the realm accrued from this bond. This gave them a unique form of power which legitimized their actions vis-à-vis the raja and the people, particularly since the Gajapati's role in temple affairs began to be intensified from the sixteenth century.

Thus, while the priests were locked in a symbiotic relationship with the raja, their own status and persona created a particular context for their interaction with society, the parameters of which were also constantly being negotiated. This interaction was dialogic, with tensions as well as corroborations. Through representation in ritual, myths, genealogies, records of landed transactions and royal proclamations, it is possible to reconstruct the priests' position in the region's social and economic networks. One can also attempt to gauge the different types of conflict between the various categories of priests, particularly those that were officially designated 'non-Brahmana'.

The struggle for authority between the temple priests and the state, or raja, was primarily articulated through the efforts of each party to gain access to, and acquire control over the deity in a variety of ways. Anangabhima, the third Ganga ruler, declared himself to be the *rautta*, or deputy, of Jagannatha[10] and his kingdom as being *Jagannatha Samarajya*, or the 'empire of Jagannatha'. The implication here is that the deity was the overlord, the ruler of the land while the raja was his feudatory, related to him through ritualized bonds of trust and obligation and the performance of certain duties on his behalf.

The declaration of the peculiar overlord–feudatory relationship implied that the raja, as Jagannatha's *rautta*, was empowered in his actions by a divine force, the highest power in the universe. Hence, it rendered the raja's authority unquestionable and omnipotent with regard to his subordinates and feudatories. Moreover, this relationship depicted the raja's absolute loyalty to his divine overlord, a personal bond that proclaimed his integrity and commitment to the interests of the lord. Moreover, there was no better means of spreading the influence of Jagannatha over the land, along with the authority of the raja. The deity's influence and the raja's authority were projected outwards as a composite entity, interlinked symbiotically in order to maximize their influence over the majority of the populace.

The temple priests had a different type of access to the deity. This was based primarily on proximity, management of festivals and other activities, and simply, the daily rituals. They viewed their bond with the deity as superior to the raja's relationship with him. The myth of Nihsankabhanudeva and the hair on the garland of Jagannatha[11] well illustrates the primacy of the priests' bond with the lord over the raja's authority. The story runs as follows. Once, Nihsankabhanudeva of the Ganga dynasty paid a visit to the sanctum of the temple and asked the attendant priest for a garland as oblation.[12] The raja had arrived at the sanctum in the dead of night during the *Navakalevara*, the festival of the 'demise' and the 'rejuvenation' of the deity.[13] Owing to the unprecedented royal visit at an odd hour, the only attendant priest was the *talachu mahapatra*, who became extremely nervous of the king's scrutiny of his duties. According to custom, the raja was to be provided with the requisite materials for worship at all times, which included offerings and fresh flowers for oblation to the deity. The *talachu mahapatra* managed to collect all the material except the flowers, which could not be procured owing to the lateness of the hour. When the raja impatiently demanded the garland for oblation, the priest, fearing the wrath of the ruler, hurriedly removed the garland from his own person and gave it to the raja as *prasada*. The raja, upon returning to his palace, noticed a long hair among the flowers of the garland and immediately summoned the *talachu mahapatra*. The priest, trembling with fear, pleaded innocence and claimed that Jagannatha himself was responsible for what had occurred. The furious raja ordered the priest to prove that hair grew on the lord's head, and imprisoned him. The priest spent the night in despair, praying to the lord. The next morning, when the king entered the sanctum, he was amazed to see long tufts of hair hanging from the deity's head. When pulled hard, the hair came out in a gush of blood. The king fell to the ground in supplication before the deity and pardoned and embraced the priest.

The story depicts a conflict between two systems of access and authority. While the king is described as wrathful and authoritarian, his anger at the priest is justified and the latter's mistake acknowledged through his great fear of the raja. The raja is viewed as operating within a given system of protocol, which emphasizes the hierarchical distance between the servitor and the deity and even the servitor and the ruler. The raja saw the priest as not simply neglecting his duty, but polluting the sacred *prasada* of the lord by offering a used garland removed from his own body, a transgression of the rules of social order. There is a questioning of the raja's authority in the servitor's transgression of the established codes of behaviour, yet he is fearful of the king's wrath. Simultaneously, the raja is checked in his assertion of his dominance by the force of a different system of order that embodies the direct link between deity and servitor that can circumvent the raja's temporal authority. Thus, the situation is pregnant with apprehension on the part of both the servitor as well as the raja.

The deity's intervention to save his servant legitimizes an alternative system of relationships, wherein the personal bond between the deity and the devotee acquires greater primacy than the fixed boundaries between status and duty, purity and pollution. The violation of the king's protocol by the priest questions the validity of these boundaries. The relationship between the priest and the deity is based on contact, intimacy and an overarching proximity, exemplified by the offering of the garland removed from the servitor's own body. There is a tantalising ambivalence in the notion of bodily contact as being polluting, especially the presence of an unclean hair of a *sebayet* in the holy *prasada* of the raja. Yet, it is that contact that signifies the servitor's intimate bond with the deity, the holiest of entities. This is a theme that runs, tangibly and intangibly, throughout the mythology of Jagannatha and comes up frequently with respect to the non-Brahmana priests, especially the *Daitas*, who were of tribal origin.[14] Thus, pre-Brahmanical forms of relating with the deity interspersed with the Bhakti model of direct personal access to the deity particularly through proximity or physical contact, combine to provide a note of dissent against the raja's temporal authority through this myth.

Indeed, the story goes beyond merely challenging the raja's perception of order, asserted through his authority. It emphasizes the superiority of the priests' bond with the deity over the raja's claim, indicating that there was an ongoing negotiation of power between the different forms of access to the deity, the raja's and that of the *sebayet*. In this dialogue of power, the *sebayet's* claim clearly had the upper hand, as is indicated by its being recorded in the temple chronicle as well as its continuing popularity in Jagannatha mythology. A space for depicting alternative visions of order appears to have been created within an established pattern of social interaction.

It is interesting to note that the story is set against the backdrop of the *Navakalevara*, the time of 'death' and 'renewal'. This is that liminal stage between the great divine time cycles, when the old images are buried and the new ones await installation. It is a moment when the established order may slip, or at least be challenged. The myth, then, is set in a period when that order may be circumvented and an alternative structure accepted.

The exclusive nature of the priests' personalized bond with the deity did not go unchallenged by the kings. The rajas continuously tried to establish their own exclusive link with Jagannatha and to circumvent the priestly monopoly of the deity. Kapilendradeva called himself the 'elected' of Jagannatha.[15] He also began the tradition of the raja being designated the *sebaka* of the deity.[16] By assuming a role that connected him directly with the deity, he was setting limits to the authority of the priests, who had thus far been the *sebakas*. It is interesting also, to note the spectrum of relationships covered in the transformation in the king's status from simply *rautta* (feudatory) to *sebaka* (servitor). The latter implies a direct, personal bond with the deity without the formal obligation inherent in the former relationship.

Purusottamadeva, Kapilendra's successor, carried this trend further and initiated the practice of *chhera pahara*, the ritual sweeping of the paths of the chariots during the annual *ratha jatra*. The practice was romanticized to the fullest in the *Kanci–Kaberi* legend, which describes the conquest of the city of Kanci by Purusottamadeva.[17] According to this legend, of which many accounts are in existence,[18] the king of Karnata, whose capital was Kanci, had a beautiful daughter named Padmavati. Accounts of her beauty reached the ears of Gajapati Purusottamadeva, and he sent a messenger to the Kanci ruler's court, requesting her hand in marriage. The Karnata king was most pleased by the proposal, but considered it prudent to make some enquiries about the Gajapati before giving his consent. He soon discovered, to his horror, that the Gajapati performed the act of a sweeper (*candala*) before the images of Jagannatha, Balabhadra and Subhadra at the annual chariot festival. The Kanci ruler was a devotee of Ganesa and not particularly sympathetic to the tradition of Jagannatha. He considered the practice of *chhera pahara* to be utterly disgraceful for a king and declined the Gajapati's offer. Purusottamadeva was most indignant at the slur on his honour and position as well as the denigration of the glory of Jagannatha by the vain Kanci ruler. He vowed to conquer and raze the city of Kanci and strike down the southern king's pride. He also decided to capture Padmavati and marry her to an actual sweeper. He prayed to lord Jagannatha for success in his endeavour and the lord appeared before him in a vision and granted him his support.

Purusottamadeva marched to Kanci at the head of a large army. During the march he was suddenly filled with doubt about the lord's promise and prayed for a sign confirming his support. Just then a milkmaid approached him and gave him a ring saying that two horsemen, one on a black mount and the other on a white, stopped by on their way southward and requested her to give it to the Gajapati. Purusottamadeva was filled with joy when he realized that the horsemen were none other than Jagannatha and Balabhadra, and, his doubts at rest at last, he marched to Kanci.

The city was destroyed and the southern ruler's armies routed in a great battle in which the gods, favouring their devotees, also participated. Purusottamadeva captured the beautiful Padmavati and entrusted her to his minister ordering him to marry her to a sweeper. Moved by the plight of the princess, the sagacious minister waited until the next *ratha jatra*, when the Gajapati ascended the dais to perform the *chhera pahara*. At that moment, the minister brought forward the Kanci princess saying that the raja was the sweeper that he had chosen for her. The raja accepted the minister's shrewd action with grace and joy.

The *Kanci–Kaberi* legend, or tradition, if one may refer to it as such, is entirely about power and status. As Bishnu Mohapatra has pointed out, it has undergone a pattern of development linked with the spread of colonialism and the formation of a modern Oriya identity.[19] He argues that the potency of the legend lies in its ability to generate meanings at diverse levels, ethical, political and cultural. It is my endeavour to draw out the issues of power, its assertion, its contestation and negotiation from this story that imbued it with a relevance that spanned four centuries.

The story focuses on the question of identity, even before it became a nationalist question. The elaboration of a separate structure of values involved the entire region. The inbuilt opposition between the unique politico–ritual structure represented by the Gajapati, and the system of social and political order stated and embodied in the southern kingdom, implies a challenge to established norms. The Kanci ruler's repugnance for the action of a *candala*, that was performed by the Gajapati appears to be an expression of an established value system, wherein certain actions, like sweeping, were considered polluting, particularly for an exalted personage like a king. The Gajapati's pride in performing his 'demeaning' task, indicated his loyalty and devotion to Jagannatha. The entire system of linkages between the Gajapati and the deity, the raja's position of privilege as the *adya sebaka* of Jagannatha is called into play here as representing an alternative to the 'established norms' of behaviour articulated by the Kanci king. The story's relationship with the *mahatmya* (greatness) of Jagannatha was a binding factor around which this alternative tradition coalesced and presented a challenge to the system of established practice. The identification of the Gajapati with the deity and his tradition, the alternative value structure that triumphed over the established order, presumed a consciousness of a separate ritual and political identity, even in this early account.

In that sense, we may see the similarity with the previous myth concerning Ganga Nihsankabhanudeva. There, too, an established order was successfully challenged by an alternative structure that transgressed accepted rules of purity/pollution. The alternative structure was sanctified through its link with the deity, a factor that overrode issues of pollution which were otherwise considered unassailable. The primacy of the bond of the *sebaka* was predominant over mundane temporal concerns.

In both legends, the situation is infused with a special, otherworldly ambience. The context for divine intervention is accorded a special significance: the incident involving the *talachu mahapatra* was set in the time of *Navakalevara*, while the *Kanci–Kaberi* myth centred around the *ratha jatra*. Both festivals imbued the occasions with a momentous quality that was removed from 'normal' functioning. A space was created for the expression of alternative structures within the parameters of established routine.

Finally, it is interesting to view the power of the devotee's claim on the deity's beneficence, a claim which is called upon and the deity is bound to respond. It is the authority of the deity that causes the displacement of social structures, yet the essential power inheres in the devotee's bond with Jagannatha, which causes the deity to act. Thus, we see that access to such linkages was a privilege that was contested and negotiated continuously.

This incident illustrates the notion of self-abasement before the deity by the king as according him great merit and strengthening his authority through the mandate of Jagannatha. The ceremony of *chhera pahara* was a direct link between the raja and the deity and largely circumvented the priests. The *Kanci–Kaberi* legend views this link as the source of great military and ideological power for the king. The tension between the Kanci king and the Gajapati hinged on the issue of *chhera pahara*, and the southern ruler's downfall is viewed as a result of his refusal to accept the link as a valid manifestation of the Gajapati's authority.

Once again, we have a situation of conflict between an established social code which debarred a king from performing the duty of an untouchable and a personal bond between the Gajapati as *sebaka*, and the deity, with the latter getting primacy. Moreover, the *chhera pahara* may also be viewed as the raja's link with the people. By performing the most menial of services, he forged a link with the lowliest of the populace, who were present in thousands on the occasion. This relationship, however, reveals a complex network of privileges that operated within certain parameters. For instance, the raja performed the menial service for the deity, who marked the apex of the cosmological and societal pyramid. Thus, his service acquired a ritual significance that accorded it an otherworldly, almost theatrical ambience. The thousands who witnessed his action did so with an attitude of awe–they did not see it as a temporary reduction of his social status, rather, they saw the performance of *chhera pahara* as an enactment of the ceremonial of his power.

The dominant theme in the above legend, in fact, seems to highlight the difference between mundane and ritual activity, the 'sacred' and the 'profane' as it were. Attention is focused here on the ritual personality of the ruler as a source of tremendous temporal power, according him great honour and authority.

THE SASANA BRAHMANAS OF PURI AND THEIR RITUAL AUTHORITY

In Chapter 1, I had discussed the establishment of a state by a chieftain as being synonymous with an act of cosmogony as well as conquest, wherein authority over territory was established as a part of the raja's persona and status. This status was reinforced through the action of *dana*, gifts of land and wealth, which enhanced the ruler's authority. The Brahmanas formed a special group of donees involved in a unique relationship with the raja as well as the community, and *danas* given to them were of potent significance in the maintenance of order in society.

Heesterman has offered an interesting insight into the

relationship between the raja and the Brahmana within the context of the Vedic sacrifice, in which *dana* played a crucial role. 'But yet: Temporal power is not completely secularized . . . it bears the imprint of the sacred, but lacks the transcendence of spiritual authority.'[20] He suggests that the Brahmana had to keep himself aloof from the temporal universe of the king in order to substantiate his own claim to a spiritual transcendence. This transcendence is viewed as central to the maintenance of auspiciousness in the community.[21] Raheja describes the gift, *dana*, given to a Brahmana by a landed chief as transmitting the community's 'evil', or inauspiciousness to him, which the Brahmana then absorbs. This unique quality possessed by the Brahmana on account of his 'pure' status also obliges him to accept the gift, hence the inauspiciousness. The following argument aims to explore the different groups, both Brahmana and non-Brahmana, within the ritual èlite linked to the temple. Their multiplex status in the community was based on their relationship with the ruler and the temple, and was frequently expressed in forms of access to material resources.

Questions about the ethnic status of the different Brahmana communities of Orissa, their origin and customs, give rise to interesting insights regarding the heterogeneity of these groups. Such issues were examined by colonial administrators in an effort to successfully classify the various categories of Brahmanas within their own parameters of region and ethnicity. Thus, terms such as 'Aryan' and 'Dravidian', used as alternatives to each other, were applied by officials to demarcate the ethnic background of Brahmana communities. 'It is worthy of note . . . that among the Brahmins of Orissa unquestionable traces may be found of the totemistic beliefs which are common among the Dravidian and semi-Dravidian groups . . . they may be due to the adoption by immigrant Brahmins of Dravidian beliefs and observances or they may show that the Brahmins of Orissa are themselves Dravidian or have undergone a considerable infusion of Dravidian blood. . . .'[22] Such reports, which have been influential in formulating official perceptions of the social order, were centred on the apparent cultural continuum from 'non-Dravidian' to 'Dravidian'. The ritual status of the *sasana* Brahmanas as a privileged category in the temple realm, with a special significance in its landed networks, has thus not been adequately debated. These Brahmanas were almost hostile to the so-called 'Dravidian' practices such as wielding the plough, common among the Brahmanas of Koraput and other areas, called *Balaramagoshthins* owing to the symbolic link with the plough-wielding deity.[23]

According to Pfeffer, the earliest wave of Vedic Brahmanas are believed to have migrated from Kanyakubja in the north into Orissa at the behest of the legendary *cakravartin*, Yayati Kesari (the Kesaris preceded the Gangas in the eighth and ninth centuries, and had their capital at Bhubaneswar), and settled in the peripheral areas of his kingdom. At the turn of the second millennium, another wave of orthodox Brahmanas came in from *Madhyadesa* (roughly in central U.P.), and with greater material means and political will supporting them, helped to develop the administrative structures of the major temple centres, viz., Jajpur, Bhubaneswar, Puri and Konarka.[24] They were granted land that was termed '*sasana*' by the Kesaris and later, the Gangas, the term indicating a royal gift that also connoted an obligation, or duty on the part of the Brahmanas.[25]

The *sasana* Brahmanas laid out the patterns of ritual and sacrifice at the Puri temple. The term '*sasana*' itself meaning to administer, these Brahmanas controlled the complex redistributive system of the temple, involving both cultivators and artisans. Divided into a number of clans, the *sasana* Brahmanas took charge of the various temple duties and *sebas* and also established and elaborate police and spy network for the smooth functioning of temple ritual. The seat of their power was the *Mukti Mandapa*, in the temple compound a great hall with sixteen pillars, each representing a major *sasana*. Built at the spot where the foundation sacrifice of the temple was believed to have been performed, this was the forum where scriptures were discussed, disputes settled and the raja's policies critically evaluated by the Brahmanas. The *sasana* Brahmanas were an authoritative group whose power in arbitrating societal and ritual conflict designated them an alternative to the raja's authority.[26]

We will now examine a text by the name of '*Sasana Karanam*', or the 'Procedure for Establishing a *Sasana*', the manuscript of which was found in Keonjhar. This text elucidates the images of order that underlay the preparation and organization of a

Brahmana settlement.[27] It describes a '*grama*' as a habitation of '*Bipras*' (Brahmanas) along with their friends and relatives who are surrounded by learned persons. Thus, it refers to a closely coordinated, ritually élite community, the laying out of whose settlement, or *gramaprakaranam*, was to be the model for development.[28]

The first section of the manuscript deals with the laying out of the settlement, the *gramaprakaranam*. This was to be done in strict accordance with the principles of *vastu*, the linear division of the streets, the shape of the dwellings and the direction of the openings all corresponding to a canonized structural ideal, the *astavarga*.[29] Then people of different castes were to be settled in their properly designated zones. The construction of *sudra* dwellings was to be carried out on all sides of the settlement. Traders were to live in the south or western direction, potters in the east or west. The butcher's house was to be constructed in the west, and the fisherman's in the north-west. The oilman was allotted the southern direction and the flower seller, the north. The craftsman was to live in the south-east, the weaver in the south-west and the blacksmith in the east or west. A ditch was to be dug around the settlement and the 'people of lower caste' (untouchables) settled beyond that. A dwelling established at a *kona* (end of a direction) was not advised, as it encouraged the proliferation of the lower castes. Tanks, temples and trees were to be placed at auspicious points. Thus, the various social and economic categories were placed at appropriate positions vis-á-vis the central focus of the settlement, the Brahmanical dwellings.

The next part of the manuscript deals with the installation of the various deities, both in the village and in the individual homes. The centre of the village was to be dedicated to Brahma, Indra and Surya were to be installed in the east, Agni in the south-east and the Matrs and Yama in the south. The presence of the various deities in their appropriate directions was meant to enhance the auspiciousness and prosperity of the settlement, while an inappropriately placed deity could bring calamity upon the village.

The remaining portion of the text deals with the ritual of establishing the *sasana* by the *yajamana*, the donor, from the demarcation of the boundaries to the laying out of the various sections. The plot of land was ritually demarcated and sanctified by appointing and worshiping the deities of each section. The earth was then ploughed and sown with appropriate seeds, which were carefully germinated and allowed to fructify, for which cows were kept in enclosures in order to provide manure. The building of the homestead was preceded by the planting of auspicious objects, including jewels and gold, within the foundation. The donor would then offer the sanctified land as *sasana*.

Pfeffer has pointed out that this text was procured from Keonjhar, an area that has a greater habitation of the plough-bearing *Balaramagosthin* Brahmanas than Puri. Hence, there are likely to be differences in ritual and practical details between the process enumerated here and the event in the Puri region. However, the settlement pattern of the houses in the Puri *sasanas*, described by Pfeffer,[30] appear to be not too different from the one prescribed in the *Sasana Karanam*.[31] More importantly, the text offers us a flavour of the images of order inherent in the creation of a *sasana*. It continuously emphasizes the *ritual soundness* of the prescribed practice, the objective of the grant being to reaffirm order, happiness and prosperity in the kingdom and in the universe. The *sasana* then, is a ritual ideal, a microcosm of the universal ordered state. It is set in a structured code of practice and ritual, the perils of breaking which are also enumerated. The installation of appropriate deities, the settling of the different castes in appropriate zones and the demarcation and the fulfilment of the needs of each homestead, are equally significant. Thus, the *sasana* illustrates the blending of economic requirements, social taboos and ritual practice in a dynamic process of conflict and interaction.

Pierre Bourdieu, in his *Logic of Practice*,[32] discussed a traditional society as unfolding according to established structures, or habitus. Habitus reproduces past conditions for present and future action, creating a 'common sense world' where practice is in harmony with experience. This practice also allows for 'regulated improvisation', wherein discrepancies are subsumed by the internal coherence of the system. In the case of the *Sasana Karanam,* which seeks to create such an idealized structure, anticipated disharmonies, such as an inappropriately placed deity or caste member are dealt with internally through ritual or punishment.

Further, in his discussion of the Kabyle home, Bourdieu observes that each object, person, animal acquires a meaning and relevance through its relationships with others, which then categorizes it within the structure of the society. For instance, the dark lower part of the house is associated with dampness, feminity, the stables, cows, darkness, sleep, sexual intercourse, birth, etc. In the process of the creation of the *sasana*, the emphasis is again on the identification of objects in order to make sense of them, categorize them and then claim them for use. For example, the most important activities are the distribution of various sections, the demarcation of boundaries (vital for the successful ordering of the settlement), the proliferation of auspiciousness and the containment of inauspiciousness through these boundaries. The land was sanctified, thus *recognized*, claimed by the *yajamana* through the impregnation of the *garbha*, fructified, and then handed over as a precious, pulsing piece of the creative universe.

The process of land donation had, as its core, a chain of obligations and reciprocity. The donation was always a gift, never a payment for services. Jens Lerche, in his paper[33] on the *jajmani* system in coastal Orissa, has constructed a model for understanding the relationships of reciprocity between the Brahmanical élite and the landed aristocracy, the Khandaits. The Khandaits are a large, heterogenous group that claim descent from north Indian Ksatriya lineages at one level, and also have strong ties in the land as well as affiliations with the non-Hindu population of the region. As in the case of the Gujars that Raheja discussed, the dominance of the Khandaits was established through their giving of *dana* to the *purohit* at a ritual function. The *purohit* absorbed the inauspiciousness of the giver that was passed through the *dana*. In this case, the receiver was obliged to accept the gift and the giver had the right to give it. Hence, the ideological dominance of the donor was ritually enforced, but the ritual dominance of the Brahmana *purohit* and the unlimited purity of his status are also acknowledged.

Thus, the material privileges as well as the obligations of the Brahmanas were embedded within a system of general reciprocity. One such embedded obligation was the institution of *tanki* (literally token), a nominal payment made by Brahmana households of a *sasana* to the principal donee as a token of respect. This amount was collectively transferred to the raja, who then gave over the amount for the ritual expenses of the Jagannatha temple, where it was called '*Sataishazari*', or the 'estate of 27000' or the household fund (*kotha bhoga*) of the lord. The Brahmanas were obliged to make the token payment which reinforced their exalted status.[34] The fund was used for ritual expenses, in which context the 'purity' of its source was considered appropriate. The network of resource redistribution that involved the raja, the *sasana* Brahmanas and the temple involved the exchange of material wealth with status, and accorded the Brahmanas their own form of access to the temple realm.

However, there were situations when conflict arose between the elements of such status and resource networks, particularly the raja and the Brahmanas. Questions regarding the legitimacy of the rulers and their authority over the Brahmana ministers often arose to challenge the political order. The raja occasionally displayed his wrath against a recalcitrant *sasana* by withdrawing its privileges.[35] This indicates that the ruler could assert his ultimate authority over the land at the cost of the ritual status of the Brahmanas. The Brahmanas, on their part, displayed the power of their connections within the temple networks, as well as their resistance to interference in the temple realm by the rulers. We have seen that the Bhoi King Narasimhadeva was murdered through a conspiracy between a Brahmana priest and the Mughal *subahdar* in 1647 (see Chapter 1). Thus the powerful Brahmanas of Puri could successfully challenge the authority of the Gajapati, as well as uphold it.

The *Mukti Mandapa Sabha* of the *sasana* Brahmanas of Puri was a functioning organization for social arbitration until recent times. In order to illustrate the normative parameters of their authority as recently as the early decades of the twentieth century, it is relevant to examine some records of disputes arbitrated by this body.[36] Many of the cases were concerned with problems regarding marriage, viz., the remarriage of widows, the feasibility of inter-caste marriage, etc. One case described a person who had lived with a 'Kandha' (tribal) woman and now wished to 'rejoin' his own caste. The *Sabha* pronounced an act of expiation for him that involved the performance of a 'sesame sacrifice' (*tila yajna*), the uttering of the *gayatri mantra* forty thousand times, and the consumption of the five products of a cow, including the dung and urine.[37] Thus, the advice of the *Sabha* was sought in problems of social relationships, especially those concerning the integrity of the caste, status and family. These disputes appear to be distinct from some others, say, which were to be arbitrated by the raja. For instance, Case No. 7 of 1960 records a complaint by a Brahmana from Kalahandi who was physically abused and manhandled by an untouchable. The *Sabha* prescribed an act of expiation for the Brahmana, to mitigate the evil effect of his contact with the untouchable. However, they expressed their inability to deal with the untouchable, who, they said, must be appropriately punished by the raja. Thus, arbitration by the *Mukti Mandapa Sabha* served to regulate the day-to-day functioning of a social structure, which acknowledged the ritual expertise of the *sasana* Brahmanas.

The *sasana* Brahmanas of Puri were a unique group in the material and social hierarchy of the region. Linked to the temple through its landed networks, they possessed a ritually dominant status, a status that was contingent upon their expertise in functions of social regulation. Their status was upheld as well as challenged through these functions, notably by the raja, who was also their chief patron.

SEBA, *BHOGA* AND *PRASADA*: THE REDISTRIBUTIVE NETWORKS OF THE TEMPLE

The ritually dominant position of the *sasana* Brahmanas, as ritual experts in the temple sphere as well as in the regional cultural matrix, was distinct from the status and persona of the *sebayets*, the different categories of temple functionaries, whose status accrued directly from their performance of services for the deity. We may once again recall Lerche's model of the *jajmani* system, this time from the perspective of the service castes and the overlord, the *saanta–sebaka* relationship.[38] The service castes were permanently attached to the Khandait households in return for an annual maintenance or *bartana*, which was a grain payment. Drawing from and moving beyond this construction, at one level the *sebayets* performed material services in the temple for which they were accorded material wealth, land, etc. At another level, the temple services involved the acquisition of a particular status, honours and privileges for the servitors, in the extensive hierarchy of the temple. The deity-*sebayet* relationship was roughly similar to the *saanta-sebaka* relationship.

The temple was a like a large 'household', where a number of personnel performed their diverse tasks, and whose positions were ordered in relation to one another. The *sebayets* of the temple performed the ritual services (*seba-puja*) and were classified into different categories or *nijogas*. It is believed that Ganga Anangabhima had introduced the *chhatisa nijoga* or the thirty-six categories of service personnel. Later this term retained only a symbolic significance as the actual number of categories swelled to two hundred and fifty.[39] In a certain sense, the *sebayets* who received payment in cash or kind for their hereditary services were not unlike the service castes that were attached to the overlords in Lerche's model. However, the performance of *seba*, ritualized service for the deity, was a unique source of influence/power/status for the servitors, whose link with the deity was qualitatively different from the *saanta–sebaka* relationship.

The notion of *seba* involved a process of conversion, the transformation of material resources into status and privilege. This process ran parallel to the more obvious practice of the temple, the offering of *bhoga* to the deity, which was sanctified and converted to *prasada* and redistributed. In that sense the *seba* too was an offering by the *sebayets,* the remuneration for which was not the annual payment in land or kind, but the status accruing from their ritual position. The temple possessing a pan-regional significance, interaction with the deity was a source of power at temporal as well as cosmic levels for the *sebayets*.

It is interesting to note that these services were not strictly hereditary, but could be acquired, either on payment of money or by other means. Among the hand-written daily accounts of the temple maintained by the *Deula Karana,* I came across a number of instances of *sebas* or even fractions of *sebas* being bought from hereditary *sebayets*. For instance, one Krishna *Maharana* and Bisnu *Maharana* together purchased half a *seba* from Tali *Maharana* (*seba* unspecified) for two *batis* of land. In another instance, one Satrughna Mahapatra, who had no son, donated his *seba* to one Damodar Mahapatra who was to be honoured with *sadi* and *candana* by the raja.[40] Thus the transaction did not focus on alienability of the *seba,* which was incidental, but on the transference of status. The point of the transactions was not the commodification of temple services—the money value was not the significant factor—but the exchange of different types of resources. The transaction involved the redistribution of access to the deity through service: access included the accompanying honours, *sadi* and *candana*, which were conferred on the *sebayet*.

Often disputes arose regarding succession to a *seba*. One incident records that Madhu *Panda* who performed *seba* in the Sitala temple, died and his *seba* was taken over by Narsingh Subudhi and others. The raja ordered that the transfer of the *seba* be postponed as there was no valid evidence of succession. This indicates that the succession to a *seba* was a tangible right, similar to inheriting property. Temple service, along with its accompanying status and privileges, was viewed as a kind of wealth, succession to which was closely monitored by the raja. This also highlights the fact that the 'proper' performance of temple functions was in keeping with the moral and material order of society, the maintenance of which was the raja's responsibility.

There were diverse patterns of remuneration in the transference of *sebas*. In one instance, Rambha *Mahari* (a *devdasi*—temple dancer) was ordered by the raja to perform extra *sebas* during a particular festival for which she received two extra *sadis*. The extra honours conferred indicated a greater appreciation for the *mahari's* efforts on the part of the raja, for which her status was, at least temporarily, enhanced. The raja's authority in awarding the servitors their due honours was in keeping with his power to accord honour and privileges in his realm (see Chapter 1).

In another incident, Banamali *Muduli* bought half a *seba*, of which he sold another half, one-fourth of a *seba*, to another *sebayet*. This appears to indicate that it was not merely the acquisition of a service, but the capacity to redistribute it, albeit only a fractional amount, that accounted for an increase in status.

By disposing of a quarter *seba*, Banamali *Muduli* demonstrated his control over that fraction of a link with the deity. In one instance, the *seba* was transferred from a *sebayet* who had no issue to one Srikara Patnaik along with some property as maintenance, for which the latter paid a sum of money for the *Kotha Bhoga*, the raja's fund for temple maintenance. Thus we see that the raja negotiated the transfer of *sebas* on occasion in order to assert his authority over the question of deciding a suitable claimant for the service. At the same time, we observe that the *sebayets* also substantiated their claim to the services, in this case by donating to the raja's fund, which pressurized the raja to act in the particular *sebayet's* favour. Thus, different patterns underlay the transactions of service redistribution that operated through the multi-layered channels of reciprocity and communication between the various participators in the temple processes.

Temple *sebas* involved transactions of status and resources within the temple sphere. While this connoted a greater proximity with the deity, it also limited the *sebayet* hierarchy and their ritual activity to the temple's physical precincts. There were other, more indirect channels of communication that linked the temple with extra-regional ritual trends and social processes. *Mathas* were one such medium for the channelization of material wealth and ritual status to and from the temple, linking it with a country-wide network of pilgrims, *sebayets* and resources. These corporate organizations had an institutionalized access to the temple's hierarchy of *sebas*, along with roots of authority in its landed property. The notion of *seba* operated in a different dimension in the context of these institutions.

Mathas were monastic establishments representing different *sampradayas*, or sects, that were situated in Puri or in the vicinity of the temple. The *mathas* originally imparted education to lay people as well as monastic novices, many of whom became sebayets in the temple. In fact, till recently, the *Parichchas* of the temple were educated at the Sankaracharya *Matha*, an influential and well-endowed establishment. The *mathas* housed itinerant *sadhus*, pilgrims and even beggars, providing free boarding and lodging. They were centres of learning and debate, where ideas and knowledge from different parts of the country converged. They were fairly cosmopolitan establishments as neither the *mahants* nor the inhabitants were necessarily local. They were well-endowed with property by their followers, much of which, was dedicated to Jagannatha and given over to the *matha* to manage. These were the *amrita manohi* lands, as they were literally meant to provide the *bhoga* (food) for specific occasions.

The *mathas*, thus were closely connected with the regular *pujas* and *sebas* by providing *bhoga* and services by the *mahants*, for which they were granted ritual privileges. For instance, the *mahant* of the Suna Gosain *Matha*, an ancient thirteenth-century establishment, still performs the *Phool Seba* each day and the *Srimukha Sringar* at the time of the *ratha jatra*.[41] Thus the *mathas* were powerful media for the inflow and redistribution of material resources, ideas and influences. Through continuous flows of *bhoga* and *prasada* the *mathas* provided the temple with a material and ideological network that reinforced its ties with the land, and spread its influence outwards well beyond regional boundaries. Each *matha* having a number of branches in other centres of pilgrimage,[42] there were constant streams of travelling monks and *mahants* between these centres, carrying with them *mahaprasada* and the influence of the Puri deities.

Through these links, other interests, such as those of different sects, also entered the temple sphere and created influence groups. The *Mukti Mandapa Sabha*, apart from the *sasana* Brahmanas, also included influential *mahants* such as that of the Sankaracarya *matha*. From the sixteenth century, the *Gaudiya* sect of Caitanya acquired considerable authority in the temple sphere, especially since the Gajapati Prataparudradeva himself became a follower of the Bhakti saint.[43] This also led to conflict, as the continuing tension between the Utkaliya Brahmanas (including, prominently, the *sasana* Brahmanas), and the *Gaudiya sadhus*, who were adherents to Caitanya's teachings and had a lot of popular support, illustrates.

The *matha*, then, lay at a peculiar point of convergence of ideology and material resources, where the food went into the temple as *bhoga*, along with the influence of the *sampradaya*, and emerged as *prasada*, to be redistributed along with the authority of Jagannatha. It is pertinent to reiterate that *mathas* and their *mahants*, especially those of the larger houses, were powerful institutions and people, controlling vast resources. The key concept here is control, not ownership, of the property. The land was granted to the *matha* 'in perpetuity', and the *mahants* had full authority over its usage. The Bhubaneswar inscription of Ganga Narasimha in 1396[44] indicates a transaction between a *mahant* of Sidhesvara *Matha* and a local wealthy man, wherein twelve *batis* (units of land) of *matha* land were mortgaged in return for 150 *madhas* or gold coins. The *mahants* clearly had the authority to make decisions regarding the alienation of the land as well.

The *mathas* were corporate institutions with their own hierarchies of management. However, they were not independent of the authority of the Gajapati, who supervised the performance of their duties as *sebayets*, as well as legitimized their functioning within their establishments. At the appointment of each *mahant*, during *abhiseka*, the raja sent *sadi* and *candana*, both to validate the incumbent's position as well as express his own authority over all institutions within his realm. During a meeting with the *mahant* of Papudia *Matha*, I was shown a *sanad* awarded by Rani Suryamani Pattamahadei, the dowager queen of Puri, in 1885 to a previous *mahant*, Jagannatha Das. The Rani granted the *mahant* the honour of performing *caamara seba* (fanning service) at the sanctum. Thus, the *mahants* were recognized as dignitaries by the raja, and awarded privileges commensurate with their position. The significance of *mathas* in the temple's redistributive networks was obviously appreciated by the raja, while their functioning was checked and monitored by him as well.

The channels of material and ideological exchange that converged on the temple, linked the hierarchy of temple personnel in an internal dynamic interaction. This dynamism also absorbed inflows of resources and ideologies from extra-regional trends and processes through linking institutions, such as the *mathas*. Through such channels, there was continuous interaction between the various groups, and the negotiation of status through such interaction. In the next section, I shall examine the manner in which the temple status accorded to a particular group of *sebayets* deviated from their 'given' status in the social hierarchy, and highlighted the space that was created through ritual service, for the expression of alternative status structures.

A discussion of such patterns of reciprocity involving material goods as well as values is incomplete without reference to the *Daitas*, a phenomenon unique to the Jagannatha cult. We have seen that through institutions like the *sasanas*, a Brahmanical élite was associated with the temple, imbuing it with the authority of ritual expertise, while deriving a high status and landed wealth from it. The *mathas*, too, reinforced the temple's rights in the land, but played a greater role in projecting its influence outwards. The notion of status was closely tied in with the performance of *seba* and ritual and underlay the functioning of the priests. Eschmann et al., have extensively discussed the tribal influence in the origin and worship of Jagannatha[45] especially the iconographic similarity to various village tutelary deities, viz., Stambhesvari, Maninagesvari, etc. I wish to examine a popular myth relating the autochthonous origin of Jagannatha in an effort to identify patterns of interaction between the *Daitas* and Brahmanical priests in the temple.

The story of Nilamadhava, the tribal deity of whom Jagannatha is believed to be an incarnation and his original devotees, the *Savaras,* has been related in several texts.[46] For the purpose of this analysis I have examined the version depicted in the *Deula Tola*, a text describing the story of the building of the temple at Puri.[47] The story delineates the context for the unique status of the *Daitas*, a group of non-Brahmanical priests believed to have been of tribal origin.[48] The pervasive presence of a tribal, hence low-caste (tribals were related with untouchables in the Hindu caste structure) group in a ritual hierarchy dominated by Brahmanical mores and caste rules, as well as their distinct niche in the landed hierarchy of the temple, is a phenomenon unique to the Jagannatha cult. Through an examination of the factors underlying their presence in the temple structure, I have attempted to explore the manner in which alternative structures and groups voicing dissent against the dominant ideologies negotiated their position in the redistributive networks of the land.

The *Deula Tola* opens with an invocation to Lord Jagannatha, the 'one who moves (*bihari*) in the Blue Mountain (*Niladri*).'[49] It describes the manner in which king Indradyumna, who was a devotee of Lord Visnu, sent his messengers in the four directions 'to find out the place where Visnu was available.'[50] The 'Pati

Brahmana'[51] who went towards the east, entered the village of the *Savaras* (Savarapalli). There he met a girl, Lalitakumari, whom he informed that he was roaming the forest in search of food.[52]

When the *Savara* chief, who had been away in the forest, returned, he offered the Brahmana food and hospitality. A few days later, he asked the Brahmana to marry his daughter, Lalitakumari. When the Brahmana pointed out that 'you are a *Savara* by community', thereby not suitable for a Brahmana, the *Savara* chief was enraged and threatened to kill him. He narrated the manner in which his 'ancestor killed Jagannatha in one arrow.'[53] The Brahmana promised to marry Lalitakumari if the *Savara* chief told him how this had happened.[54]

The *Savara* said that generations ago, when the Mahabharata war was recently over, Lord Narayana (Krishna) was reclining on a swing made from the *siali* creeper, when the *Savara's* 'father' (ancestor), mistaking his foot for the mouth of a deer, shot at it with an arrow. Realizing that he had injured Krishna, the hunter ran to Arjuna the Pandava and brought him to the lord's side, where Krishna breathed his last. Attempts to cremate his body being unsuccessful, the gods advised the Pandavas to float the body in the ocean, as it was destined to be later worshiped as the *Daru Brahma*, the holy log.

After hearing this account, the Brahmana married Lalitakumari who subsequently became pregnant.[55] The Brahmana gradually became aware that the *Savara* chief went out every night and returned, smelling of '*karpura* and *candana*', camphor and sandalwood, which indicated his performance of ritual worship. Through his wife, the Brahmana contrived to question his father-in-law about his activities. The *Savara* was furious with his daughter for obliging him to disclose his secret, and reluctantly allowed the Brahmana to accompany him, provided he went blindfolded so that he would not know the way. Lalita gave her husband some oilseeds which he dropped along the path as he was led blindfolded. When the Brahmana beheld the deity, he was overcome with rapture. That day the lord refused the offering of *kandamula* (fruit and roots) that the *Savara* placed before him. On being questioned by the anguished devotee, the lord replied that the time had come for him to leave his forest abode and appear in a temple (*deula*) in a wooden image (*daru rupa*). 'Your worship ends now and his (the king's) will now be carried on.'

After the Brahmana and *Savara* returned, the former began to stay increasingly preoccupied and pensive. He informed his wife that he was missing his relatives and desired to meet them. At this point, Lalitakumari revealed that she was aware that he was a messenger (*duta*) of king Indradyumna and that he had contrived to gain access to Jagannatha by befriending the *Savaras*. She agreed to help him since she had been an *apsara* (celestial dancer) in her previous birth, who had appeared in human form in order to make Jagannatha accessible to the world. With her support, the Brahmana returned to his king.

Indradyumna was overjoyed at learning the whereabouts of his deity, and immediately cleared the forest preparatory to marching to *Niladriparvata*, where the deity's shrine was located. Performing all the requisite oblations and pilgrimages at the shrines along the way, the king reached, '*Sri Nilakandara*', the auspicious cave. At this point, he suddenly became intoxicated with pride at his achievement in having gained access to the deity, and the lord vanished. The Brahmana *duta* (Vidyapati) suggested that the *Savara* chief may have hidden the deity, and pointed out the tribal village where he lived. The enraged king surrounded the village with his soldiers and captured the chief. The distressed *Savara* prayed to the lord for help, and Jagannatha appeared to the king in a vision, admonishing him for tormenting 'my *Savara*'.[56] He advised the king to build a temple for him on the *Niladri* hill. The raja immediately released the *Savara* and did as ordered.

A number of varying issues and trends emerge from this account of the first section of the *Deula Tola*. The focus of the connection between the deity and the forest-dwelling *Savaras* is intimacy, depicted through physical proximity. The means to gain access to this intimate link was viewed as an equally close relationship, symbolized by the Brahmana's marriage with Lalita which led to his discovery of the deity's whereabouts. When the Brahmana had been initially questioned by Lalita regarding the reason for his visit, he had said that he was roaming the forest in search of food. Here, the twin metaphors of food and sexual intercourse, symbols of intimacy epitomized by the bond of marriage, recur in the account of the *Savaras*' link with the deity.

In another version of this legend authored by Saraladasa, a fifteenth century poet of Tribal origin, Jagannatha was worshiped by the *Savaras* as *Sabari Narayana* (Narayana of the *Savaras*), who was married to a tribal woman, Sriya, who used to cook for him his favourite food, burnt cakes (*poda pitha*, one of the most popular items of the *mahaprasada*) and meat.[57] The intimacy of the bond between the 'simple' forest dwellers[58] and the deity, presents an alternative image of devotion and worship to that represented by Brahmanical ritual and social structures. The deity's origin amongst the forest-dwellers is like a nostalgic memory of a simple past in the face of a more complex and sophisticated present.

Interestingly, the death of Krishna leading to his reincarnation as the holy log (*daru brahma*), is also attributed to the tribal hunter, Jara. The linkages of food and sex are further reinforced through the link of death, wherein the deity is killed (or sacrificed) by the hunter in order that the deity be transformed into the supremely accessible image of Jagannatha, the lord of the world. Moreover, when the tribals 'lose' their deity to the king, there is also a sense of retribution for the 'sin' committed by their ancestor, Jara, by killing Krishna, although the course of events is depicted as preordained.

The notion of the events being preordained is interspersed with the existence of a strategy on the part of the king and his messenger. The Brahmana's marriage to the *Savara* woman and the means by which he gained access to the tribal deity, was carried out primarily to fulfil the king's ambition of worshipping the rare form of Visnu. Yet when the Brahmana lied to his wife about his desire to visit his relatives, she countered his deception by revealing that she was aware of his status as the king's messenger and of his plan to acquire the deity. Thus, all the tribals were not innocent participators in their own betrayal—there is a sense of awareness of the treachery underlying royal strategy to gain control over their customs.

This notion of treachery is greatly magnified in Saraladasa's version, wherein Brahmana/Vidyapati is depicted as having seduced the tribal chief's daughter and with her assistance, having contrived to worship Lord Nilamadhava. Further, the king's fury at the deity having vanished led to his slaughtering the entire tribal settlement, save the chief. There is sympathy for the tribals in this account—they are viewed as bewildered victims of a king's ambition. The closeness of their bond with the deity was voiced by Jagannatha himself, who appeared to the king in a dream and cursed him for killing his 'kinsmen'. The treachery and violence of the king and his messenger is set in contrast to the innocence and devotion of the *Savaras*.

The theme of the *Savaras* being the kinsmen of the deity is a pervasive one in temple ritual and cosmology. According to Saraladasa's account, lord Krishna promised the hunter Jara, that he would be his kinsman in another incarnation, following which he appeared as Nilamadhava/Jagannatha. The notion of kinship as establishing the *Daitas*' unique status in the temple hierarchy, is an alternative to the dominant pattern of status relations in this realm, which are usually based on caste, landed or ritual position. The *Daitas* represented the accommodation of kin-based tribal social relations within the parameters of a caste-based Brahmanical ritual structure. This process of accommodation maintained the *Daitas*' distinct status as a separate category of personnel.

The *Daitas* occupy a separate category in the *Chhatisa Nijoga*, the thirty-six categories of temple functionaries. The *Jagannatha Sthalavrttantam* records a grant of six *batis* of land to ' . . . a *Savara* servant of Jagannatha, Ugrasena *Daita*'. They have their own niche in the redistributive networks of the temple, being endowed with land and wealth and possessing a status commensurate with their ritual services. During the *Nava-kalevara*, the ceremony of rejuvenation, when the images are renewed, they perform a unique service that is indicative of their position as the deity's kinsmen.[59] Their intimate relationship with the deity is highlighted by the fact that when the old images are buried, they shave their heads and perform the *shradha*, as if mourning for a dead relative. They are responsible for transferring the mysterious *brahmapadartha*, the divine essence, from the old images to the new ones. At the time of the annual *ratha jatra,* they take away the images to the *anasara tati*, or the 'relatives hut', similar in design, according to Eschmann, to the altar houses found in tribal villages.[60] The 'return' of Jagannatha to his kinsmen, the *Savaras*, is marked by the discontinuation of the Brahmanical ritual and *mahaprasada*, only fruit and berries being offered as *bhoga.*[61]

In the eighteenth century, we observe an increased interaction between tribal groups and caste Hindu society. Tribal leaders were converted to tribute-payers by the Marathas and other inter-regional powers, who also initiated large-scale recruitment of labour from these groups.[62] Tribal areas that were 'opened up' to the economic mainstream of caste-based agrarian society saw the imposition of social bondage on the tribal people and their entry into the caste hierarchy at a low level. Systems of inter-caste dependence that ensured tribal bondage to caste Hindu society were maintained through a network of economic and religious rights and obligations.[63] I have discussed, for instance, the manner in which the raja of Keonjhar secured the service and tribute of the *Bhuiyans* and *Juangs* by associating them with temple service (see Chapter 1).

In Orissa, there has been a greater proximity between tribals and caste-based society as compared to other parts of the country, although separate cultural identities have been maintained by both. F.G. Bailey, in his study of a *Kondh* village in Orissa[64] informs us that according to a *Kondh* legend, for 'nine centuries' (a metaphorical expression indicating a long time) the *Kondhs* of Baderi remained a tribe and did not become a caste. They were 'protected' by various factors, such as their remoteness from the political and cultural mainstream. However, with the advent of colonial rule, the policies of 'reform' which led to the Meriah wars[65] introduced the subjection of the *Kondhs* to the Oriya *tehsildars*, middlemen of the rajas and the colonial rulers.

Traditionally, however, high-caste Oriyas regarded the tribes as dependent allies, more different than inferior. The defeat of tribal chieftains by Hindu rajas was a common motif in the legends surrounding the founding of new states, as we have seen with the state of Dhenkanal earlier.

The tribal people, too, did not fully accept caste Hindu dominance. Through numerous myths and legends illustrating the theme, they regarded them selves as originally on par with caste-based society, as warriors who were displaced through treachery. The tribes paid tribute to the Hindu rulers, but could easily withdraw their allegiance, and considered themselves essentially independent. This notion is echoed in Saraladasa's retelling of the Indradyumna legend where the tribes were subdued through treachery, but not obliterated, and their cultural identity as a separate group survives within the temple sphere.

Thus we see that the temple was an arena for the enactment and resolution of social conflicts, where status and ritual identities were created as channels for mobilization of divergent groups. The links of reciprocity between the raja, different social groups and institutions like the *mathas* were focused on the temple. At the core of these relationships lay the notion of access, especially access to the deity, a focal point in relation to whom all positions and hierarchies were structured. We have seen that the ritual intimacy of the *Daitas* with the deity accorded them a ritual status on par with most Brahmanical priests. Thus the temple sphere had its own hierarchy of status, with space for circumventing dominant norms.

RATHA JATRA

> The Brahmins at certain times carry the image (of the deities) in procession upon a carriage of sixteen wheels . . . and they believe that whoever assists in drawing it along obtains remission for all his sins.[66]

In this section, I wish to explore the *ratha jatra*, one of the thirteen annual festivals of Jagannatha and the one that is most significant. The festival, involving months of preparatory activity and subsuming numerous smaller-scale ceremonies and events, provided a space for social and ritual structures to interact. The raja, the Brahmanas, the *Daitas*, the *mathas* and other institutions, played their roles in the event through which they also negotiated their own status in the temple realm. With the carefully orchestrated ritual providing a backdrop, voices of dissent against dominant norms struggled to make themselves heard. This event also became an occasion for spaces to be created to express alternative forms of authority. Ritually it was a powerful and dangerous time, a moment symbolizing the enactment and validation of all cosmic and creative processes. However, it was also a moment when those processes could be subverted or circumvented. I propose to explore this moment of anxiety, fervour and riotous abandonment that the *ratha jatra* represents, even today.

As a festive event of extra-regional significance, the *jatra* has been the subject of lengthy and colourful descriptions by foreign travelers and visitors. Through an examination of such impressions, I have attempted to extract the diverse notions of order and authority and the structures of cultural dominance and subordination that formed these perceptions. It is pertinent to observe, however, that these accounts did not emerge from a cultural vacuum. They represented varied interests and motivations which became particularly relevant at a later date, during the crystallization of a colonial discourse in the region.

My exploration of the *ratha jatra* is primarily through the lens of the different impressions recorded by various writers. Hence, I have emphasized those aspects that create the most prominent impressions, the lush visual imagery, the mass participation of the public. I have not dwelt on an analysis of ritual or of the particular roles played by different social categories. It is my intention to experience the festival through accounts of the different sensations that it evoked in the minds of witnesses. The context of these accounts will be examined in a subsequent chapter.

The festival begins with the *Devasnana jatra* on the full moon day of *Jyestha* (May-June), when the deities are bathed with one hundred and eight pitchers of water. This is followed by the period of *Anasara*, when the deities are 'hidden' from the public for fifteen days and the images are repaired for their glorious presentation during the *ratha jatra*. The *Niti* of the temple describes the primary ceremonies of the *jatra* thus:

> On the morning of the second day of the bright fortnight of Asadha, after completion of pakhala puja—Thakura (raja) comes from his palace, recites prayers, offers puspanjali to the Deities and prays for permission . . . supatis are spread . . . the Badathakura, Subhadradevi and lastly, Paramesvara are carried in pahandi at the same time around the ratha and placed on Patatuli. Then, three dayena garlands . . . are offered. . . . The yatra bhoga is offered in Sodasa Upacara with sounds of madala, mahuri, ghanta and waving of chhatra and chamara. After performance of customary seva on the ratha, thakura [raja] receives the prasada from the body of the deity. Similarly after finishing chherapahara of Nandighosa . . . then thakura places pata muchula on his head and pushes the Taladhvaja ratha from behind. The Ratha Yatra starts. When rathas move, Chherapahara of the space in front is done and chandan water is sprinkled. Plantain trees are planted on two sides of the danda and jars filled with water are placed . . . gates of mango trees are made and rain of flowers is above. The prostitutes sing songs and dance. Various musical instruments are played upon.[67]

The *ratha jatra* was a part of temple ritual and performed regularly since before the advent of the Gangas into this region. The *Anargharaghava Nataka* of Murari Mishra refers to the 'yatra' of the god Purusottama in the tenth and eleventh centuries, before the construction of the present temple.[68] After Jagannatha was declared the state deity by Ganga Anangabhima in the thirteenth century, the festival acquired an increased significance. There is sculptural evidence from the thirteenth and fourteenth centuries, of a temple car built like a chariot bearing a deity at a temple near Dhanmandal in Cuttack district.[69]

The *jatra* itself commences on the second day of the bright half of the month of *Asadha* (July–August) and lasts for about nine days. It is preceded by a ritual cleansing of the deities, the *snana jatra*, and every twelve years or so, the old images are discarded and new ones installed at the *Navakalevara*, held just prior to the *ratha jatra*. In that sense, there is an internal ritual rejuvenation of the deities, primarily for the purpose of *darsana*. The crux of the event is the public display of the images, when the gods themselves emerge from their sanctum and make themselves physically accessible to the people. The notion of making contact with the divine images through *darsana* and even physical touch is central to the multitude of pilgrim devotees. Caitanya, Jagannatha Dasa and other Bhakti saints and poets, have been described as rushing to embrace the deity in a fervour of devotion.[70]

The theme of contact between the deity and thousands of assembled devotees is a powerful undercurrent in all descriptions of the event. A number of writers and travellers over the past five centuries have recorded their impressions of the festival. François Bernier writes in the sixteenth century:

> . . . at this festival is collected an incredible concourse of people . . . a superb wooden machine is constructed . . . with I know not how many grotesque figures nearly resembling our monsters . . . satyrs, apes and devils. This machine is set on 14 or 16 wheels like a gun carriage and drawn or pushed along by . . . fifty or sixty persons. . . . The first day on which this idol is formally exhibited in the temple, the crowd is so immense and the press so violent that some of the pilgrims . . . in consequence of their long journey are squeezed to death. The surrounding throng gives them a thousand benedictions and considers them highly fortunate to die on such a holy occasion . . . and while the

chariot of hellish triumph pursues its solemn march, persons are found . . . so blindly credulous . . . as to throw themselves on the ground in the way of its ponderous wheels which pass over and crush to atoms the bodies of the wretched fanatics. . . .[71]

A detailed description of the power of mass emotion, a collective expression of fervour and the desire for sheer physical contact with the deity on the part of the devotees, is contained in the account of Andrew Stirling, Persian Secretary to the East India Company Government in 1820:

On the appointed day, after various prayers and ceremonies have been performed within the temple, the four images are brought from their thrones to the outside of the Lion Gate—not with decency and reverence, seated on a litter or vehicle adapted to such an occasion—but a common cord being fastened around their necks, certain priests to whom the duty appertains, drag them down the steps and through the mud, while others keep their figures erect and help their movements by shoving them from behind, in the most indifferent and unceremonious manner, as if they thought the whole business a joke! In this way, the monstrous images go rocking and pitching through the crowd, until they reach the cars. . . . On the other hand, a powerful sentiment of religious enthusiasm pervades the admiring multitude of pilgrims assembled without when the images first make their appearance through the gate. They welcome them with the loudest shouts of joyful recognition and stunning cries of Jye Jagannath, victory to Jagannath; and when the monster Jagannatha himself, the most hideous of all the figures, is dragged forth the last in order, the air is rent with plaudits and acclamations. . . . After the images have been lodged in their vehicles, a box is brought forth containing the golden . . . feet, hands and ears of the Great Idol which are fixed on the proper parts with due ceremony . . . thus equipped and decorated, it is worshipped with much pomp and state by the Raja of Khurda, who performs . . . the ceremony of the Chandalo, or sweeping, with a richly ornamanted broom. At about this period . . . bands of villagers enter the crowd dancing and shouting . . . each carrying in his hand the branch of a tree. They are the inhabitants of the neighbouring Pergunnahs . . . called Galabetiahs, whose peculiar duty and privilege it is . . . to drag the Raths. . . . At each pause, the Dytas or charioteers of the god advance forward . . . with wands in their hands, throwing themselves into a variety of wild and frantic postures, address some fable or . . . jokes to the multitude . . . often their speeches and actions (are) grossly and indescribably indecent and obscene![72]

The *pahandi*, when the images were brought out to be placed in the chariots amidst deafening outcry and were pushed, 'shoved' and jostled by the fervent crowd, is vividly described by Stirling. The significance of contact, epitomized by physical touch, is pre-eminent at this time. The moment of *darsana*, the revelation of the deity, is an epiphany of sensations from the first sight to the physical touching. The power and divinity of Jagannatha is transmitted to the devotees through sensation and is amplified through their participation. On the other hand, the roughness with which the deities were 'shoved', the 'wild and frantic' gestures made by the *Daitas* waving their phallic wands, and the 'grossly . . . obscene' jokes indicate a powerful infusion of grotesquery into the charged situation. William F.B. Laurie, representing evangelical interests in India in the early nineteenth century, cuttingly denigrates the event:

> . . . the entire scene of the Ruth Jatra savours, to an incredible extent, of the ludicrous, the barbarous and the awful. The eager expectation, the unceasing din of a great multitude, the acclamations of 'Victory to Jagannath!' which rend the ear when the images are brought forth, or rather, *rolled* forth, by means of iron handles fastened in their backs, and exposed to the stupid gaze of the delighted people. . . . The ponderous machines are set in motion, they creak while the creatures strain the cables in the midst of their joy and madness. Then they are 'All around, behind, before, with frantic shout and deafening roar; and the double, double peals of the drum are there and the startling bursts of the trumpet's blare; and the gong that seems, with its thunderss dread to astound the living and waken the dead.'[73]

Laurie's description of the festive fervour of the event as 'ludicrous' and 'barbaric' recalls the grotesque images of carnivals in post-Renaissance Europe, conceptions of which appear to have influenced his account.[74] Impressions of noise, chaos and an underlying, uncontrolled violence indicate the collapse of established norms of behaviour. These are corroborated in the account of Thomas Bowrey, a seventeenth-century English traveller and trader. 'In the middle of that great Diabolical Chariot, is placed their great patron Jno. Gernaet, having the foremost hand open, fairly to be beheld by many of the people . . . but more than one half are pressed down by the crowd. . . . And which is the stranger and more incredible, many of them come a great many miles to end their days here, under the wheels of this ponderous, but, accounted by them, holy arke.'[75]

Death, either accidental or intentional, under the wheels of the *ratha*, was believed to deliver the devotees from the cycle of rebirth. This left a powerful impression upon witnesses, and was a recurring theme in most of the descriptions of the festival. Bakhtin has argued for a regenerative view of death as being an integral part of the grotesque. Indeed, he sees death as being 'pregnant', in that it gives rise to new forms. He views death and birth as a continuous process, celebrated in popular culture through grotesque images.[76] The deaths of pilgrims crushed under the chariot wheels during the *jatra* was viewed as a marvellous occurrence by the people, not as a dismal end to existence but as the doorway to a better existence. Thus death, in this particular context, was celebrated.

This celebration acquired grotesque dimensions through the popular expression of modes of behaviour that were not in accordance with established values. The grotesque is a transgressive mode, according to Bakhtin, hence its emphasis on the protruding organs, the mouth, the nose and the phallus, epitomized in caricature. The twin processes of transgression/transformation may be seen in the phallic imagery and uncontrollable, even violent fervour displayed by the devotees and the functionaries.

Impressions of the devotees' 'ludicrous' behaviour, the telling of 'obscene' jokes by the *Daitas*, also depicts elements of the carnivalesque. They imply the subversion of the dominant, or 'official' norms of behaviour, at the core of which lies laughter, or the mockery of authoritarian structures.[77] At another level, the simultaneous chanting of *mantras* and the bawdy shouting of obscene jokes, marks the convergence of ritually dominant symbols and popular, profane forms of expression. Mutually distinct linguistic and cultural forms come together and interact in a moment charged with tension. This was a time for the re-examination and reaffirmation of the moral and cosmic order. Distinct categories came together while maintaining their differences, their interaction implied that the existing relations between social categories may not remain so. This was the source of tension inherent in the festival.

The subversion of 'official' norms of behaviour in a ritual context has been viewed as an attempt by the lower strata of society to resist domination by higher groups and values.[78]

The expression of such resistance through ritual occasions, particularly at festivals, also contained them by setting limits to their enactment. The ritualized expression of transgressive behaviour at the *jatra* was in itself a means to restrain it, the ceremonial creating checks on its uninhibited display. Moreover, particular groups performed particular acts, for instance it was the *Daitas* who used obscene language, and the Brahmanas who chanted the mantras. The ritual thus contained behaviour within the parameters of social groups, each category performing activity that was 'appropriate' to its ritual function. Therein lies the difference between the *ratha jatra* and the Bakhtinian carnival.

However, the power of resistance to official norms made its presence felt, owing to its public expression. Indeed, the uninhibited sexual innuendo and incipient violence at the *ratha jatra* was not merely accepted by the crowds—it was celebrated as a part of social regeneration symbolized by the festival as a whole. The *jatra* was a time for the renegotiation of norms, its cyclical nature indicating a return to the past in order to structure the future. We may once again recall the Bakhtinian image of the constantly evolving grotesque body, continuously swallowing and regenerating itself.[79] In that sense, the role played by transgressive behaviour as a part of the celebrations, though ritualized, questioned established structures in the process of regenerating them.

The most prominent aspect of the festival was the lavish display of visual imagery. The event was literally a visual feast, and had impressed witnesses as such. The *Baharul Asrar*, the travelogue of Mahmud bin Amirwali Balkhi in 1626, provides a picturesque account:

> The car consisted of ten wheels, the circumference of each being 20 *zira*, the length of the chariot being 60 yards and the breadth being 50 yards. The height from the ground to the top would be more than 80 *arrah* (cubit). The idol known as Jagannath was installed at the top pedestal and the tower of the chariot was decorated with coloured silk. Nearly 500 devotees, including . . . Brahmans, Rajas and Zamindars from different parts of the country offered their services for making the procession ready. About 100 *kalabantas* and *natis* were engaged for reciting devotional songs to Hari and Govinda and when the procession moved, they also accompanied (them), singing and dancing all the way.[80]

The central focus of the *jatra* was the vision of the deities as they made themselves accessible to the public. This was an event of great power, compounded by its being the culmination of an arduous pilgrimage. The festival was thus territorially situated within a sacred space, the *Sankha Ksetra* (the area of the town in which the temple is situated is believed to be in the shape of a gigantic conch) a divine kingdom, as it were, and closely tied in with ideologies of kingship. This is illustrated by the pivotal role played in the ritual proceedings by the raja, traditionally the deity's representative (*rautta*), who possessed a unique and powerful persona owing to his participation in them. Kulke points out that the scene of the festival depicted in the Dhanmandal temple showed that the chariot was preceded and followed two *chhatras*, symbols of royal authority.[81] Such umbrellas are now used by the Gajapati when he comes to perform his *sebas* at the festival.

The crux of the link between the raja and the deity was the exclusive *chhera pahara*, the ritual sweeping, the Gajapati Maharaja *seba* par excellence. Formally established by Purusottamadeva in the late fifteenth century, the *seba* publicly affirmed the direct link of the raja with the deity, circumventing the authority of the priests. The *seba* also involves the raja pushing the cars after sweeping the road, signalling the start of the journey to the Gundica temple. This indicates the power of the Gajapati over the ritual functioning of the temple and the movement of the deity, a display of his authority over the Lord of the World. This is an interesting variation from the ubiquitous theme of the raja publicly deriving authority from the deity.

The particular *sebas* performed by the Gajapati as his unique privilege were a powerful media for the public dissemination of his authority. At this festive occasion, when divinity revealed itself before thronging crowds, the notions of power and royal status acquired a new dimension. Foucault has argued that the king was a visible and concrete embodiment of political power in a monarchic state.[82] The presence of the raja as a participator in the ceremonies, as a physical embodiment of his authority, was a demonstration of that power. The presence of thousands of devotees served to enhance the king's power in a process of affirmation that linked the people with the ruler. Foucault suggests that power was not simply seized, but was acquired or

NOTES

1. Raheja, *The Poison in the Gift*, 1988, pp. 18-19.
2. Kulke, 'Royal Temple Policy', pp. 125-55.
3. S.C. De, *Descriptive Catalogue of the Copper Plate Inscriptions of Orissa*, Bhubaneswar: Superintendent, Research and Museum, 1961, pp. 1-23.
4. Kulke, 'Royal Temple Policy', pp. 125-38.
5. De, *A Descriptive Catalogue*, pp. 24-55. See also Kulke, 'Royal Temple Policy'.
6. See Introduction. Also see H. von Stietencron 'The Advent of Visnuism in Orissa: An Outline of its History according to Archaeological and Epigraphical Sources from the Gupta period upto 1135 AD', in Eschmann et al., pp. 61-77.
7. De, *A Descriptive Catalogue*, pp. 1-25.
8. Korni Plates of Codagangadeva in Kulke, 'Royal Temple Policy' p. 134.
9. The *Chhatisa Nijoga* is the collective term used in the *Madala Panji* for the hierarchy of priests. The actual number of categories has, since then, grown far beyond the original thirty-six. Groeme's report on the internal management of the temple accounts for two hundred and fifty categories in 1806, whereas the current Record of Rights reports one hundred and nineteen categories, as certain *sebas* have been discontinued. The presence of non-Brahmanical priests within the ritual hierarchy of the temple illustrates the acknowledgement of different social segments of the populace within the parameters of the temple and the cult. It was also a source of tension and a contest for power within the priestly hierarchy.
10. See Chapter 1. Anangabhima laid the foundation of the ritual link between the state and the Jagannatha cult through this declaration. He also called himself the *putra* of Purusottama, Rudra and Durga represented in the three images at Puri. 'Draksharama Inscription', *South Indian Inscriptions*, vol. IV, no. 1329. See also Kulke, 'Early Royal Patronage of the Jagannatha Cult', in Eschmann et al., pp. 150-1.
11. *Rajabhoga Itihasa* of *Madala Panji*, ORP Ms. 49, p. 29.
12. For a description of this myth, see G.N. Dash, 'The Evolution of Priestly Power', in Eschmann et al., pp. 165-8.
13. See G.C. Tripathi, 'Navakalevara: The Unique Ceremony of the "Birth" and "Death" of the Lord of the World', in Eschmann et al., pp. 223-65.
14. A number of myths relate Jagannatha with his tribal origins through food habits and marital alliances, all expressions of intimacy. See, for instance the popular story of Sriya Candaluni, wherein Goddess

Lakshmi, is believed to have assumed the form of a tribal woman in order to validate the great significance of the tribal peoples in the worship of Jagannatha. R.P. Mohapatra, *Temple Legends of Orissa*, Bhubaneswar: Orissa Sahitya Akademi, p. 39 (hereafter *Temple Legends*).

15. Kulke, 'Jagannatha as State Deity', pp. 199-208.
16. Ibid.
17. R.P. Mohapatra, *Temple Legends,* pp. 30-5.
18. See Bishnu Mohapatra, 'Ways of Belonging: The Kanchi Kaveri Legend and the Construction of Oriya Identity', in *Studies in History,* 12, 2, 1996, pp. 203-21 (hereafter 'Kanchi Kaveri').
19. The different versions of the legend beginning with the sixteenth century poem by Purusottama Das have been examined by Mohapatra, who suggests that the flood of literature pertaining to this tradition in the late nineteenth and early twentieth century indicates the coalescence of an ethnic identity in Orissa in this period. The legend became a potent symbol of an Oriya consciousness at a time when the regional community was threatened by ethnic and linguistic racism, particularly the imposition of the Bengali language in Oriya schools. This trend later fed into the politics of nationalism, becoming synonymous with 'Oriya' glory. Mohapatra, 'Kanchi Kaveri'.
20. J.C. Heesterman, *The Broken World of Sacrifice*, Chicago: University of Chicago Press, 1993, p. 5.
21. Raheja, *The Poison*, pp. 25-34.
22. S.L. Maddox, 'Final Report on the Survey and Settlement of the Province of Orissa, 1890-1900', vol. I, Cuttack: Board of Revenue, p. 154.
23. See G. Pfeffer, 'Puri's Vedic Brahmins', in Eschmann et al., pp. 421-37 (hereafter 'Puri's Vedic Brahmins').
24. Ibid., p. 426.
25. Ibid., p. 423. The notion of the acceptance of the gift being an obligation, is in keeping with the argument that the Brahmana was obliged to accept *dana* in order to remove the community's inauspiciousness and ensure its well-being, as discussed.
26. It must be pointed out that the spheres of authority arbitrated by the *sasana* Brahmanas and the raja were usually distinct, with an internal logic of differentiation. The Brahmanas generally dealt with issues pertaining to the transgression of ritual rules, particularly related to purity/pollution and caste conflicts. The raja arbitrated in problems of discipline, particularly among temple personnel, in keeping with his role in maintaining the temporal order. Our view is, of course dominated by the politically circumscribed status of the raja following colonial intervention.

However, it is probable that their jurisdictions may have clashed at times, the Brahmanas being authoritative enough to challenge the raja's judgement.

27. According to Pfeffer, this text illustrates the practices of an older group of Brahmanas, the *Balaramagosthins*, quite distinct from the Puri Brahmins. Pfeffer, 'Puri's Vedic Brahmins', p. 426.
28. *Sasana Karanam*, tr. Sri Upendra Dhal, ORP Ms. 689, Heidelberg: The Orissa Archive, South Asia Institute, pp. 1-2 (hereafter *Sasana Karanam*).
29. *Dhvajo dhumrasca simhasca / sva vrsa khara eva ca / gajo dhvamaksa tathaitani / bhagani kramaso vidhuh // Silpi Patha*, ORP Ms. 151, p. 24.
30. Pfeffer 'Puri's Vedic Brahmins', p. 424.
31. *Sasana Karanam*, pp. 5-8.
32. Bourdieu, 1990, pp. 270-83.
33. Lerche, 'Dominant Castes'.
34. Pfeffer, p. 429.
35. Ibid., p. 430.
36. Nirmal Kumar Bose (ed.), 'Data on Caste: Orissa', *Anthropological Survey of India*, Memoir no. 7, Calcutta, 1960, pp. 189-90 (hereafter 'Data on Caste').
37. 'Mukti Mandapa Sabha of Brahmins, Puri', in ibid., pp. 183-4.
38. Lerches.
39. 'The Report of Charles Groeme, Collector, Puri, regarding the establishment, customs etc. of the temple of Jugunnath, 10 June, 1806' (hereafter 'Groeme's report'), in Mukherjee, ed., *A Critical Study*, 1984, p. 42ff.
40. 'A collection of the daily accounts of the Jagannatha temple maintained by the *Deula Karana*, collected under the Orissa Research Project, Heidelberg' (hereafter 'Daily Accounts').
41. Personal conversation in the temple, December 1996.
42. Papudia *Matha*, a small seventeenth century establishment situated a few hundred feet from the *Simha Dwar* (the main gate) of the temple, had 254 branches all over the country. I was informed by the chief *mahant*, Sri Ramakrsna Das, that although many of these had broken away from the control of the main Puri branch, others had affiliated themselves with larger *mathas* in other places.
43. See Mukherjee, 'Caitanya in Orissa', in Eschmann et al., pp. 309-19.
44. *Epigraphia Indica*, 32, p. 229.
45. A. Eschmann, 'Hinduization of Tribal Deities in Orissa: the Sakta and Saiva Typology', in Eschmann et al., pp. 61-79.
46. See A. Eschmann, H. Kulke and G.C. Tripathi, 'The Formation of the Jagannatha Triad', in Eschmann et al., pp. 169-96.

47. *Puri Deula Tola*, composed by Krishnadasa, trans. M. Sharma Biswas, Cuttack: Prabhati Pustakalaya, ORP Ms. 663.
48. This link is now largely symbolic, the community from which the *Daitas* are selected being of mixed Karana (Kayastha) and Brahmana descent, settled in Puri. Their relationship with any of the current tribal communities of Orissa is negligible.
49. *Puri Deula Tola*, p. 1.
50. Ibid., p. 4.
51. A category of temple functionary who are believed to be half tribal and half Brahmana. In other versions of the story including the one described in the Skanda Purana, the messenger was named Vidyapati, who married the daughter of the tribal chief Visvavasu. The Pati Mahapatras or Pati Brahmanas are believed to have descended from this union.
52. The deliberate suppression of the true reason for his visit suggests that there was a strategy to 'acquire' the deity by the king/Pati Brahmana, through subterfuge if necessary. This is borne out later by the secrecy and treachery by which the Brahmana gains access to the deity and leaves the village to inform the king. The worship of the deity by the tribal chief was also cloaked in secrecy until the king arrived and took it over. The acquisition of Jagannatha by the king, therefore, involved the opening up of a 'secret' tradition, making it accessible to the people at large. This is a major factor that legitimizes the forcible taking over of the cult through accounts such as *Deula Tola*.
53. *Puri Deula Tola*, p. 5.
54. Here again, the Brahmana's condition for marrying the tribal woman in exchange for information about Jagannatha, illustrates the strategy that was required to gain access to the secret deity. The transgression of ritual marriage norms wherein it was considered polluting for a Brahmana to marry a tribal woman, was viewed as a price willingly paid by the loyal messenger. At another level, the entire story is about the intimate interaction between tribals and caste Hindu society, an interaction epitomized by the marriage of the ritually 'impure' tribal woman and the Brahmana. Ritual norms were thus circumvented in order to create alternative structures of social interaction at an intimate level, symbolized by marriage, represented in the unique rituals of the Jagannatha cult.
55. *Puri Deula Tola*, p. 8.
56. Ibid., p. 16.
57. This account, described in the *Vana Parva* of the Oriya *Mahabharata* composed by Saraladasa in the fifteenth century, presents a somewhat different perspective from the Puranic versions, including the *Deula Tola*. Saraladasa's account appears to be more

sympathetic towards tribal customs and people. This is partly explained by the fact that Saraladasa was himself of a low caste, being known as 'Sudramuni'. See A. Eschmnann, 'A Vaisnava Typology of Hinduization and the Origin of Jagannatha', in Eschmann et al., pp. 99-103.

58. Their 'simplicity' was emphasized through statements like 'I am a *Savara* of the forest. I do not know how to speak'. *Deula Tola*, p. 8 as well as the offering of fruit and roots to the deity by the *Savara*, indicating his simple devotion. These images also reinforce the oppositional nature of the two groups, the forest-dwellers and the Brahmana/king, by acknowledging the latter's greater sophistication and military authority.
59. Tripathi, in Eschmann et al., pp. 223-63.
60. A. Eschmann, 'Prototypes of the Navakalevara Ritual and their Relation to the Jagannatha Cult', in Eschmann et al., pp. 264-83.
61. Stietencron, p. 12.
62. Bayly, *The New Cambridge History of India* II I, Cambridge: Cambridge University Press, 1987, pp. 30–1.
63. Jan Breman, *Patronage and Exploitation*, New Delhi: Manohar, 1979.
64. F.G. Bailey, *Tribe, Caste and Nation: A Study of Political Activity and Political Change in Highland Orissa*, Manchester: Manchester University Press, 1960, p. 7 (hereafter *Tribe, Caste and Nation*).
65. Attempts by British administrators to eradicate allegedly barbaric practices, including human sacrifice, led to the systematic breaking up of the tribal ritual systems.
66. S.C. Mahapatra, *Car Festival of Lord Jagannatha Puri,* Puri: Sri Jagannatha Research Centre, 1994, p. 49 (hereafter *The Car Festival*).
67. ORP, Mss. 429, trans, S.C. De.
68. S.C. Mahapatra, *The Car Festival of Lord Jagannath Puri*, p. 46.
69. Ibid.
70. Mukherjee, 'Caitanya in Orissa', Eschmann et al., p. 311.
71. François Bernier, *Travels in the Moghul Empire AD 1656-1668,* New Delhi: Munshiram Manoharlal, 1983 (hereafter *Travels*).
72. Stirling, *Orissa,* pp. 135-40.
73. William F.B. Laurie, *Orissa, the Garden of Superstition and Idolatry*, London: Johnstone and Hunter, pp. 17-18 (hereafter *Garden of Superstition*).
74. See Simon Dentith, *Bakhtinian Thought: An Introductory Reader*, London: Routledge, 1995, pp. 225-53.
75. Sir Richard Carnac-Temple (ed.), *Thomas Bowrey: A Geographical Account of Countries Round the Bay of Bengal, 1669-1679.* Cambridge, 1905, p.16 (hereafter *A Geographical Account*).
76. Dentith, *Bakhtinian Thought*, pp. 68 ff.

77. Ibid., p. 71.
78. Dilip Menon, 'The Moral Community of the *Teyyattam*: Popular Culture in Late Colonial Malabar', *Studies in History*, 9, 2, pp. 187-217.
79. Dentith, *Bakhtinian Thought*, p. 244.
80. Quoted in S.C. Mahapatra, *The Car Festival of Lord Jagannath Puri*, pp. 50-1.
81. Kulke, 'Rathas and Rajas', pp. 69-70.
82. Foucault *Power/Knowledge*, pp. 78-108.
83. Dreyfus and Rabinow, eds., *Michel Foucault*, pp. 144-7.
84. See Chapter 1. See also Kulke, 'Rathas and Rajas'.

CHAPTER 3

Cultural Impressions: Early Constructs as Precursors to Colonial Policy

We have seen in the previous chapter that the Jagannatha temple and its related institutions were the subject of varied portrayals by numerous foreign travellers, traders, soldiers and administrators. The corpus of images relating to the *ratha jatra* that were portrayed in the various accounts, were a cultural resource that contributed to the construction of certain stereotypes regarding local institutions. I will now take up the accounts of certain European travellers of the sixteenth and seventeenth centuries and explore the context of their particular experiences, as well as their implications for policy formation in the colonial period.

Between the fifteenth and eighteenth centuries, there were large-scale social, economic and political changes in Europe that were chiefly instrumental in shaping policy and perceptions of Asia and the Orient. By the fifteenth century, the Italian city-state, a commercially and politically dominant entity in the Mediterranean, was losing ground. It was superseded in the sixteenth century by territorial nation states, rich in land and manpower, which could effectively maintain trained and paid armies.[1]

The establishment of the nation state was accompanied and augmented by a new dimension to the European élites' self-perception and their understanding of the world. Voyages of discovery undertaken to establish trading contacts brought amazingly large amounts of wealth and resources into Europe. They also brought a changed sense of what Louise Pratt has termed 'planetary consciousness', an awareness of their own self in relation to 'other' cultures, particularly those of Asia, Africa and the New World.[2] It is no coincidence that the sixteenth and seventeenth centuries saw a tremendous increase in scientific exploration that frequently accompanied commercial ventures in these regions, leading to large quantities of documentary material on the areas. Apart from facilitating the successful commercial exploitation of these lands and cultures, such documentation was viewed as increasing Europe's knowledge of other cultures. In the sixteenth and seventeenth centuries, knowledge, as an 'ordering apparatus', increasingly became a source of power, particularly for the urban élite in Europe. This benign form of domination, which authorized Europeans to reconstruct different societies according to their norms of order, later legitimized the political and economic penetration of such societies by European imperialism.

I have examined the travel writings of Thomas Bowrey, an English sailor, who visited Orissa and the surrounding region in the second half of the seventeenth century, and those of François Bernier, whose brief but influential account of Jagannatha Puri is a valuable impression of prevailing customs. While emerging from a cultural matrix with certain common dominant trends, the accounts offer distinct perspectives at many levels. While Bowrey, an English sailor and trader, concentrated on a description of the eastern coastal region, Bernier's perspective centred on the Mughal empire, and he viewed Orissa as a far-flung outpost of the empire. Bowrey's interest in and interaction with local commercial processes, personnel and products highlights his preoccupation with trading, whereas Bernier's points of reference are the local aristocracy and dominant institutions, including the Jagannatha temple. Both Bowrey and Bernier, however, in their writings, reflected the European ideals of order and authority in the context of which they viewed local society. I have also incorporated the views of other travellers whose experience of Orissa and Jagannatha contributed to the projection of the particular image of the land that was later inherited by colonial administrators.

In the first section of my argument I have examined the theme of Indian institutions being portrayed as having 'deviated' from a Eurocentric norm. European bourgeois ideals of property, the state and social institutions are reflected in the travellers' description of their experiences in this regard. In the second section, I have explored a deeper and more totalized penetration of local cultural forms by a dominant European ethnocentrism, not unlike the patriarchal subordination of the feminine. The 'feminization' of Indian society contributed to its image as subordinate and dependant, both perceptions that validated colonial political and economic expansion in the eighteenth and nineteenth centuries. The portrayal of the social, ritual and political institutions encountered by the travellers provided areas of reference for the formation of impressions about the subcontinent in Europe, so that they became linked within the realm of a literary or textual discourse.

Writing, or 'the making' of a text, is in itself an exercise in 'thick description'. What the sixteenth century European traveller in the Indian subcontinent was faced with, a multiplicity of conceptual structures, blended, overlapping, knotted together and even disparate, is not too different from the situation confronting the specialized modern ethnographer. His method of grasping the issues, of 'experiencing' the culture through his own 'otherness', was a type of fieldwork—'interviewing informants, observing rituals, eliciting kin terms, tracing property lines . . .'.[3] His account was an original cultural study, explicating the 'symbolic system'[4] to a foreign audience in a form that was intelligible to them and validating dominant ideologies of their economic and political environment.

This last notion itself generates questions that are seminal to our argument—namely, the role of the ethnographer/traveller and his method in decoding and recoding, to paraphrase James Clifford, the symbolic system. The image of the ethnographer is one of a 'trickster', one who does not lie but never tells the whole truth; who, while professing to 'speak for' his subjects, actually translates their realities within the parameters of his own motivations, prejudices and patronage.[5]

The descriptions focus on the institutions of status and resource distribution in Indian society, much of which was perceived by the Europeans as falling within the familiar category of 'religion'. The question of the relationships between power and status, kinship and caste, temporal authority and sacredness are of paramount importance to scholars today. The theory that the political and economic domains of Hindu life are largely encompassed by the religious, or the centrality of purity—pollution to status, as proposed by Dumont has been rejected by

Dirks. His perspective mediates between what he views as the artificially created discrepancy between the political and the religious, and goes on to explicate the ritual nature of kingship in pre-colonial India, and its centrality to social structure, especially with respect to ties in the land.[6] This argument also highlights the linkages between status and material resources, a hitherto problematic question.[7]

I would like to point out the limitations of a pan-Indian construct and stress the significance of regional variations with respect to my field. I have already discussed in detail the ritual nature of the Gajapati kingship as well as the significance of the temple and its priests in the processes of political formation in the region. I view both the Gajapati as well as the temple priests, especially the powerful *sasana* Brahmins, as vital nodes in a network of ritual, material and political linkages that energized the region. The question of centrality to this system, either for the raja or the priests, was subservient to the notion of status as accruing from a share in the network.

To return to the question of how European travellers confronted this complex reality that varied every few hundred miles, the earliest direct observers of Indian social systems, were the Portuguese. Bernard Cohn has argued that the account of Duarte Barbosa in the early sixteenth century emphasizes the centrality of the Brahmanas and the significance of ritual pollution with respect to the untouchables.[8] This view dominated much of Europe's understanding of Indian society for the next three centuries, and, I would add, even beyond. Cohn divides the debates over Indian society in the eighteenth and nineteenth centuries into two broad arguments, the perspective of the missionaries and that of the Orientalists. The latter constructed a view of Indian society that was derived from the *dharmasastras* and other Hindu classical texts, regarding them as an accurate and universally applicable representation of contemporary social reality. The missionary view, which developed slightly later, in the early nineteenth century, heaped venom on Hindu society and condemned all its institutions. However, the Orientalists and the missionaries, though ideologically disparate, were in accord over the fact that religious ideas and practices underlay all social structure, and the primacy of the Brahmanas in maintaining that structure. Both groups accepted the *varnasrama dharma* theory as central to Hindu cosmology.[9]

Kate Teltscher, in her detailed analysis of European writing on India in the seventeenth and eighteenth centuries, sees their depiction of Indian society as affirming their own images of order and authority. The descriptions of their forays into alien lands was meant to confirm the prestige and primacy of their home cultures. The world was to be mapped out, subordinated, in a manner of speaking, for the greater glory of England or France. The cultural differences that they encountered in their travels were portrayed as deviations from the norm, which inhered in their own cultures. I propose to examine the initial ethnocentrism of the early travellers before it hardened into colonial prejudice which infused administrative institutions in the nineteenth century.

It is out of such a cultural matrix that the European travellers, including John Bowrey and François Bernier emerged, and encountered India. Their perspectives, while possessing some similarities, are also distinct at many levels. While Bowrey typifies the English mercantilist sailor, Bernier's account reflects a more élitist perspective, his close interaction with the Indian aristocracy, and his interest in local political and sociological phenomena. Of the two, Bernier's description is the more introspective, considering multiple motives rather than deciding on simplistic explanations. The accounts can be examined at two different levels. First, they are interesting from a purely experiential perspective, for the vivid visual and physical images that they depict, for the flavour of a foreign culture that they present to their audience. Second, we may discern notions of order and state authority that underlie their accounts, that are derived from their perceptions of their home governments and societies. The European structure was the norm, from which India was a deviation. This was the case, partly because the accounts catered to the home audience with certain ideal values. Often, we see that the presentation of the 'other' crosses the limits of simple deviation, and the authors relish their descriptions of alien exotica, be it the local fauna or simply the 'fackeers'. In some cases, we see a shifting of the home ideal as the authors become more involved in their subject's complexities, and describe events in their own terms, not simply for home consumption.

WESTERN NORM, EASTERN DEVIANT

Bowrey's description of the region he designates 'Orixa' is enclosed within his account of the 'Choromandel Coast':

> The Kingdome is of noe great Extent, but is an indifferent pleasant Countrey, Subject to the Great Mogoll (Aurangzeb) for the most part but not altogeather [sic], by reason of Severall Radjas who (before the Mahometan conquest of the Hindus) possessed this Kingdome, some of which are not yet subdued and brought under the Moorish Yoke, but inhabit the Mountains and the woods, and some, yea, a Considerable part of the plaine land, more especially neare to Point Palmeris, the Entrance into the Bay of Bengala, where, for above 100 miles, the land is divided by Rivers and Rivulets into Islands, and thereby become invincible.[10]

Such a description inspires particular images of ordering and circumscription of the land and ecology, the state and the people. The 'Kingdome' of Orissa, at one level, was an officially designated *subah* of the Mughal government since 1590 (see Chapter 1). The division of what was mostly the Gajapati kingdom into *Mughalbandi* and *Gadajata* sub-regions by the Mughals, had already caused considerable territorial re-structuring. The extension of administrative authority over the coastal areas by the Mughals was frequently contested by the different rajas, as we have seen. Bowrey's description, however, gives a geographical and politico-ethnic unity to an officially imposed category.

The significance of an area being viewed as a 'region', a composite physical, social or politically integrated space, has multiple connotations, as shown in area-specific studies of different regions in India. For instance, Lodrick has examined the 'idea' of Rajasthan as comprising such a space, from various perspectives.[11] As an 'instituted region', such as a *subah*, it can be created at 'the stroke of a pen'. Some areas are denoted regions for purposes of organization and analysis by scholars and administrators alike. Both these categories are imposed, providing a perspective from outside the area, looking at and into it. Bowrey's description presents Orissa to a European state and reading public in a form that was intelligible to them, while also attempting to articulate the particular nature of his experiences. Thus, we have a 'kingdome': a circumscribed, integrated geopolitical entity, which is 'of noe great extent', indicating that it was well within the Europeans' capacity to understand and appropriate. Bowrey's travels were primarily to establish trading contacts, hence his perspective is strongly navigational, mapping out the territory for maximum accessibility. It has been discussed that European 'knowledge-making apparatuses'—particularly navigational accounts of travels in the seventeenth and eighteenth centuries—were instrumental in extending European influences, commercial and ideological, to the 'utmost bounds of the earth'.[12] The language of appropriation in Bowrey's account is filled with metaphors of conquest—the 'Radjas' who 'possessed' the 'kingdome' were not fully 'subdued' under the 'Moorish yoke'—indicated his view of the land as awaiting acquisition.

Thus regarding the compartmentalization and ordering of land in preparation to its being appropriated by European commercial and later, imperialist expansion, it is pertinent to recall Foucault's argument for the European construction of its cultural 'other'. According to this, knowledge, a sixteenth century 'episteme', involved an infinite accumulation of confirmations to justify the analogies of existence. Hence, the whole world had to be explored in order to validate the resemblance between the 'microcosm' and the 'macrocosm', categories through which the entire universe was 'ordered'.[13] From the seventeenth century onwards, there was a separation between a powerful (and invisible) 'spectator' culture, before the dispassionate and totalizing gaze of whom the rest of the world was objectified. This separation deepened as knowledge brought the world closer together, bringing the 'other' nearer to the 'spectator' for exploration and analysis.

The construction and validation of a European ideal based on analogy that formed the basis of travel writing in the pre-colonial period, is explored in this section. Through the travellers' impressions of property, kingship and religious belief in 'Orixa', included the way they formulated the above categories, I hope to gain an insight into dominant political and cultural trends that later crystallized into colonial policy. I believe that the roots of imperialist domination lay in the comparison of experienced cultural forms with the European ideal, a link that reduced the forms to a visible and permeable 'order' that could be recorded, transported and displayed before the home audience.

Power and Property: the Enumeration and Appropriation of Wealth

As a part of the demarcation of Indian coastal boundaries by Western sailors, the temples at Puri and Konark acquired an enhanced significance for Bowrey and other travellers. Their initial visual impressions of the temples were from their ships, looking inland.

> We had a view of a great and celebrated Pagoda, which looks quite white, and which is called Jagernate . . . situated on high ground rising from the centre of a large wood . . . so that it is visible from a long distance. We were told that the Gentues had a particular reverence for it, and that those of Coromandel, Orixa, Golconda and Bengala went on pilgrimage thither. . . .[14]
>
> We sailed in sight of the Black Pagoda and the White Pagoda, the latter is that place called Jaggrenaut to which the Hindoues from all parts of the country come on pilgrimage. . . .[15]
>
> At 12 this noon (31st Jan 1681) the white pegodo (alias Jagrenett) . . . bore North dist. per judgement 17' at this bearing. . . . Jagrenett makes in three pegodas, the S. most the highest, the midle one somewhat lower, the N. most the lowest, the tops of each being blunt and very white; on each side are buildings and seemeth to be within a large compound, and small trees on each side which are not discernible at a great distance.[16]

This perspective is particularly appropriate in the light of our earlier discussion regarding the externality of the European spectator culture to their objects of exploration and analysis. From the sea, the travellers saw the 'celebrated white . . . Pagoda', set on raised ground for their inspection, as it were, and comprising three structures, the sanctum, *Natamandapa* and *Jagamohana*. Moving closer, Bowrey's account discusses Jagannatha with allusions to other temples, in architectural and material detail.

Many, yea, most of theire Pagods, are very stately buildings of stone of curious workmanship of the same, representing all Sorts of musick and dances to theire Gods, and are Surrounded with cloysters of marble. . . . Supported with Pillars of the Same . . . with walks to the great gate of the Pagod, as alsoe to the great Pond or tanke, where they frequently wash themselves all over before they assume to Enter the Pagod. The Entrance . . . I have often Observed, are most rare and Admirable worke, vizt. a man on horsebacke cut out in one Entire piece . . . all of marble, and which is more rare, I have Seen within Some of these great Pagods, a large Cart and 2 horses, with all their appurtenances, cut out of an entire Stone . . . and these they often bow to in representation of theire God Jno. Gernaet, beinge as he is, Upon some festivals, carried about in a large triumphant Chariot, most rarely carved, painted and gilded, and drawne by men of which in Order.[17]

Moving 'inward' from the external perspective of the sailors, Bowrey's account depicts an insight into the structure of the temples, physical and ritual. He displays his knowledge of the customs, and explicates the significance of the idols. He assumes the position of interpreter for the culture to the Western audience, a position that gave him power over both Indian conditions and European conceptions. The totalizing perspective of this generalized account reduces Jagannatha along with other shrines into the same structural and ritual category. Images of the exotic, ' . . . the most rare and admirable' statues as well as customs, objectifying and fusing the animate and inanimate together, were a common motif in seventeenth century travel writing. Accounts of Eastern exotica were often lifted word for word from earlier writings by subsequent travellers, the repetition serving to validate their authenticity.[18] Bowrey thus presents the 'delicacies' of Orissa to a European reading public, enumerating and reinforcing popular images and curiosities.

As guidelines for European traders, such accounts included prolific descriptions of wealth and sumptuousness.

The four most celebrated Pagods are Jagrenate, Banarous, Matura and Tripeti. Jagrenate is one of the mouths of Ganges whereupon is built the great Pagod, where the Arch Bramin, or chief Priest among the Idolaters, keeps his residence. The great Idol that stands upon the Altar in the innermost part of the Pagod, has two Diamonds for his Eyes, and another that hangs about his neck, the least of those Diamonds weighing about forty carats. About his Arms he wears Bracelets, sometimes of Pearls, and sometimes of Rubies; and this magnificent idol is called Resora. . . .[19]

The temple's fabulous wealth was viewed as an indication of the region's vast resources that could be commercially exploited. Minutiae regarding the size and shape of the deity's ornaments have overtones of appropriativeness, as if the temple treasure was being evaluated as a resource as well. At another level, such descriptions tend to highlight the fact that the land and its resources were already under the European control, as they had been penetrated by classificatory and documentary processes, 'knowledge-making apparatuses'. Pratt has argued that European commercial interests entered non-European societies under the overarching umbrella of 'scientific exploration', particularly from the eighteenth century onwards. Following the creation of ordering mechanisms like the Linnean classificatory system, science and commerce worked hand in hand to create 'commercially exploitable knowledge'. The 'innocent' yet powerful 'eye' of scientific knowledge surveyed and documented alien lands in a form of conquest, that Pratt denotes as being 'anti-conquest'.[20]

At one level the appropriation of travelled lands through documentation was highlighted in these accounts. At another level, local customs and institutions of property and inheritance were also examined as deviations from the European norm. Both Bowrey and Bernier formed the impression that all property belonged to the Mughal emperor, and estates reverted to him on the death of the owner. Bowrey wrote that '. . . if any of them die, theire estates, in full falls to the Kinge, none of his Seed dareinge to claim any of it by right or title. . . . '[21] Bernier's account corroborates this view: 'It must not be imagined that the Omrahs or Lords of the Mogol's Court are members of ancient families, as our nobility in France.The king being the proprietor of all the lands in the empire, there can exist neither Dukedoms or Marquisates nor can any family be found possessed of wealth arising from a domain, and living upon its own patrimony. . . .'[22]

Forms of access to and control over property that the travellers encountered were viewed as a deviation from a preconceived norm. This deviation was emphazised through the language of negation— ' . . . there can exist *neither* Dukedoms *nor* Marquisates . . . ' (italics mine). European institutions of landownership were thus designated as being the norm. The local system was compared and subordinated to European forms of property ownership; its 'inferiority', thus denoted, opened up possibilities of its 'improvement' through colonial intervention. The image of an omnipotent and tyrannical monarch who held the nobility in thrall, was contrasted with a free European land-owning class, in control of its own patrimony. Thus, the first seeds of Oriental Despotism were sown.

The description of lavish wealth on one hand and the inability to control wealth by the local landowners on the other, is overlaid by an aura of unreality. The trappings of luxury apparently available to the landowners and landed institutions appear to be unsubstantiated by any degree of power over it. Teltscher has discussed Thomas Roe's denunciation of Jahangir's court as a 'theatrical sham', wherein the display of wealth was ritualized, but was thought to be divorced from 'real' power.[23] The superficiality of great wealth unchannelized by local entrepreneurship brought out in the travel writings, leaves open possibilities of European commercial and political expansion. This vision of great Eastern treasures, teetering on inadequate political foundations, later legitimized their takeover by Western enterprise.

Rebellious 'Radjas'—Order, Authority and the Ideal of Kingship

The travellers' view of the local state and forms of kingship reflect their adherence to the paradigms of the European monarchies. They were driven by the ideal of the nation-state, that of a powerful monarch at the centre supported by a hereditary nobility. To some extent, they found this theme reflected in the Mughal court. In Orissa, however, the situation was quite different. Bowrey's view of 'Orixa' is of a small stretch of land inhabited by independent 'Radjas' that lay between the powerful kingdoms of Golconda and the Mughal territories, in short, the *Gadajata* states of central Orissa. He sees the local populace as ' . . . a very poore, Idolatrous people . . . very low Spirited, Save those Radjas and their armies who live by the Sword, and will not pay homadge to any kinge or Emperour in the Universe.'[24]

Here, we see the absence of an all-powerful monarch to whose authority the 'radjas' should ideally submit, according to Bowrey. Contrast this with the Bowrey's comment on the emperor's supposed control over property, wherein European 'free' ownership of property was upheld as an ideal. In this case, the monarch's presence is viewed as necessary to the maintenance of order in the land.

An exhaustive project of 'ordering' was central to the development of science in Europe in the seventeenth and eighteenth centuries.[25] The complex of science, rationality and a totalizing knowledge is vested in the notion of power as being invisible, all-knowing and all-encompassing. Echoes of this complex find expression in Bowrey's notion of the state as an ordering presence, to whose authority the individuals must submit. The 'rebellious' chieftains of Orissa appear disorderly in this context.

Images of 'disorder' abound in Bowrey's description of the rajas and their lands: ' . . . it is a very troublesome kingdome for travellers, the kingdome not being Settled Under one Government, both parties make many pretences to injure the poor travailer . . . .[26] Predominant among these was the perception of the absence of a large, homogenous administrative structure in the region, as the travellers encountered numerous small chiefdoms ruled by the *Gadajata* rajas. We have discussed the political ferment and shift in relations of power in the sixteenth and seventeenth centuries, after the Gajapati state was divided into *Mughalbandi* and *Gadajata* states (see Chapter 1). The rhetoric of 'rebelliousness' could be applicable to the *Gadajata* rajas by the Mughal *subahdars* at Cuttack, as they frequently resisted their taxation and efforts to 'control' them. The role of the Mughal *subahdar* was not a simple one, as we have seen. They were involved in local conflicts of authority and sought to control institutions of power, including the raja and the temple. Thus the balance of power between the *subahdar* and the Khurda raja continued, possibly supported through the exchange of large sums of money.

Bowrey's description of the rajas as rebellious, thus articulates the dominant view of the Mughal administration. There is another angle to this depiction as well. The rajas as well as the terrain were viewed as 'troublesome', difficult to penetrate and control. This reflects the perspective of the European complex of science/commerce/power that sought to 'conquer' difficult areas and situations in order to validate their control over them. The association of local rulers with the topography, flora and fauna, reinforced the separation between the rationalist Western spectator and a de-humanized, naturalized East. The Linnean perspective underlay such assumptions, particularly the theory of racial classification of Homo Sapiens as a species.[27] The fusing of the rajas with their territories, reducing them to a single complex in order to explicate the difficulty in 'controlling' them, depicts such a juxtaposition of local institutions with their natural surroundings. Such reduction primarily served to remove the rajas from Western normative qualities of human agency and enterprise—they were equated with nature and 'instinct'. Thus, their authority over their land was also indirectly questioned.

The validity of visual scrutiny, what was empirically verifiable and immediately available, was central to European scientific discourse in the seventeenth and eighteenth centuries. The visible sign that makes known the vast design of nature, was central to the evolution of European science.[28] Thus, the local institutions of kingship were de-culturized in the travel writing, their ritual and political contexts were 'invisible' to the European spectators.

The notion of order depicted in Bowrey's account, signified by a totalizing and uniformly powerful monarchy is derived from a Western paradigm, but is also responsive to the travellers' interests in India. Such a state was portrayed as being desirable since Bowrey discovered the land to be 'troublesome' for travellers owing to the many estates and the chieftains who taxed the travellers as they passed through their territories. Extraction of tribute, often by force, by local chiefs and 'little kings', in return for safe passage through their lands, was a part of the complex of royal authority in many parts of India.[29] It was an assertion of their power over the wealth passing through their territory, as well as their assurance of its protection.

Alternative views were expressed by different travellers in order to explain the political reality that they encountered. Central to these was the theme of 'disorder' and degeneration in the state structures. Whilst Bowrey regarded the rajas as anarchic within a preconceived order, which he based on European ideals, another sixteenth century traveller, Thevenot, on the other hand, attempts to explicate what he perceives as the political degeneration of the region. 'The country was kept in far better order under the Patan kings, (I mean) before the Mahometans and Moguls were Masters of it, because then they had Uniformity in Religion. It has been found by experience that disorder came into it with Mahometanism, and that diversity of Religions hath there caused disruption in Manners.'[30]

Here we observe the expression of another widely held view of the structural and political events of the time. The *Madala Panji*, the temple chronicle, which had been regularly composed since the reign of Ramacandradeva I, records the 'disorder' caused in the scheme of temple functions by repeated 'foreign' (*yavana*) particularly Muslim invasions, notably that of *Kalapahar* in 1568. The glorification of the Gajapati regime and the social 'degeneration' caused by its collapse, articulated in the *Madala Panji*, is echoed in Thevenot's comment. The local Brahmanical perspective is intertwined with the European–Christian notion of religious uniformity as being fundamental to an idealized image of the past, from which the present is viewed as having degenerated.

Thus we see that while the travellers were focused on the superiority of the Western state as a political and social paradigm, their accounts express a totalizing and penetrative attitude to Indian conditions. The Western scientific and rationalist discourse acquired an appropriative dimension in the context of the travelled lands, which were thus marginalized.

Western Rationality v. *Eastern Credulity*

The travellers' attitude to the social and ritual institutions that they encountered, was a curious combination of incredulity, empathy and distaste. The ideal of Protestant Christianity was a dominant theme in their evaluation of Indian phenomena. In this respect, they found much to denigrate in the religious practices that they observed. 'Theire irreligious religion, is wholly composed of nothinge Save Idolatry, intermixed neither with Judaisme nor Mahometanisme, but quite averse from them both (Savinge in theire burnt offerings and Sacrifices). More especially from Christianitie. They neither circumcise, nor baptise, but yet doe believe there is a god in heaven.'[31]

In his effort to demonstrate the degree to which Hindu customs were alien to the Christian ideal, Bowrey utilized the very categories of comparison that he was seeking to separate. Thus, rather than diverging completely, Hindu belief is placed further away on a continuum from the ideal, viz., Protestant Christianity. Although Hindus are believed to possess some common core of resemblance to the ideal, since they '. . . doe believe there is a god in heaven . . .', they are seen as having deviated from it. The notion of resemblance was particularly significant in the construction of Western theories of knowledge in the sixteenth century.[32] This assumption fixed the linkages between two belief systems in an 'object–image' relationship, thereby indicating the superiority of the former and the subordinate identity of the latter. The separation of Hindu belief from Christianity was important for the establishment of the latter's dominance, in order to bring the passive, subordinated system closer to the 'scrutinizing gaze' of the Western observer. Yet, the link between the two was necessary in order to articulate the deviance of Hindu belief from the established Christian norm. The cultural 'other' of European Christianity was constructed as its flawed image.

The link between the dominant and 'inferior' cultures was maintained largely through the denigration of the latter's customs and practices. Mandelslo, a German contemporary of Bowrey, expresses his verdict on the Hindus in even more caustic terms. 'They are a sort of very ignorant people, who refer themselves, as to matters of Religion, to their Bramans. They believe, that in the beginning, there was but one God. . . . '[33] Here, as in Bowrey's comment, we note the centrality of the Christian notion of monotheism to the argument, an effort to extract this core concept as the root of Hindu belief as well. The references to rituals, burning of lamps, prostration at temples, etc., are discussed as deviations from that central monotheistic norm. In fact, the association of idolatry and temples with the worship of the devil, are almost Biblical, hence the reference to the great 'Pagod' and 'Jno. Gernaet' as 'diabolicall'.[34]

Bowrey appears to be impressed by the manner in which the 'Brachmans' held the rest of society in thrall. He regards them as the chief controllers of ritual affairs, in which the people were unduly immersed, leading to their neglecting warlike activities. The Brahmans controlled 'Jno. Gernaet', in which deity the greatest number of Hindus were seen to have complete faith. 'The Brachmans are their Priests, but I am sure, and without all controversie, very Diabolicall ones.' He goes on to describe the 'splendid' manner in which 1,000 or 1,200 Brahmanas were maintained at the temple, and the 'cunninge' ways they had of extorting large sums of money from credulous devotees. The terms used to describe the Brahmanas' duplicity, viz., 'bewitchinge' and 'sorcery', indicates that the entire populace was kept in the dark by this one group, which carried out a unified and premeditated deception over generations. Bernier elucidates this point:

> The Bramens encourage and promote these gross errors (of voluntary suicides under the *rathas*) and superstitions to which they are indebted for their wealth and consequence. As persons attached and consecrated to important mysteries, they are held in general veneration and enriched by the alms of the people. So wicked and detestible are their tricks and impostures that I required the full and clear evidence of them . . . ere I could believe that they had recourse to similar expedients.[35]

Indian rituals were seen as extreme versions of certain Christian practices by the Europeans, an aspect that was perceived as validating their relevance.[36] Ideals of austerity and vegetarianism, encountered in India by the travellers, were also inherent in Christian monasticism. In the seventeenth century, Roberto de Nobili, the Jesuit missionary, assumed the persona of a Hindu *sannyasin*.[37] On the other hand, the representation of local beliefs as being ridiculous or 'absurd', reveals another kind of tension that emerged in the accounts, the deepening rural–urban divide in Europe. Pratt has argued that the penetration of agricultural processes by the 'systematizing' efforts of an urban bourgeoisie in Europe in the seventeenth and eighteenth centuries led to a marginalization and 'primitivization' of the peasantry.[38] Their 'modes of thinking and acting' were trivialized and subordinated by the scientific/commercial/urban cultural complex. In terms of the yardstick of 'development', they were regarded as little better than the inhabitants of the Amazon, a conquered and colonized people. In this respect religious practices encountered by the travellers were regarded as primitive, denoting the 'undeveloped' state of local belief systems.

Representations of temple images and Hindu ritual practice as 'Diabolicall' in the accounts, recall the Christian association of pagan customs with the devil. Bernier was struck by what he viewed as monstrous and grotesque carvings on the *rathas* during the annual festival. 'A superb wooden machine is constructed . . . with I know not how many grotesque figures, nearly resembling our monsters which we see depicted with two heads, being half man and half beast, gigantic and horrible heads, satyrs, apes and devils. . . . '[39]

Images of the grotesque formed a part of folk humour and festivity in Europe during the Renaissance. In his analysis of the 'carnivalesque' in folk culture, Bakhtin describes the comic and jovial figure of the devil, who was not regarded as terrifying or alien by the people.[40] The repressive response of 'rational' Christianity to such images caused their appearance as caricatures to mock established structures, their laughter sardonic rather than spontaneous. The travellers' reference to the 'credulity' of the Hindus and their 'submission' to the Brahmanas' authority, trivializes local belief in a manner similar to the marginalization of European peasants by the urban intelligentsia. The description of the Brahmanas as 'diabolical' with repeated references to their 'sorcery', recalls Christian denigration of pagan beliefs as 'diabolical', which had given rise to the carnivalesque representations of the devil in folk culture. The primitiveness of the populace is seen as enhancing the power of 'diabolical' characters, like the devil and the Brahmanas.

The image of a group of 'cunninge' Brahmanas who controlled the credulous people was strongly focused on their acquisition of wealth through their ritual machinations. Bernier pointed out that suicides during the *ratha jatra* were encouraged by Brahmanas in order to enhance their wealth and prestige. The juxtaposition of material resources with 'superstition' is in keeping with the combined impetus of European science and commerce, expanding its field of influence. Pratt has argued that there was an 'ideological dialectic' between scientific and commercial enterprise, which sought to 'mirror and legitimate each other's aspirations'.[41] The hostile references to the control exercised by Brahmanas over social and ritual institutions, particularly those that were storehouses of wealth like the Jagannatha temple, indicates the desirability of their replacement by European rational culture and commercial enterprise.

Accounts of the 'credulity' of the local populace and the intellectual 'backwardness' of the people served to enhance the significance of European rationalist and scientific discourse. Incidents highlighting the superiority and the uniformly applicable authority of Western science were popular 'asides' in the travel narratives. For example, Bowrey relates that during a lunar eclipse, he had asked some Brahmanas if they, or their god, Jno. Gernaet, could predict the next such occurrence, and was amused by their reply that only god could do it.[42] Foucault has pointed out the significance of representation in science in the classical period in Europe. Scientific processes of ordering carried an essentialist notion of simple elements underlying all natural phenomena, their combinations progressively increasing in complexity. Thus, all nature could be uniformly reduced to 'simple' formulae, and the universe could thus be perfectly ordered and comprehended.[43] Alternative perceptions of natural phenomena were thus subordinated by an overarching, totalistic 'scientific' construct that was articulated in the writings.

According to Bowrey, since Copernican astronomy and the discovery of the solar system in Europe had demystified cosmic phenomena, local belief in 'god' as connected with eclipses was simply an expression of ignorance. The ideal of Western science was believed to hold the only 'true' explanation, whose validity was viewed as superior to local 'credulity'. Familiarity with the scientific ideal also invested Bowrey with the power of knowledge, both about cosmic phenomena and over the 'ignorant' Brahmanas, who were seen as deprived of the privilege of knowing the 'truth' on account of their credulity.

Bowrey's account of Hindu society in Orissa created and maintained certain stereotypes, which also influenced the colonial administrators at a later date. He believed the 'Ourias' to be extremely poor and 'low-spirited', despite the rebellious 'radjas'. The image is one of an oppressed, meek and credulous populace inhabiting an indifferent country, whose 'wildness' attests to their lack of initiative and industry.[44] Their being conquered by the Muslims corroborates their lack of martial skill and strength. He claims that Orissa had very few towns, hence the extent of trade and skilled craftsmanship was also limited.

The crux of these arguments lay in the submissiveness of the populace, which was epitomized by their adherence to the caste system. Bowrey describes Hindus as being extremely particular about observing caste rules, which he terms laws, especially eating taboos. He appears to be struck by the notion of ritual pollution and a fall from the caste status through contact with an untouchable.[45] He describes in detail the social ostracism resulting from such an occurrence, until the lost status is regained through a pilgrimage to Jagannatha. The temple maintained groups of Brahmanas who attempted to extort large sums of money from the supplicant while granting him his earlier status. Thus, the caste structure was seen to maintain a materially exploitative group of 'cunninge' priests, whose hold over the credulous people was virtually absolute. There is an underlying sense of incredulity at the prevalent belief system that undercuts its validity in the eyes of the audience. The elaborate hierarchy of social purity and status is regarded as essentially futile, with an inadequate rationale behind the strict adherence to rules.

Repeated references to the submissiveness of Indians in the accounts reinforced their image as a culture waiting to be subordinated. This is validated by accounts of their submission to the 'Mahometan Yoke', a fact that corroborates their inability to govern themselves. An image of the weak and childlike Hindu, in need of guidance and support, calls out to the European cultural model of a rational government. The epithets used to denote the people of Orissa—'poore', 'idolatrous', 'low-spirited'—are the polar opposites of the contemporary Western self-image as enterprising, rational and pioneering. Here again, we see the construction of Europe's cultural 'other' as a subordinate entity, a fact that validated its domination later.

As part of their 'weak' character, Hindus were believed to be cunning in business and not averse to cheating. 'They are generally a very Subtile and Cunninge Sort of men, Especially in the way of merchandising. . . .'[46] Here again we see the enumeration of the Western norm of 'professional' behaviour, from which the merchants and their practices were seen as deviations. Such impressions reinforced their 'low-spiritedness'. Also associated with their 'weakness' was the Indians' antipathy to bloodshed and their non-martial disposition. Mandelslo proclaims: 'They believe in the Immortality and Transmigration of Souls, upon which persuasion they abhor the effusion of bloud. Accordingly, there are not to be found any Robbers or Murtherers among them, but on the other side, they are generally Lyars and Cheats, in which good qualities they exceed all the other Indians. . . .'[47]

The apparent licentiousness and aberrant behaviour of the

society is explored by Bernier as well. He agonizes about the peculiar 'discrepancy', as he sees it, between the normal reserve of the temple dancers and their 'indecent postures' during festive celebrations, when, he feels, they were accessible even to the 'naked and hideous' *fakirs* who surrounded the temple.

In front of the Chariot, and even in the Deuras or Idol temples, public women during festival days dance and throw their bodies into a variety of indecent and preposterous attitudes, which the Brahmins deem quite consistent with the religion of their country. I have known females celebrated for beauty, and who were remarkably reserved in their general deportment refuse valuable presents from Mahometans, Christians and even Gentile foreigners because they considered themselves dedicated to the ministry and to the ministers of the Deura, to the Brahmins and to those Fakires, who are commonly seated on ashes all around the temple. . . .

Bernier further recounts in detail a ceremony at the Puri temple wherein a 'beautiful maiden' is selected by the 'wicked' Brahmanas to be the bride of Jagannatha, and is kept in the temple sanctum for a whole night, when the deity is believed to consummate their union through sexual intercourse. Actually, Bernier says, one of the Brahmanas, or 'imposters', enters through a small back door, and 'enjoys the unsuspecting damsel'.

The superior knowledge of the Western observer, demystifying a situation that is opaque to a people blinded by credulity, is highlighted here. The participants in the ceremony are divided into the 'wicked' Brahmanas and the 'unsuspecting' people, whose collective 'innocence' is personified by the young virgin. The large and varied hierarchy of temple priests is reduced to a single monolithic category, the Brahmanas. The imposition of value-laden categories disregards, even trivializes the ritual. It introduces an element of strategy into the performance of local ceremonies, wherein it appears that the sole aim of the Brahmanas is to dupe the people into satisfying their whims. The presence of the traveller as providing insight into the 'essence' of the situation provides a point of reference for the opposition between the 'knowledgeable' West and the credulous East.

Images of duplicity, lack of courage and motivation and blind submission to exploitation built up the 'Ouria' Hindu as the negative 'other' of the 'strong', rational, pioneering and penetrative European cultural ideal. This impression of passivity is occasionally contradicted, for instance in the case of the *ratha jatra*, Bowrey alludes to the suicides under the chariots' wheels as ' . . . a most Noble, Heroick and Zealous death'. The image depicted in these epithets is completely at variance with the 'passive' nature of Indians that was popularly depicted in the accounts. In her analysis of eyewitness accounts of widow burning, Lata Mani has argued that the ambivalence expressed by European spectators towards what they viewed as a 'horrifying' custom comprised two major issues. At one level, the element of 'horrible fascination' which compelled the observer to witness the burning was a voyeuristic objectification of the women, who were viewed as 'beautiful' and 'courageous', and the 'tragedy' of their death was described in allegorical terms. At another level, their subordination to tradition indicates their inherent passivity, and validates their role as victims.[48] In the case of the *ratha jatra* the hint of admiration for the pilgrims' nobility and heroism is ambiguous: it places their courage within a contextual framework of violence and irrationality and portrays the suicides as passive victims of a 'Diabolicall' tradition.

Such contradictory portrayals reinforced an essentialized perspective of a Euro-centred ideal associated with positive and dynamic qualities, while the 'East' was homogenously regarded as representing passivity, credulity and negativity. The 'East' was constructed as Europe's negative 'other' through the accounts, which also linked the two domains in a relationship of dominance and subordination.

FEMININE EAST—MASCULINE WEST

Images of the feminine constitute a unique genre within the complex of the travellers' impressions. Colonialist, racist and sexist discourse converges in depictions of women in Indian society, as well as in the travellers' view of the land, customs and attitudes that they encountered. Women were depicted by both Bowrey and Bernier as illustrations for their impressions and the reinforcing of stereotypes regarding the passivity, licentiousness and exotica inherent in local culture. Their objectification and appropriation by the penetrative gaze of a masculine and dominant West laid open the society for exploration and subordination in the accounts. Bowrey described at length the women dancers and performers who were a part of the festivity and ritual at the Jagannatha temple. 'Hundreds of women are here maintained to dance on theire festivals and days of Sacrifice and offerings, with all varieties of musick that Asia affordeth to play before theire Gods, vizt. pipes, drums, trumpets, with varieties of stringed instruments, with multitudes of Voices very delicate to hear and behold were it acted in a better Sence, and not onely so in theire Cathedral Pagod, but in all Others, as many as theire Abilities will Extend to the maintenance of, and for theire activities of body are much admired by all spectators. They are, for the most part, very Straight handsome–featured and a well-limbed people.'[49]

The *ratha jatra*, as we have noted, was accompanied by a number of *devadasis* and acrobats, folk dancers, both male and female, whose performance enhanced the auspiciousness of the festive moment. The *devadasis* or *maharis*, as they were known in Orissa, were consecrated to the temple from an early age by their families, who usually belonged to the neighbouring villages of Puri. Often, they were simply the daughters of *maharis* themselves. They were involved in temple services, viz., the waking and rocking to sleep of the deity each day, when they would sing and dance as part of the ritual. They also performed special services at important festivals like the *ratha jatra*, when, at the time of the *Pahuda*, or return of the deities from the Gundica temple, they would represent goddess Lakshmi in a sexually explicit dialogue with the *Daitapatis*, the part-*Savara* priests who spoke for Jagannatha. The acrobats and dancers who accompany the procession to this day, are usually part of travelling troupes that gather at Puri on such occasions.

Bowrey further goes on to comment about the unmarried status of the dancing women and their freedom in choosing their sexual partners. 'These dancinge Women have a privilege above all Others in these Easterne parts, which causeth such multitudes to Endeavour to attain to Such Employs, where they may Enjoy Earthly pleasure Enough, without any Scandall to themselves or relations. They are wholy at theire own choice whether they will marry or noe, or live Subject to any one man and have the liberty to be made use of by whom they please; therefore I think Seldom or never that they leave this life to retire to theire homes and lead a Chast [*sic*] life, or to marry, whereby theire pleasure is very uncertain. . . .'[50]

The account is accompanied by a sketch of the dancers, who are shown as performing against a backdrop of swaying coconut palms. The figures are essentially feminine, but have an androgynous quality. They are frozen in mid-posture, as if captured by the viewer's eye. They all face forwards, as if performing for an audience. The trees are laden with fruit, imparting a festive and luscious quality to the occasion. This composite image of people amidst their 'natural' surroundings, brings out the totalizing, feminizing and voyeuristic attitude of the European observers. The performers are identified with nature as being uninhibited, both in terms of a 'free' interaction between the sexes, as well as in the presentation of an 'authentic' performance for the Western audience.

The androgynous qualities inherent in the dancers associates them with a passive, childlike innocence, lacking in self-awareness, sexual and political, that are essentially regarded as a male concern. This may be viewed in the context of the Enlightenment in Europe that brought in an awareness of the finitude of the universe, which was centred on the dominance of Man over nature.[51] Man, a masculine principle, embodying dominant human traits, became an object of his own exploration. All nature was centred on him, yet he was transcendent to it by virtue of his superior knowledge. The people shown in the sketch are devoid of masculine self-awareness and therefore are associated with nature, to be explored and analysed. The theatrical quality accorded to the event presents it as an unreal phenomenon, a stage act for the consumption of the Western public.

Bowrey's account also depicts a mingling of Western fantasy with Christian disapprobation of the dancing women's public lives. Couched in an exotic backdrop of heathen festivity amidst coconut palms, as the sketch indicates, the dancers are seen as physically alluring and innocent of more evolved social mores. The image of their liberty to 'Enjoy Earthly pleasure' with no thought of the 'Scandall' to themselves or their families titillates the voyeur as well as inferiorizes those who enjoy an unrestrained sexuality. Their freedom to 'live subject to any one man' yet be able to 'be made use of by whom they please', is the extension of the Western and predominantly male fantasy. This image of social liberty and sexual freedom is set against the Protestant ideal, which is for all good women 'to retire to theire homes and lead a Chast life. . . . ' This, in fact, appears a dull and constricting option to the self-determination and excitement apparently inherent in the dancers' lifestyle. Thus, the accounts create an exotic, fascinating and sinfully desirable picture to titillate the home audience.

At another level, the sexually unconstrained view of the women, to 'be made use of ' by different people is extended, by inference, to the entire society and opens the way to its subordination by the patriarchal, 'masculine' West. The ideal of male superiority inherent in the travel accounts denigrates the image of sexual freedom in women, regarding them as being in need of control and supervision.

Ania Loomba has discussed the designation of women and racial 'others' as the biological and natural 'inferiors' of the dominant male European ideal. Non-Europeans are regarded as inhabiting the same symbolic space as women, both are associated with 'nature' and primitivism. Both are viewed as passive and childlike, hence their 'innocence' and lack of self-awareness. They are continuously described as 'lacking'—in initiative, intellectual powers and perseverance. Alternatively or simultaneously, they are viewed as being outside the normative parameters of the dominant male ideal, as 'dangerous', 'treacherous', 'emotional', 'wild', 'sexually aberrant', 'lascivious' 'animal-like', etc. The operation of 'patriarchalism', according to Loomba, particularly of white colonialism, extends the control of Man as 'father' over women, and white man as 'father' over Black men and women.[52] Thus, the androgynous figures in Bowrey's sketch are bereft of the full human and sexual identity that is inherent in the culturally dominant white male.

Interestingly, the image of lascivious temple dancers is offset by the alternative lifestyle of the married Hindu women. Bowrey regards them as oppressed by a 'jealous husband', with no future to look forward to except to be burnt as a *sati* on the death of their spouses, which practice he depicts as being popular among the 'Gentiles of Hindoustan'. He describes in detail the horrifying end to one such widow, and condemned the 'Satyrical Priests' who brought it to pass.[53] Thus, an image of two extremes is created: on the one hand the free public women who did not conform to the travellers' norm of chaste, married, family women and on the other, the women brutalized by marriage and eventually murdered in the cause of fidelity. Both alternatives were viewed with disapprobation. Both images depict a lack of control, the former involving unbridled pleasure and freedom, the latter denoting unmitigated pain. The lack of control once again depicts the dark side of Hindu society, the evil aspect inherent in an idyllic, amoral paradise. It also indicates the Hindus' inability to guide their own passions and destinies, thus highlighting the steadying influence of rational Western culture.

We have seen that the travellers' view of the institutions that they encountered was influenced by their own cultural matrix, as well as the exigencies of catering to the demands of a particular political and commercial audience. Their opinion of the caste hierarchy was essentially one of class-based tension, where knowledge was the key to the exploitation of the masses by the Brahmanas. The Brahmanas were regarded as greedy and deceptive, and along with their affiliation to the temple, that magnificent storehouse of wealth, solely engaged in amassing riches. The accounts do not penetrate the complex structures for the management and redistribution of temple property. In fact, the travellers emphasize the obvious riches, especially the jewellery, gold and silver belonging to the deity. They do not refer to the vast landed property of the Jagannatha temple, managed by the *mathas* and other institutions. The travellers' collective misconception regarding the absence of private property, and all lands reverting to the monarch, further fuelled their inability to note the varying forms of usage and control of property. They did not comprehend the rights of the rajas to taxes, gifts, honours and obeisance, all equally important, or the temple privileges of Brahmanas and their respective obligations.

The travellers' accounts of the Jagannatha temple and its related institutions is overlaid, on one hand, by their perception of idolatry which of a blind submission to an 'ignorant' faith by a credulous populace. The references to the deity's image as 'monstrous' echo the Christian denigration of pagan practices. On the other hand, the descriptions of the wealth of the temple coupled with images of the 'wild' rajas and an 'unstable' state structure indicate an attitude of appropriativeness that later influenced colonial penetration of the temple realm.

The accounts of Bowrey and Bernier both set their experience of Hindu society against a preconceived norm, the European ideal of religion, the state and social behaviour. Their description of Hindus as cunning, weak and lacking martial skills and courage indicates that they do not conform to the European male ideal. Coupled with their wealth and sumptuous lifestyle and the images of licentious public women, an impression of an indolent, morally weak, and in a subtle way, feminized society is created, wherein all the above standards are initially defined by Western stereotypes. This impression was probably a Western fantasy as well as a motive for commercially exploiting an easy target. The notion of a weak and helpless people, a feminine stereotype, open to tyrannical foreign rule and requiring guidance and protection from a militarily powerful, rational and commercially successful force, embodying typical masculine qualities, went on to form the rationale behind colonial expansion later.

It has been argued that the travellers' accounts make use of familiar metaphors, including repetitions of famous incidents, Christian tropes and literary images to validate their experiences.[54] However, underlying their descriptions, there were processes of self-definition, explorations of their own identity, their position vis-à-vis the vast unfamiliar spaces that they were traversing. The extension of European commercial and political control over these areas later fixed categories and oppositions that were initially fluid, into a rigid colonial matrix.

NOTES

1. Fernand Braudel, *The Mediterranean and the Mediterranean World in the Age of Philip II*, vol. 2, London: William Collins Sons and Co. Ltd., 1972, pp. 657-60 (hereafter *Mediterranean*).
2. Pratt, *Imperial Eyes*, p. 15.
3. Geertz, *Interpretation of Cultures*, p. 10.
4. Ibid., p. 17.
5. James Clifford and George Marcus, eds., *Writing Culture*, Berkeley and Los Angeles: University of California Press, pp. 6-8 (hereafter *Writing Culture*).

6. Nicholas B. Dirks, *Hollow Crown*, pp. 4-5.
7. This connection is reversed by Murray Milner, who returns to a Brahmana-centred social construct and attributes the high status of Brahmanas to their denial of materialistic values and temporal power. Milner, *Status and Sacredness.*
8. Bernard Cohn, 'The Study of Indian Society and Culture', in B. Cohn, ed., *An Anthropologist among the Historians and Other Essays,* New Delhi: Oxford University Press, 1987, p. 139 (hereafter *An Anthropologist*).
9. Ibid., pp. 145-6.
10. Carnac-Temple, *A Geographical Account*, pp. 128-9.
11. Deryck Lodrick, 'Rajasthan as a Region: Myth or Reality?', in Karine Schomer, Joan L. Erdman, Deryck O. Lodrick and Lloyd I. Rudolph eds., *The Idea of Rajasthan: Explorations in Regional Identity*, New Delhi: Manohar, 1994.
12. Pratt, *Imperial Eyes*, pp. 29-30.
13. Foucault, *Order of Things*, pp. 28-32.
14. Schouten quoted in Carnac-Temple, *A Geographical Account* p. 12.
15. Ibid.
16. Ibid.
17. Ibid., p. 7.
18. Teltscher, *India Inscribed*, pp. 1-10.
19. Tavernier in Carnac-Temple, *A Geographical Account.*
20. Ibid., pp. 5-8.
21. Ibid., p. 127.
22. Bernier, *Travels*, p. 211.
23. Teltscher, *India Inscribed,* pp. 20-1.
24. Carnac-Temple, *A Geographical Account*, p. 130.
25. Dreyfus and Rabinow, *Michel Foucault*, pp. 18-19.
26. Ibid., p. 131.
27. Pratt describes Linnaeus' classificatory scheme, which had divided people into five major categories: (a) Wild Man—Four-footed, mute, hairy; (b) American—Copper-coloured, choleric, erect, etc.; (c) European—Fair, sanguine . . . governed by laws; (d) Asiatic—Sooty, melancholy, . . . governed by opinions; (e) Africans—Black, nose flat . . . governed by caprice. Pratt, *Imperial Eyes*, p. 32. The juxtaposition of physical characteristics with attitudes and dispositions led to the formation of enduring racial stereotypes that were validated by their 'scientific' basis, and also thus universally applied.
28. Dirks, *Hollow Crown*, pp. 65-74.
29. Foucault, *Order of Things*, pp. 26-8.

30. Surendranath Sen, ed., *Indian Travels of Thevenot and Carreri,* part II, National Archives of India 1949, p. 68.
31. Carnac-Temple, *A Geographical Account*, p. 15.
32. Foucault, *Order of Things*, pp. 17-20.
33. Carnac-Temple, *A Geographical Account*, p. 15.
34. Ibid.
35. Bernier, *Travels*, p. 336.
36. Teltscher, *India Inscribed*, p. 27.
37. Ibid., p. 74.
38. Pratt, *Imperial Eyes*, p. 35.
39. Bernier, *Travels*, pp. 304-6.
40. Mikhail Bakhtin, *Rabelais and His World*, trans. Helen Iwolsky, Bloomington: Indiana University Press, 1984, pp. 40-1 (hereafter *Rabelais*).
41. Pratt, *Imperial Eyes,* p. 34.
42. Carnac-Temple, *A Geographical Account*, p. 34.
43. Foucault, *Power/Knowledge*, pp. 15-21.
44. Ibid., pp. 128-30.
45. Ibid., pp. 11-12.
46. Ibid., p. 9.
47. Carnac-Temple, *A Geographical Account*, p. 15.
48. Lata Mani, 'The Female Subject, the Colonial Gaze: Reading Eyewitness Accounts of Widow Burning', in T. Niranjana, P. Sudhir, and V. Dhareshwar, eds., *Interrogating Modernity: Culture and Colonialism in India*, Calcutta: Seagull Books, 1993, pp. 273-90 (hereafter 'Reading Eyewitness Accounts').
49. Carnac-Temple, *A Geographical Account*, pp. 13-14.
50. Ibid.
51. Foucault, *Power/Knowledge*, pp. 29-35.
52. Loomba, *Gender, Race*, pp. 45-8.
53. Carnac-Temple, *A Geographical Account*, pp. 36-7. Bernier, too, was struck by the cruel custom. See Bernier, *Travels*, pp. 310-12.
54. Teltscher, *India Inscribed*, p. 18.

CHAPTER 4

The Temple, the Raja and the Colonial State

On all occasions when the subject of that valuable acquisition, the Province of Cuttack, is under consideration, the important possession of the Temple of Juggernaut must stand in a prominent point of view. In a political light its value is incalculable, and even as a source of Revenue to the State it will be found of great consequence, as under the protecting influence of the British government, the number of Pilgrims will so greatly increase that it becomes difficult to make any comparison between the amount the tax formerly yielded and what it may now be reasonably expected to produce, it may be nearly eight lacks than two per annum.[1]

The entry of the East India Company administration into the Orissan *Mughalbandi* was focused on their acquiring control over the Jagannatha temple. The twin objectives of ideological dominance and revenue exaction as defined in the above statement—' . . . In a political light its value is incalculable and even as a source of Revenue to the State it will be found of great consequence . . .'—largely motivated policy formation by colonial authorities. In the process, however, issues of power and dominance, legitimacy and authority were reconfigured and relocated, particularly in the interaction between the British administration and the traditional Gajapati kingship.

In this chapter I have examined the manner in which authority was negotiated between the two contending domains of power, the militaristic dominance of the Company administration and the ritual hegemony of the Khurda raja in the region. Access to the temple and its redistributive networks formed a focus for the enactment of the conflict, wherein the old regime was deconstructed and the raja was recontextualized within a new and uniquely colonial discourse. This discourse was articulated through the penetration and appropriation of traditional networks of authority and status by the Company regime, as well as its simultaneous rationalization through plethoric documentation. By closely analysing three texts that played an important role in the evolution of the government's policy towards the temple, I have explored key notions that dominated the official discourse; viz., the implications of the 'discipline' that was sought to be imposed, the significance of documentation as an exercise in control and the articulation of conflicting values vis-à-vis local institutions.

The development of colonial policy in India also had another side to it, viz., an ongoing critique/debate in England concerning the Company's activities in India. Accounts of Indian conditions by English writers in the seventeenth and eighteenth centuries served to structure a variety of stereotypes that formed a part of the colonial discourse. Chief among them was the notion of 'Eastern mismanagement', the inability of Indians to successfully govern themselves.[2] The image of sadistic, indolent and incapable Indian princes who were defeated by a 'handful' of 'upright and disciplined' British soldiers[3] offset the inherent weakness of the Indian regime against the strength and stability of the British forces. According to this view, which also fitted in neatly along with other notions of Oriental Despotism, the Indians were virtually asking to be colonized.

The 'improvements' brought about by the 'rational' and 'benevolent' colonial regime were illustrated, for example, through accounts of the 'pacification' of the *Santhals* by Augustus Cleveland in the 1770s. Here, the paternalistic benevolence of Company officials in conjunction with a trivialization of tribal custom justified the most intimate penetration of local institutions by official machinery. The writers' air of authority in successfully classifying and documenting the nuances of social institutions indicates their legitimization of power through knowledge. This is most aptly demonstrated through pictures of Indian life by European artists like Baltazard Solvyns and William Hodges. Hodges' idyllic portrayal of a blooming post-famine Bengal in the 1770s linked British benevolence with Mughal beneficence.[4] Solvyns' depiction of concubines and Hindu marriage ceremonies, both of which were restricted to 'outsiders', was a triumphant violation of customary privacy in the name of 'scientific rigour'. The revelation of 'forbidden' aspects of Indian society to the voyeuristic gaze of a colonial observer, served to intensify their domination, especially in their own view. Indian society was charted, mapped and demystified with dehumanizing thoroughness under the shadow of military power.

The military penetration of Orissa was coterminous with the production of a quantity of documentation, recording and reducing territory, custom, ritual and socio-economic relations to textual categories that were intelligible to the new administrators. The numerous reports and texts that questioned local institutions and processes also served to objectify them. The process of 'reformulation' of Indian culture, argues Cohn, occurred through such questioning and explanations that were also motivated by forms of colonial coercion.[5] The colonial administration's ambivalence towards institutions that they observed as being 'violent' and 'unlawful' may be viewed in the context of an underlying violence that characterized the colonial assumption of power as a whole. This was the crux of the voyeuristic observer status that was adopted by the administration, as articulated in eyewitness accounts of *sati*, also discussed in the previous chapter.[6] Power was vested in the observer. Indians were used as illustrations, never participants. They were represented as devoid of agency and the right to choice.

Their objectification in colonial discourse also removed the government from obligations and accountability. The entire mass of bureaucratic documentation was an exercise in the appropriation of local institutions by the colonial regime, their penetration by official 'knowledge'. Simultaneously, such documentation rationalized its own violence with respect to the institutions, making the correspondence a 'mask of force' as it were.

THE DESTRUCTION OF THE OLD REGIME

The penetration of the temple–state network in Orissa by the Company administration involved the redefinition and negotiation of prevailing structures of power. Although the British had claimed territorial authority over the larger province of

Bengal, Bihar and Orissa, they were yet 'outsiders' to the world of the temple and the ritual kingship. At one level, the Company administration were an important force in a larger conflict over power which also involved the Marathas and the Bengal Nawabs. At another, they increasingly desired to gain control over the temple and its redistributive networks, at which point they had to contend with the Khurda raja and his ritual linkages with Jagannatha.

The Gajapati regime was destroyed by the colonial government during their acquisition of authority over the temple. This involved the military subjugation of the Khurda raja as well as attempts to subvert his ideological authority in the temple sphere. With a view to developing the temple's revenue potential through the pilgrim tax as well as appropriating the Gajapati's position of ritual dominance in the region, the Company administration initially attempted to actually replace the raja in the temple sphere.

In order to gain insight into the form and degree of authority acquired by the British within the larger power structures that subsumed the region, it is necessary to review their interaction with the other trans-regional political powers that were active in the area, primarily the Marathas and the Bengal Nawabs. The Marathas had taken over the administration of the *Mughalbandi* of Orissa following a treaty with Alivardi Khan of Bengal in 1751. The treaty had been negotiated over a period of protracted conflict over the territory between the two powers. The Marathas had also attempted to extend their influence in the temple sphere, thus indicating their awareness of its significance in validating political structures in the region. A *sanad* issued by Janoji Bhonsla in 1743 authorizes a Gaudiya *mahant* of Puri, Basudeb Goswamy, to collect taxes from the *Gadajata* rajas and 'other zamindars' in the region.[7] The Marathas had made several political forays into Orissa.[8] Janoji's order to the *mahant* to collect taxes from the local rajas may well have been in anticipation of the extension of his own power over them, utilizing the validating authority of the ritual cesses.

The Company had acquired the *Diwani* of Bengal, Bihar and Orissa in 1765. Prior to this, they had played a major role in the conflict between the Nawabs and the Marathas, being alternately consulted by both sides and their affiliates. In 1762, the Nawab, in a letter to the British resident at Patna, negotiated the maintenance of British troops at Cuttack in order to repulse the Marathas.[9] In 1764, Chimna Sau, the Maratha *subahdar* at Cuttack, professed friendship with the British, and requested joint action between their respective troops in order to 'settle' the province.[10] The British waited for an opportunity to become principals in the conflict, and thereby gain leverage in acquiring control over Orissa.

Following their acquisition of the Bengal *Diwani* which accorded them only a nominal authority over the *Mughalbandi*, the Company administration had yet to contend with the prevailing dominance of the Marathas. They attempted to negotiate the cession of Orissa by the Marathas, for which they were prepared to pay an annual tribute. Janoji Bhonsla, the Maratha ruler, refused to part with ' . . . the Jaggernaut Pagoda and all the duties collected from the pilgrims. . . .'[11] The Company government offered to keep a Maratha representative at Puri only '. . . for the preservation of the religious ceremony annually performed by the pilgrims of the Jaggernaut Pagoda . . .'.[12] Thus, the temple became the crux of the negotiations between the two political powers in their attempt to control the region. We have seen that Janoji attempted to extend Maratha influence in the region through the temple's networks of patronage. It is obvious that the British officials had at least an inkling of the temple's ideological significance for the region, as a place of pilgrimage. This may have prevented them from forcing the issue with the Marathas, although they were militarily superior at this point. They realized that authority over the temple would help them legitimize their control over the state. In this context, Cornwallis wrote to Malet, the British resident at the Maratha court in Poona, that ' . . . it may be wise . . . to encourage a spirit of pilgrimage among the Hindus . . . to the Company's dominions . . .'.[13]

When diplomacy failed, the Company administration prepared itself for a military showdown with the Marathas. A lot of planning and effort were invested in the formulation of a policy to gain influence over the temple at all levels of the bureaucracy, beginning from Governor General Wellesley himself. Col. Harcourt, his Military Secretary, in a despatch to Col. Campbell, Commanding Officer of the Company's troops, exhorted him to ' . . . employ every possible precaution to preserve the respect due to the Pagoda and to the religious prejudices of the Brahmins and the Pilgrims. You will furnish the Brahmins with such guards as shall afford perfect security to their persons, Rites and ceremonies and to the sanctity of the Religious Edifices. . . .'[14] A letter from Jagannatha Tarakapancanana of Triveni, a famous 'Pundit' of Bengal, was forwarded to the temple priests at Puri, assuring them of the benevolence of the British government. An abstract of the letter sent to John Melville, Commissioner at Cuttack in September 1803, states that:

> . . . from the knowledge he (Jagannatha Tarakapancanana) possesses of the character of the English, he is enabled to assure that they ('Ramcaund' and other temple Brahmanas) need not be afraid to form a connection with the British Government which is distinguished for its particular benevolence to its subjects. Thus satisfied of this themselves, they must exert all their power of persuasion to inspire the respectable characters in that quarter with the same degree of confidence. . . . [15]

The British government sought legitimation from what they considered were influential reference points within the temple sphere, a corroboration of their suitability by a well-known Brahmana. They also hoped to influence ' . . . the respectable characters . . . ' of that sphere, presumably a social and political élite whom, they believed, would validate their rule. At another level, the pilgrim tax was viewed as instrumental in gaining the confidence of the 'suspicious' Brahmanas: 'The Brahmins with characteristic suspicion were doubtful whether the English would keep faith on this vital point (the imposition of the pilgrim tax) and were eager that by the re-establishment of the tax, levied by former rulers on the pilgrims, the interest of the new rulers might be brought in, and of their veracity to their former promise renewed and corroborated as it were, a public and manifest seal to the engagement.'[16]

The policy of conciliation of local traditions, elaborately constructed and delicately transmitted to the Brahmanas, who were viewed as influential representatives of the temple, comes across with a large amount of theatricality. To the Company government, the preservation of indigenous custom was a political exigency, necessary in their conflict with the Marathas. Moreover, the conciliation of the temple community would result in its yielding a large revenue as pilgrim tax, an outcome that was also validated through a longstanding precedent, as it was 'levied by former rulers'. The rationale for imposing the tax also included the eagerness of the Brahmanas to continue it, although they were seen as viewing the government's commitment to supporting temple practice with 'characteristic suspicion'. The pilgrim tax was thus presented in official accounts, as a statement of the government's support of the temple.[17] The fundamental objective underlying the conciliatory policy, was making a powerful public statement. Hence, the use of popular symbolism was considered essential.

The priests responded to the Company administration's overtures by issuing a formal letter welcoming the Company's administration into Puri and declaring that Jagannatha himself had named the new rulers as his guardian. Commissioner Harcourt was presented with a petition inscribed on gold leaf, written in the traditional formal style of ritual documents that further affirmed the priests' support for the colonial government. John Melville reported that: ' . . . I merely state these circumstances to your lordship what a Brahmin this day, told me is a fact. That the Brahmins at the holy temple consulted and applied to Juggernath to inform them what power was now to have this temple under its protection; and that he has given a decided answer that the English Government was in future to be his guardian.'[18]

The rhetoric of truth, veracity, benevolence and respect for local institutions, qualities that the government wished to project, reinforced their image as suitable guardians for the temple within the parameters of their own official discourse. The presence of the 'suspicious' Brahmanas who simultaneously needed to be placated, is a disturbing, uneasy element in the correspondence, indicating the tensions arising from the interaction of alternative systems of power. Yet, the image of potential local resistance to British incursion in the form of 'suspicious' Brahmanas, was created by British official accounts, and also successfully overcome, within those accounts. The real, and much more potent challenge to their authority lay elsewhere. The Gajapati, as a major focus of territorial and ideological power, could not be ignored by the Company administration for long.

The Company had assumed the direct administration of the temple in 1803, through which they hoped to strengthen their influence in Orissa. They did not, however, take into account the Khurda raja, 'the fallen, but still revered descendant and representative of the ancient native sovereigns . . .'[19] who still symbolized the Gajapati kingship of Orissa. The raja had lost most of his territory to the Marathas earlier, especially the four crucial *parganas* of Limbai, Rahang, Serain and Chabiskud, which included the *Sriksetra*, the area of the temple. Anxious to regain his lands, Mukundadeva II of Khurda agreed to allow the movement of British troops through his territory on condition that the four *parganas* be restored to him as well as a payment of Rs. 100,000 to be made to him by the Company.[20] Subsequently, the raja was paid only a fraction of the promised sum, and when he sent his *Diwan* to the Commissioner's office at Cuttack, his claim to the four *parganas* and to the remaining sum of money was flatly turned down. Disappointed, the raja and his *Diwan* entered into negotiations with the Marathas and certain tributary chiefs and tried to regain their influence within the temple in an effort to revive the power and influence of the old state.

A letter from Melville throws light on the tension between the Gajapati's ritual authority in the region and the intrusive, militarily dominant Company regime. 'I have been assured that the Cuttack government (under the Maratha *subahdar*) offered to all tributary Rajahs to relinquish a whole year's revenue, if they would assist in preventing the English from obtaining possession and the Khoordah Rajah who is more powerful than all the rest put together . . . considered the offer to be ridiculous and assured them at the same time that whenever the English got the fort of Cuttack, he would acknowledge the British government as superior.'[21]

The initial correspondence between John Melville, Commissioner at Cuttack, and the Khurda raja reveals the Company administration's desire to acquire complete control over all the provincial rajas under a mask of guarded cordiality. Despite the neutral tone of the Company's invitation to all tributary rajas to ally with them against the Marathas, there was an underlying hint of awareness of the Khurda raja's special position of ritual authority in the region, indicated by the statement—'. . . the Khoordah Rajah, who is more powerful than all the rest put together'. The raja's ambivalence towards the new entrants into the power struggle is highlighted by his repudiation of the *subahdar's* offer, yet he was not favourably inclined to unquestioningly accept British supremacy. This feeling was compounded by the taunt that he would only accept British authority after they took over the Barabati fort at Cuttack, which was still outside their control. This fort had been the traditional stronghold of the Gangas and the Gajapatis, and was a symbol of their power and kingship. The raja, at this point appeared to be negotiating the most advantageous situation that could be afforded to him, given that the Marathas were a threat to his position of ritual dominance in the temple sphere.

Another letter written by Melville to the raja in 1803, describes the Company's notion of 'friendship' as it was extended to him, involving the safe passage for British troops through his territory as well as the provision of 'guides and intelligence' by him.[22] More importantly, the raja was not to open any dialogue with the Marathas nor allowing them into his realm. According to Melville, the raja's '*vakil*' declared himself a 'friend' of the Company by agreeing to these terms. Till this point, the negotiations between the Company and the raja bore some semblance to a dialogue, with both parties retaining their independent political identities. The raja was still a ruler, albeit a defeated and subordinate one. Subsequently this position was changed when the entire material basis and resource network of the raja was subverted.

It is interesting to examine the description of British incursion into Orissa from another angle, the account recorded in the *Katakarajavamsavali*, the royal genealogy of the Puri kings that was loosely a part of the corpus of the *Madala Panji*.[23] According to this text, in the tenth regnal year of Raja Mukundadeva, a chief of the Hunas known as 'Engrej' came from the 'southern country' and presented one lakh silver coins to the raja. Subsequently, the Marathas fled and the Huna chief entered the Barabati fort and took possession of the 'kingdom'. Thereafter, the raja opposed the British owing to the 'ill-counsel' of some of his 'wicked ministers' and in the ensuing conflict, the Khurda fort was occupied by the British. The raja eventually made his peace with the English authorities, but his ministers were executed by them. The raja was 'ordered to stay', (Sanskrit: *sthapita*) at Midnapur, but was later brought back and 'interned' at Puri (Sanskrit: *raksita*).

Keeping in mind that the text essentially legitimized the sovereignty of the Gajapati dynasties, the sense of continuity and lack of conflict in succession from the time of Ramacandradeva I till the rule of Mukundadeva depicted in the text endorses their authority. So also does the notion that the British 'presented' the raja with one lakh silver rupees, in keeping with his status, although the reality was more problematic. Thereafter, we notice a change in perspective, and a paradoxical duality enters the account. On one hand, the text also legitimizes British rule over the region, regarding the objections of Jayi Rajaguru as 'ill-counsel' by 'wicked ministers'. At another level, there is an undercurrent of resentment against the raja's incarceration, both at Midnapur and at Puri, even after he had made his peace with the English. His position as temple administrator was not regarded in a positive light, rather there is a sense of his being forcibly detained. The text was compiled in the beginning of the nineteenth century, when Company administration of temple affairs was at its most direct. Thus, the Company is regarded as yet another ruling power in the region, victorious over the raja. Yet, the position of the raja was not that of a defeated ruler in the past, and his being installed in the temple was a cause for uneasiness.

Following the advent of British troops into Puri and Cuttack in 1803, the raja attempted to exercise a measure of his traditional authority over the temple functionaries. While the negotiations with the Company were in progress, the raja's *Diwan* wrote to Morar Pandit, chief *Pariccha* of the temple appointed under Maratha rule, threatening him with punishment for oppressing the Oriya Brahmanas who were under him.[24] The raja spoke for the interests of his people in his 'own' realm. As the traditional '*svamin*'[25] of the land and its resources and people, the raja also felt that he possessed the requisite authority to punish the erring *Pariccha* in conformance with his traditional role as arbitrator in temple conflicts (see Chapter 1.) His action was challenged by the Company administration, who refused to recognize his authority over temple functions. However, the Collector of Puri, Thomas Fortescue, in turn, wrote to Morar Pandit asking him to pay the annual *nuzar* prestation of nine gold *mohurs* and ten rupees to Mukundadeva.[26] The British officials were careful not to immediately disrupt traditional temple practices.

The Company government had started to establish their own channels of communication with temple personnel, and sought to circumscribe the raja's influence in this sphere. The region was effectively under the military domination of British forces, and their administrative apparatuses, particularly the Boards of Revenue at Cuttack, were in the process of being established. The raja's assertion of authority over temple functioning was a challenge to their structures of power and governance. Fortescue's action in abolishing the raja's authority over the temple while simultaneously granting the payment of the annual *nuzar*, was a bizarre misunderstanding of the prestation's role in validating the raja's supreme authority over the temple. It was also an attempt to acquire control over temple disbursements, except that the particular sum was not an ordinary payment, but a recognition of the raja's role as *adya sebąka* in the temple. This was a tangible instance of the clash between two systems of authority, the raja's ritual role in the temple realm and the military dominance of the British government. Attempts by the government to penetrate the sphere of temple functioning on its own terms, added a dimension of complexity to the charged situation.

In July 1804, following the raja's appointment of a 'mokuddum' of the village of Batgam, situated within his territory, the Company government responded violently, claiming it to be 'an act of presumption and unprovoked aggression'.[27] The raja's appointee was not to be 'allowed' to exercise 'any authority whatever in the village'. Despite the village being in the raja's territory, his authority over its administration was being severely restricted by the new government, whose administrative networks were gradually manipulating traditional landed structures. Along with the exercise of punitive authority to enforce their policies, the decisions of the Company government were encased in a particular rhetoric of bureaucratic control, which demarcated relations of power and hierarchies of control. Thus, the raja's act was defined as 'presumption' and 'unprovoked aggression' in official correspondence, being viewed as a transgression of boundaries created through the correspondence itself.

Since the beginning of his dialogue with the Company government, the raja had sought to retrieve the four *parganas* of

Serain, Rahang, Limbai and Chabiskud, having forfeited them to the Marathas. When the government prevented him from issuing orders in his own territory, the raja attempted to reassert his hold over the confiscated lands by claiming his annual tribute of sheep and goats from the areas. This was a traditional practice: the Gajapati was entitled to a number of cattle from these *parganas* at the time of the annual *ratha jatra*. In October 1804, armed retainers of the raja carried away 144 heads of cattle from some villages near Pipli as tribute. The Company administration responded swiftly. The raja was taken into custody and his territories confiscated. A circular was issued regarding the expulsion of the 'late Rebellious Tributary Gurjat Rajah of Khoordah from the Territories of Khoordah by the British troops and the annexation of that country to the Territories of the Honourable Company in the Province of Cuttack'.[28]

An inherent dissonance in the patterns of behaviour of the raja and the government authorities calls for an analysis of the multiple factors underlying their respective actions. At one level, the raja's collection of 'tribute' from the disputed areas over which he desired to assert his power, was prompted by the curtailing of his authority by the Company administration. The government's response in imprisoning the raja was the characteristic way of putting down a rebellion. Yet where was the rebellion and who was it directed against? The British government had effectively replaced the *subahdari* at Cuttack, and was thus entitled to tribute from the Gadajata chiefs, including the raja. His collection of ritual dues, strictly speaking, was not under their jurisdiction. However, the problematic nature of their relations with him and the dues being realized from the disputed *parganas*, placed his action in the light of a challenge to their authority over the region. Hence his dismissal and the annexation of his territory, the 'normal' punishment meted out to a rebellious chief.

A feeling of unease remains regarding the ritual nature of the raja's action, that cannot simply be explained by the cause and effect nature of the above analysis. The tribute was collected at the time of the annual festival, a moment of power within the sacred time cycles, when the significance of the raja's action was redoubled. The raja thus acted within a particular system of authority, within which his claim acquired a sacred dimension.

In his analysis of the divergent representations of the Bhils and their 'wildness' in colonial and subsequent historiography, Ajay Skaria states that *dhads*, or raids made by Bhils from the forest on neighbouring villages, are best understood as multiple claims to power.[29] The *dhad* was carried out as a political act, meant to repudiate or challenge other chiefs by the Bhil 'raja', or it could be a demand for '*haks*' (dues) by the raiders. These '*haks*', established through the raids, were essential for the maintenance of power, particularly of kingship, as all Bhil men were ideally styled 'rajas'. Keeping this scenario in mind, the Khurda raja's action in carrying away the cattle may then be viewed as a metaphor for the assertion of his power over his territory, at a sacred moment when his authority was doubly validated.

The colonial government regarded the raja's action as directed against their institutions of state. The rhetoric of 'rebellion', its connotation as a deliberate act violating their authority, was recreated several times over through numerous retellings in the official correspondence, until it assumed the status of a separate discourse. The raja's removal was the characteristic punishment for rebellion—his subsequent incarceration and the resulting controversy among colonial officials was an alternate construction of political power.

The raja, Mukundadeva, along with Neelakantha Mardaraja, zamindar of Harispur, was imprisoned at Midnapore. From his place of confinement, Mukundadeva wrote to the Governor General, praying for his indulgence, and blamed his 'Mookhtiyar' the *Diwan* Jayi Rajaguru for his actions. The *Diwan* was subsequently executed.[30] As a prisoner of the British government, the raja became a focus of a bureaucratic refiguring of power relations and the formation of an official discourse on authority. Different opinions were voiced regarding his fate. Harcourt wanted him 'exterminated'.[31] The circular regarding his expulsion, which was to be 'hung up in the most public places', named him 'the late Rebellious Tributary Gurjat Rajah of Khoordah', a string of epithets that parodied the list of honorific titles that usually preceded the raja's name. The use of the term 'rebellious' and 'tributary' inverted the connotations of power and sovereignty that were claimed by the use of the *birudas*, or honorific titles. This public pronouncement of his 'disgrace' in the scheme of the Company government, contradicted the aim of the notion of 'extermination' that Harcourt had advocated—it ensured that the raja would continue to exist, in life as well as in official documentation, being classified as 'rebellious'.

The existence of the raja as a prisoner of the government was testified to repeatedly by the minutiae regarding his maintenance that were continuously documented. A letter from Fortescue to Groeme, one of many, directs him to 'make such advances of cash for the maintenance of the prisoners Mukundeo late Rajah of Khoordah and Neelkanth Murdraj late Zemeendar of Hurreespur committed to your charge as may appear to you necessary and proper.' One may recall Foucault's image of the *Panopticon*—the modern prison as representing the altered notion of punishment in post-eighteenth century Europe. The earlier form of the *Supplice*, a public spectacle involving extreme torture of the condemned prisoner, expressing power relations that were defined in terms of the subject's link with the monarch, gave way to a tightly-knit grid of surveillance and the exercise of power over human bodies. The monarchical focus of power had disintegrated into a diffused, 'synaptic' regime of power, where it was exercised from within the social body rather than from above it.[32] Applying the notion of surveillance as a form of official control, the raja's incarceration decontextualized him from his politico-ritual framework and placed him under constant scrutiny by the Company administration. This enabled the bureaucratic mechanisms of the administration to control his physical form, while alienating him from his persona as raja. He was shorn of his royal status and ritual infrastructure, and reduced to dependence on the government.

The plethoric documentation regarding his 'maintenance' as a prisoner fiscalized the basis of his existence, reducing its fundamental premise to a fixed expenditure that was his link with the new regime. The documentation introduced a new discourse of power regarding the forms of control exercised by the colonial regime over traditional institutions in the region. The raja was circumscribed and classified by official accounts, a process wherein the basis of his authority and sovereignty was eroded. The sanitization of the raja's punishment with its underlying image of 'humaneness', the diffusion of power to surveillance through 'maintenance', effectively caused the erosion of the raja's contextual matrix of status and privilege.

He was 'remodelled', so to speak, through his interaction with the colonial regime, a process that facilitated the penetration of the traditional networks of power and status by colonial forces.

The Company government obviously found the raja's 'spiritual suzerainty' a hindrance in their quest for control over the temple. A strong case was built up in contemporary and subsequent official accounts, of the raja's 'rebellion' against the government. The annexation of Khurda is said to have occurred 'on account of the treachery on the part of the Rajah of Khoordah who after promising his aid and passage of troops from the Madras side, joined the Marhattas and was the cause of much trouble . . .'.[33] The continuous rationalization during documentation of policy in an effort to build an overall image of a benevolent government, commonly characterizes much of the colonial correspondence.

The 'treachery' and 'rebelliousness' that the Khurda raja was accused of, amounted mainly to his being a stumbling block before the Company's ambition of establishing complete control over the region, military and ideological. However, they succeeded in alienating the indigenous institutions from their resource bases to some extent by directly replacing the old leadership. The question is, were they aware of the depth of the relationships between the institutions and the interlinking processes, and were their actions directed towards these links at all? It would appear that the British government did not yet fully comprehend the nature of the material and ideological framework that bound the raja with the temple, or else they may not have decided to recall him into the temple sphere. In the next section, we will observe how those very institutions were modified to suit the requirements of the administration. They were remoulded, so to speak, and replaced from where they had been removed. The action of 'remoulding' put the colonial government under great stress as well, which gave rise to another type of conflict.

The Raja Reinstalled within the Temple: Colonization of the Sacred Kingship

The policy of support and conciliation initially followed by the colonial government with respect to traditional institutions in Orissa, is exemplified in Harcourt's Despatch to Campbell[34] where he was advised to take every precaution to safeguard the temple and its accessories. The new government was not, in any way, to interfere with the functioning of the system as it had prevailed, nor were they to allow '. . . any person . . . to enter the Pagoda without the express desire of the Bramins'. At the same time, they were directed to ' . . . be careful not to contract with the Bramins any engagement which may limit the powers of the British government. . . '. The delineation of a structure of authority surrounding the temple by the government, had multiple implications, even within their own official discourse. First, the temple was circumscribed and classified in colonial correspondence as an entity separate from other administrative areas. Second, the boundaries of this entity were demarcated and controlled by the colonial government, who, by not allowing 'any person' to enter the temple without the 'express desire of the Bramins', introduced a hierarchy of power related to accessibility within temple functioning. By extending the jurisdiction of the 'Bramins' (this itself was an ambiguous category) to controlling entry into the temple precincts, and by according to themselves a hegemonistic authority to articulate the Brahmanas' 'desire', they sought a niche of access and control in the processes of temple management, access which was otherwise denied to them.

The correspondence also highlights a separate motivation underlying the government's policy of conciliation, viz., the effort to prevent the formulation of 'any engagement' with the Brahmanas that 'may limit the powers of the British government'. A struggle for dominance between the temple management and the kingship had characterized the formation of the peculiar temple–state nexus in Orissa (see Chapter 1). However, the language of negation that is prominent in colonial correspondence, the avoidance of linkages with temple management rather than participation in them as in the case of the Gajapati kingship, created a divided structure of authority. The view of power as a fractured entity, with temple-related functions being viewed as separate from the administration of the state, caused the formulation of a new economic and political discourse and the 'hollowing' out of institutions in the sense proposed by Dirks.

A case in point is the issue of allocation of resources to the temple for its functions, a responsibility that the new government had immediately assumed on taking over the administration. The appointment of the Board of Commissioners at Cuttack and a Collector of revenue at Puri in 1803 illustrated the alacrity with which the new rulers had laid down bureaucratic machinery to control revenue structures.

The Company administration's desire to extend full control over the temple was made clear at the outset and they took over the administration directly, with the appointment of a Board of Commissioners. However, the new rulers soon found themselves at a loss regarding the peculiar problems and disputes that they encountered in the temple. On 30 June 1804, the temple *Paricchas* submitted a petition to the Board requesting money and other articles necessary for the performance of a purificatory ceremony. A bird of evil omen had alighted on the head of Goddess Bimala and defiled her sari. In order to avert the consequent calamity, complex rituals were required to be performed. The Board of Commissioners cautiously criticised this request as a 'direct attempt to impose upon and extract money from the government'[35] although they sanctioned the sum.

The new rulers were aware that their policy of conciliation as well as their status as non-Hindus, allowed them minimal control over the internal management of the temple. The temple's redistributive framework included 'cause and effect' linkages between material, cosmological and ideological factors, wherein physical defilement of a divine image resulting in a cosmic calamity could conceivably be remedied by very material means, a situation beyond their comprehension. The situation of inauspiciousness, symbolized by the defilement of the divine image, marked the convergence of a set of 'special' circumstances that required a ritual response. This was a paradigmatic occurrence, almost mythic in its context, indicating that a ceremony had to be performed at this moment which was imbued with power that could be destructively unleashed. Many such illustrative incidents are known in the mythology of the region, depicting the prevalence of a set of special circumstances, such as the dove attacking a hawk at a certain spot, where a powerful kingdom was to be founded. The symbolic power infused in the particular situation could be transferred to the resulting circumstances, positively or negatively. The negative impact of the situation was sought to be nullified by the priests.

Colonial correspondence regarding the matter depicts, more than ever, the schism between the worldview of the new rulers and the temple management. The government's reaction emphasized their focus on the sanctioning of money for the performance of the ritual: their reaction hinged on this issue. The Board of Commissioners, in their message to the Collector, stated that, 'Although the Board are anxious on all occasions as far as may be with propriety and due regard to the maintenance of the interests entrusted to them, to yield to the religious prejudices . . . of the priests and Bramins of the temple of Juggernaut; yet they cannot but view the above transaction in any other light than a direct attempt to impose upon and extract money from the Government. . . .'[36]

The new government's alienation from the cultural matrix that rationalized the temple's ritual functions is obvious here. While categories of 'propriety' and 'regard' for local customs are stated as characterizing official policy, the temple's belief system is referred to as 'prejudices', thus creating alternative contextual frameworks to view the situation. The new government's tolerant attitude towards prevailing institutions indicates a paternalistic patronization of local belief, with an underlying conviction of its falseness. Once again, we get a sense of a theatrical event that the government reluctantly endorsed, but could not participate in, either physically or ideologically.

There appears to be a conflict between two systems of belief. Foucault discusses the relationship between power and truth in Western society, wherein 'power never ceases its inquisition and registration of truth'.[37] The 'production' of truth is seen as essential to the production of wealth, in other words, a particular construction of 'truth' is viewed as the means to legitimize the acquisition of a particular entity, 'wealth'. The *Paricchas*' request for funds was not accepted as a valid channel for gaining access to wealth, thus was viewed as 'extraction'. The temple's networks of material and ideological exchange wherein the mythic, cosmic and physical worlds were interrelated dynamically through reciprocal linkages, was alien to the new government's understanding of the situation.

Despite their disapproval of the *Paricchas*' request, the Board of Commissioners sanctioned the money. On one hand their own policy of conciliation dictated that local institutions were to be appeased. At another level, their acquiescence further alienated them from involvement and understanding of temple functioning, and highlighted the separation of official opinion from policy implementation. The contradictory response also highlighted the different perspectives present within the bureaucratic complex that voiced varying interests. Thus, colonial policy, subsuming divergent opinions, came to acquire its own rhythm and momentum, constituting an independent discourse.

The interaction between the colonial bureaucratic machinery and the redistributive networks of the temple involved the clash of alternative structures of power, as we have seen. This also resulted in the appropriation of temple functions by bureaucratic processes and the consequent resistance within the temple sphere. Following their assumption of direct administration of the temple, the Company officials sought to gain an insight into its affairs by systematically documenting the different functions and personnel. As they could not enter the precincts, they acquired 'reliable' information from senior priests and collated the material, constructing an account of the institution that could be circulated among the different levels of the bureaucracy. One of the earliest and most prominent of such accounts was the report on the 'internal' management of the temple compiled by Charles Groeme, submitted in 1806. The primary focus of this report was the establishment of an administrative framework to facilitate the collection of the pilgrim tax and the efficient management of temple accounts.

The colonial government's desire to increase their control over temple functions, coupled with Groeme's description of 'confusion' and 'embezzlement' in temple accounts led to the formulation of Regulation IV in 1806. This document ordered the levying of the pilgrim tax, as well as the appointment of an assembly of 'pundits' to manage the 'internal economy, the conduct and management of the officers and entire control over the priests . . .'.[38] The 'pundits' were to be appointed by the Governor General on the recommendation of the Puri Collector and the Board of Commissioners. While this regulation is said to have 'legalized' the Company's control over the temple, it was, in fact, the establishment of an indirect control and the first step towards separating the government from the temple. The document stated that:

> The superintendence of the Temple of Juggernath and its interior economy, the conduct and management of its Officers and the entire control over the priests, Officers and servants attached to the idol and to the Temple, shall be vested in an Assembly of Pundits or learned Brahmins, who, on all occasions, shall be guided by the recorded rules and institutions of the Temple or by long and established usage. The Assembly of Pundits shall consist of three members to be recommended by the Collector of Pilgrim Tax through the Board of Revenue to the Governor General in Council. In the selection of persons to fill the situations, it shall be the particular duty of the Collector to consult the opinion of the most respectable Hindoos.[39]

The temple along with the functioning of its 'interior' economy was circumscribed as an area that was outside the direct jurisdiction of the colonial government. Its management was to be carried out by an assembly of Brahmanas, however, the government reserved the right to control their appointment. The juxtaposition of temple management with revenue affairs is prominent in this regulation, wherein the appointment of the 'pundits' was to be made through the direct recommendation of the Revenue Collector. Thus, the temple was largely subsumed by the overall function of revenue management of the colonial government. Yet, it was a separate space, to which direct access was denied to the new government. The withdrawal of direct administration and the appointment of a team of 'pundits', however, was an insidious form of penetration of the temple sphere by the government.

As early as 9 October 1806, a debate began over finding a 'more satisfactory individual' in whom the 'control of the Jagannatha Temple consistent with the usages of the Temple can be properly vested'.[40] James Hunter, Collector of Pilgrim Tax at Puri, recommended that the temple administration be handed over to the Khurda raja.[41] In January 1807, the Secretary Revenue Department at Calcutta, informed the Board of Revenue, Cuttack, that the Governor General had decided to release the Khurda raja from his confinement and reinvest him with the control over the temple 'which he formerly possessed'.[42] Charles Buller, Settlement Commissioner at Cuttack, also insisted on his appointment. Thus, Regulation IV of 1809 appointed the Khurda raja as superintendent of the temple in whom control over the priests, the internal economy and management of affairs was vested. This ended the direct administration of the temple by the Company administration.

The re-establishment of the raja as temple superintendent truly marked the colonization of the old regime. The raja was not accorded his prior status of Gajapati, nor was his territory, that had been confiscated by the Company government, returned to him. The context of his position vis-á-vis the temple had been subtly altered by the colonial administration, and the raja did not simply step into the place that he had vacated a few years ago. That is not to assume that the raja's status in the temple sphere had remained unchanged over the centuries prior to the advent of the British. We have observed that the Bhoi dynasty had to continuously strive to maintain its ritual credentials as Gajapati amidst waning political authority. Yet this conflict was within a particular symbolic framework that assumed the legitimacy of his ritual identity. The entry of colonialism created a new language of discourse, and involved the restructuring of the traditional framework of status and privilege. As Dirks, in his analysis of the encounter between the colonial government and the traditional kingship in Pudukottai, puts it, '. . . the cultural systems of state and temple were irrevocably altered . . .'.[43]

The raja was placed in charge of the 'internal economy' of the temple, the 'management' of the priests and other functionaries and all 'internal' affairs. The temple was apparently viewed in isolation from the status and privilege networks that linked it with the land and the politics of the region. The raja was not viewed as the centre of these networks by the colonial government, but was to be 'guided by the recorded rules and institutions of the temple or by established usage'.[44] Hitherto, the raja's authority in making decisions and arbitrating disputes was vested in him by virtue of his position. Although the raja acted within a system of custom and tradition, the tensions and patterns of which were known to him, his administration of justice was akin to divine justice in its spontaneity. The notion that he be guided by 'recorded rules' illustrates the colonial administration's preoccupation with precedent as a basis for justice and the authority of written records, a characteristic feature of European law. Thus, the internal authority of the raja was redefined in colonial terms.

Moreover, the raja's appointment was conditional to his discharging his duties with 'integrity, diligence and propriety'. The Governor General reserved the right to dismiss him on charges of 'misconduct'. The rules of behaviour that were to govern the raja's conduct within his realm were defined by the colonial government, who sought to circumscribe his actions within the framework of their own assumptions. The creation of a colonial context to the raja's current position in the temple, involved both the desire of the government to manipulate the raja in order to achieve maximum leverage in the temple sphere, as well as the raja's resistance to these attempts. According to the traditional cosmological framework of Jagannatha, it was highly incongruous that the *adya sebaka* of the lord of the universe could be dismissed for misconduct by the Company administration.

The first decade of the raja's management of temple affairs has often been described as a period of 'dyarchy',[45] indicating the Company's manipulation of the raja's position. It was a time when the maximum shifts and adjustments in policy matters took place, as the two systems of authority, the indigenous and the foreign, attempted to fit together. In that sense, it was a seminal period for the formulation of the colonial discourse, as the contact and conflict between the two systems as well as the resultant modifications, were at their peak.

The interaction between the two systems created an ideological space, within which the raja, in his dual role as Gajapati and an official representative of the new regime, began to consolidate his authority. In 1810, when the raja of Khimedi (Parlakhimedi) arrived at the temple for his annual pilgrimage, the Khurda raja denied him entrance for *darsana* and prevented him from procuring *mahaprasada*, considered to be the staple food for pilgrims. In a letter to the Collector at Cuttack, Samuel Busby, Collector, Puri, complained about the Khurda raja's behaviour in 'detaining' and 'insulting' Padmanabha Narayanadeva of Khimedi, who had apparently arrived for his pilgrimage along with his aged mother and three wives. The Khimedi raja had apparently paid his tax as per regulations, and therefore, Busby felt, the Khurda raja had no right to prevent him from having *darsana*. The Khurda raja responded to Busby's questioning and stated that the visiting chief had not applied for his permission to enter the temple, as was the customary courtesy. Busby called the *Deula Pariccha* and other senior priests and confirmed the veracity of the raja's claim. However, he denied its validity as it appeared to him a purely ritual matter, with 'not the least connection with the pilgrims'. Moreover, Busby asserted, that since the region was under the control of the British government, the Khurda raja had no right to issue 'original passes' on his own authority.[46]

As Gajapati, the raja still wielded an enormous amount of power through his link with the temple. The visiting rajas that came for their pilgrimage, according to custom, informed him in advance whereupon he arranged for the provision of various privileges that were in keeping with their status vis-à-vis the temple. There had been rivalry between the rajas of Parlakhimedi (Khimedi) and the Khurda dynasty over the title of Gajapati since the sixteenth century. The visiting chief, by not applying to the Khurda raja for permission, had deliberately transgressed the traditional courtesy due to the Gajapati while fulfilling the terms required for *darsana* according to the new regime. This was, in fact, a challenge to the authority of the Khurda raja, who responded by denying the visiting chief access to his realm, the temple. The Khimedi raja also bore his royal insignia into the temple precincts without informing the Gajapati, thereby flouting his authority in his own territory. The Khurda raja was employing his authority as the protector of the divine order of the temple, which had been transgressed by the visiting chief (see Chapter 2).

Busby reports that the raja influenced the cooks (*swars*) and prevented them from preparing the *mahaprasada*. 'Upwards of four to five thousand souls are now starving for want of customary Mahaparsad.'[47] Within the symbolic networks of the temple, food represented the dynamically charged channels of reciprocity that connected the various spheres of authority. The Khimedi raja's transgression of customary parameters of status and privilege, had repercussions throughout the temple realm in the language of symbolic reciprocity, a 'disturbance' of the balance of authority that was represented by the disruption of the *mahaprasada* preparation. The extent of the Gajapati's authority over all aspects of temple functioning, including his ability to cause five thousand pilgrims to starve, was not appreciated by Busby. The unique contradiction between the civil officials who were 'responsible' for temple administration and the raja, who, on one hand, was appointed by the government and answerable to it and on the other, was a ruler and the deputy (*rautta*) only of Jagannatha, arose from the conflicting claims to power of each over the other.

In the ranks of the Company's government, we observe a mixed reaction to the raja's misdemeanours. The officials who were on the spot and in contact with the raja, tended to react explosively. Busby was 'distressed' at the plight of the Khimedi raja, and displayed sympathy for his claim, particularly since the Khurda raja's action undermined his own authority whilst the Khimedi raja's approach enhanced it. In another such incident during the visit of the Raja of Khandpara, Richardson, Settlement Commissioner of Puri in 1814, called the Khurda raja 'an unfit person . . . to conduct the affairs of the temple' and suggested that a deputy superintendent be appointed.[48] Trower, Collector of Cuttack, threatened to suspend the Khurda raja for preventing the raja of Khandpara from entering the temple. This was the response of those who were in direct interaction with the raja. The reaction of the distant authorities, such as those in Calcutta, on the other hand, was cautious, based on perhaps what the raja represented to the Company administration; control over the temple and an ideological handle for the region. His presence in the temple also saved the Company from growing criticism about its link with idolatry. Hence, the frequent complaints against the raja were consistently ignored.

Thus, it will be noticed that the reinstatement of the raja did not take place at all, as the original context of his role vis-á-vis the temple, had changed. He was placed within a colonial context and his authority was confined and 'systematized' in accordance with that context. His appointment, originally meant to draw upon his traditional links with the temple, actually proceeded to redefine those very links to suit colonial requirements. Yet we observe that the context itself was still in a process of evolution, and a variety of pressures influenced its formulation.

CRYSTALLIZATION OF COLONIAL THOUGHT

Official perceptions of the Company government's policies regarding the administration of the temple in the first decade of the ninteenth century were full of conflicting trends. At one level, they were conscious of replacing the Marathas, a Hindu power in a predominantly Hindu state. The notion of conciliation of local traditions and personnel was projected through official records, as was the image of the Company government as a benevolent protector of the temple. At the core of this policy lay the issue of the pilgrim tax and the larger revenue that the temple was expected to yield under the 'benign and efficient' supervision of the colonial government. Charles Groeme, appointed Collector of pilgrim tax at Puri in 1804, was commissioned to investigate the temple's internal management and accounts. In June 1806, he submitted his report, a document that played a pivotal role in the restructuring of colonial relations between the temple and the state. Through its emphasis on minute documentation and detailed categorization of temple transactions, Groeme's report was instrumental in the establishment of a new bureaucratic structure and administrative machinery in the region. The report of George Webb, Groeme's successor, submitted in December 1807, supplemented Groeme's account with a detailed survey of temple accounts and disbursements.

The plethoric writing of administrative reports, minutes, memos and detailed correspondence following the taking over of the region by the colonial government constituted the formation of a separate discourse, establishing relations of power and control. In the colonial context, textuality has been described as a 'masked' use of force.[49] Colonialism as a discourse, is viewed as interpellating colonial subjects by incorporating them in a particular system of representation, i.e. through texts. The production of knowledge and strategies of representation were symbiotically related to forms of plunder and the acquisition of wealth. Thus the discourse of textuality established forms of control over the region by the bureaucratic apparatuses of the new regime.

I will now examine in detail three documents that were crucial to the evolution of the official discourse at this time, viz.,

Harcourt's Despatch to Campbell and the reports of Charles Groeme and George Webb. These illustrate the complex opinions, perspectives and trends that characterized official discourse and resulted in the 'colonization' of the temple–state realm along with its ancillary institutions. Three predominant themes characterize this process: the notion of discipline as defined and imposed by the colonial authorities on the temple and its institutions, the significance of the representation of indigenous processes through official accounts, and the particular ambivalence in official attitudes towards local institutions, signified in the Compact ideal of Wellesley. I have further explored the significance of the evangelical view of the temple's link with the state and the manner in which this played a role in restructuring the relations between the Company administration and the temple sphere.

The Rhetoric of 'Discipline' in the Administration's Relations with the Temple Sphere

The penetration of temple institutions by the new regime operated, to a great extent, through the imposition of 'discipline' over various sectors of its functioning. This notion was projected through multiple injunctions, to 'conform' to British authority, to 'order' the seemingly chaotic temple management, to 'fix' and 'classify' incomes and expenditures. In his message to Lt. Col. Campbell, commanding the Northern Division of the Madras Army, Lt. Col. Harcourt, Military Secretary to the Governor General, enumerated Lord Wellesley's policy of appeasement of local institutions. 'You will use every possible means to conciliate the inhabitants.' Yet, there was an underlying menace in the injunction, that those who ' . . . shall not act against the British authority' shall be left unmolested.[50] Particular attention was to be paid to the affairs of the pilgrims, and they were to be accorded ample 'protection'. The 'Bramins' were recognized as deriving considerable profit from the pilgrims and the temple, yet their 'rapacity' was to be left unchecked, their 'religious prejudice' to continue without hindrance. Simultaneously, Campbell was instructed not to enter into any arrangement that would limit the Company government's authority in the temple sphere and the region. Another suggestion of the new government's military dominance was made through the posting of an armed force near the temple, presumably for its 'protection'.

The threat of coercion against those who did not conform to British authority underlay the conciliatory rhetoric of the Compact policy. The focus of official correspondence was the prospect of increased revenue from the pilgrim tax, a major factor in the relatively peaceful taking over of the *Mughalbandi* by British troops. This does not indicate that there was a total absence of violence in the manoeuvre—there are references to 'what might have been taken as a prize to the Army' in the government records, indicating that some degree of raiding did take place.[51] However, large-scale plunder, as had taken place in other states, such as Seringapatam, did not occur in Puri. Force was also indicated as a means for the establishment of dominance by the Company government through the directive to not enter into any engagement that would limit their authority. The unlimited use of power, military and ideological, was a desired outcome of the 'conquest'. To reinforce its newly established authority, the Company government posted an armed force near the temple, the focal point over which control was desired. Thus, military coercion was an option kept alive by the new rulers while pursuing their conciliatory strategy.

Following the initial military take-over of Puri and its environs, the new government began to install more comprehensive and penetrative measures of asserting their control over local institutions. The pilgrim tax was a focal point in the establishment of a relationship between the temple and the new government, even in 1803. Wellesley's policy initially advocated its abolition as it was viewed as a form of oppression by the new rulers. The initial abolition of the tax was also carried out in order to improve their image vis-à-vis their predecessors, the Marathas, who were viewed as oppressive and tyrannical, particularly with reference to tax collection. However, this state of affairs was, even then, viewed as temporary and the collection of the tax under the systematic and 'civilized' Company administration was expected to yield unimaginably high profits.

Charles Groeme, in his report on the internal management of the temple, described the '. . . confusion that exists in every department of the temple. . . .'[52] He eulogized the period when the Khurda raja controlled temple affairs. 'During that period when the affairs of the temple were under the immediate control and management of the Rajah of Khoordah, even the slightest deviation from the prescribed duties were severely fined or . . . given corporal punishment. . . .'[53] Jagannatha Rajaguru, the second *Pariccha* of the temple and Groeme's chief informant, had formerly been the revenue officer of Khurda under the raja. Hence, it may be inferred that he had a vested interest in seeing the raja restored to his former position in the temple.

An important factor that preoccupied Groeme was the lack of 'discipline' in the temple management and the neglect of their duty by the *sebayets*. 'The Deul Purchas who were guilty of neglect of their duties were always liable to be dismissed from their offices by the Khoordah Rajah. . . . Any servant of the temple who were guilty of an enormous offence, whether toward god or man . . . was dismissed from the situation. . . . '[54] Groeme's statement indicates a vacuum within the sphere of authority, resulting in the subsequent chaos and 'mismanagement'. The report repeatedly states that in former times, maximum attention had been paid to the detailed performance of the different *sebas*, a situation which had since degenerated. Groeme viewed the ordered system of the temple as comprising multiple tiny rituals whose correct performance would maintain the entire complex, in fact, a mechanical entity.[55]

The detailed classification of temple functions that was demanded of Groeme by the authorities, was in itself, a form of discipline that was sought to be imposed. The systematization of the functions, restoring order out of chaos, as it were, was aimed at making sense out of unintelligible rituals and processes. The categories that constituted 'sense' were thus formulated from a Western perspective, and sought to accommodate prevailing conditions within their parameters. The figure of authority that was represented by the raja, according to Groeme, incorporating powers of arbitration and punishment, was seen as necessary to the successful running of the temple. This indicated that the new rulers were obliged to provide such a disciplinary figure, in keeping with the temple's 'traditions'. The numerous bodies of arbitration, the *paricchas*, the *Mukti Mandapa Sabha* and others, were not viewed in their separate contexts with their disparate areas of functioning, but were hierarchically ordered. The raja was placed at the top of the hierarchy.

The classification of temple functions into numerous disparate rituals, viewed as mutually exclusive events, dispersed official authority over their representation. It allowed the mechanisms of control, embodied by the classificatory exercise, to penetrate every section of temple functioning. One may recall Foucault's theory of the dispersal of power over each segment of the social organism in a modern state, so that surveillance and discipline, rather than punishment become the modern apparatuses of control. The 'fixing' of categories of ritual, *sebas*, and forms of material and ideological exchange, also led to Groeme's definition of their transgression as 'embezzlement', 'mismanagement', etc. The issues of 'discipline' and 'duties' coalesced around the problem of the 'embezzlement' of temple properties by the *sebayets*. Groeme reported widespread siphoning off of materials for temple *bhogas*, pilgrims' offerings by the *pratiharis*,[56] and land produce by the *mathadharis*.[57] Groeme's use of the term 'embezzlement', apart from displaying an appropriative claim over temple functions by the government, immediately imbued it with criminal connotations and placed it within the context of a particular structure of legal rhetoric. Through his allusion to the *sebayets'* actions as embezzlement, Groeme drew up certain boundaries, between 'right' and 'privilege', 'status' and 'official position', that had not previously existed in the system.

Within the context of the colonial definition of order, what was outside its parameters, was not valid, or 'right'. Thus, the writing of classificatory reports caused a particular structure of categories and relationships to be imposed upon the earlier networks of status and reciprocity. Groeme saw the structure of rituals and functions as fixed, and their performance as the 'duty' of the personnel. The *seba* itself was not so much a 'duty', as Groeme terms it, but a 'right' or a 'privilege'. We see this from the fact that fraction of *sebas* were purchased eagerly by various functionaries in order to increase their access to the temple sphere.[58] The right to a *seba* entitled the servitor to a certain status, and was a form of power. Its 'misuse' as Groeme sees it, was also an expression of that status. Thus, we see that the *sebayets* often threw 'impediments' in the way of the regular performance of the various ceremonies of the temple[59] a situation most offensive to Groeme. The smooth running great 'engine' of the temple was often derailed by its own drivers! Groeme did not realize that the objective of the *sebayets* was not the unhindered and efficient performance of the *sebas*: their status and position accrued from the expression of their authority in the temple realm, and occasionally this involved blocking the complex ceremonies.

Similarly, the report of George Webb, Collector at Cuttack, was a detailed enumeration of all the disbursements and transactions of the temple for a period of six years, from 1801 to 1807. The list of pilgrim tax collections and a comprehensive account of the temple lands, particularly those under the management of the *mathas*, was 'regrettably' delayed, as the Commissioners indicated to the Governor General. It was a massive effort, nevertheless, minutely detailed and well illustrates the concern of the administration about the expenditure incurred by the temple.[60]

Webb's report is a classic illustration of a concerted effort made by colonial authorities to penetrate the fiscal institutions of the temple. His report involved a detailed ordering of the temple's networks of material and ideological reciprocity that led to a homogenization of the diverse relationships in landed relations. Following his examination of the various categories of land endowments, Webb modified and 'tightened' the revenue collection. For instance, he claimed to have ascertained that the 'actual' value of certain villages paying *tanki* (quit rent) was far above what was actually given.[61] The collections from land allotted for *khanjas* or fixed amounts were included within the *jumma* (revenue) of the entire district, and disbursed from the central district treasury.

Thus, the relations of revenue collection between the *sebayets* and the landholders were reformulated, and ritual collections subsumed as generic revenue. The awarding of lands under *tanki*, or quit rent, was an honour accorded to privileged personnel under the traditional regime. Evaluating it as general revenue was a destruction of the landholders' privileges and status accruing therefrom. Here again, we see the imposition of a particular framework of landed relations reinforced by an overarching militaristic authority, which caused the alienation of pre-existing relations of status and privilege.

The recommendations of Groeme and Webb must be seen in

light of a larger debate on the government's role in temple administration and policy formation. The regulation of temple functions was fraught with internal tensions amongst the colonial bureaucracy, and the imposition of control and 'discipline' on the related institutions was viewed from different perspectives. In January 1809, a draft despatch was sent by the Court of Directors of the Company to the Board of Control at Calcutta, deeming it 'improper' for a Christian government to 'interfere in matters which cannot be proper or competent for that government to regulate'. Participating in the daily functioning of a 'Hindoo' temple was viewed as a 'direct invasion of the most revered . . . institution'.[62] Robert Dundas, President of the Board of Control, replied to this missive in the most scathing terms:

> The Board are sorry that they are not able to accede to the position laid down in para 14 in respect to the temple of Juggernath. . . It appears to the Board . . . to be the duty of the Magistrate (and as such, in no wise inconsistent with the principles of our religion) in a country in which the worship of the Hindoos must be suffered to prevail under its protection, to interfere so far in the . . . superintendance of the religious establishments of that people, as may be necessary for the maintenance of tranquillity or for the preservation of peace and government order among the Hindoos themselves.[63]

The Court of Directors, however, was adamant. 'The Court beg leave respectfully to state that they still deem it their duty to propose the prohibition of such things beyond the care of the police, the administration of Justice, the collection of a tax requisite for the due attainment of these ends. . . . '[64] The debate culminated in Regulation IV of 1809, wherein the Khurda raja was appointed temple superintendent in charge of its internal economy and with full control over the priests. Thus, it is evident that the framework being imposed for the regulation and control of temple institutions was not a one-dimensional entity, but was negotiated between divergent opinions and motivations. The 'ordering' of temple functions involved a reorganization and reformulation of Western institutions such as 'justice', the police, etc., and their application in a uniquely colonial context, within the parameters of current exigencies.

Loomba has analysed colonial processes of data-gathering, documentation, etc., leading to policy-formation, as corresponding to the relationship between the discursive and material practices of imperialism.[65] The writing of texts describing indigenous institutions was focused on the exploitation of such institutions as sources of revenue. To this end, rituals and processes were 'ordered' and classified, as well as being alienated from their ideological and material contexts. A new structure of relations and categories of functioning were imposed upon them under protection of a military dominance. This was a new 'order' that was fixed and perpetuated through plethoric correspondence.

The Politics of Representation: Creation and Control of a Cultural 'Other'

The production of knowledge about prevailing institutions and practices by the colonial government involved their penetration through strategies of representation. Gathering of information, its ordering and presentation to Western official authorities fed into the processes of establishment of apparatuses of power and control. Indigenous institutions were reconstructed within the parameters of colonial administrative requirements as being completely alien to Western norms, a perspective that linked the two in a perpetual relationship of oppositions. The detailed classification and documentation of resources and personnel was also framed in the language of appropriation, as wealth capable of being exploited.

The initial two years of Company administration, when temple expenses were actually defrayed from the general revenue, resulted in a change of policy on the part of the government. In March 1805, the Governor-General instructed the Board of Commissioners to initiate tax collection in order to meet temple expenses and for its repair and maintenance.[66] In a letter to Charles Groeme, Thomas Fortescue, Secretary to The Board of Commissioners, instructed him to obtain 'such information in regard to the Establishment (of the temple) and customs thereof as shall enable you to form a report on the same . . .'. Groeme was required to ascertain the extent of the following: 'The lands appropriated to the Temple, the resources and revenues thereof and the amount of the annual demands established by custom or otherwise on certain pergunnas villages and castating [*sic*] as correctly as possible the period of their origin and generally all information descriptive of the resources of the Temple.'[67] While the pilgrim tax was a primary economic motivation to maintain their link with the temple, the process of classification and documentation of temple functions and processes was in itself a form of penetration of this realm by the new authorities.

In colonial terms, the acquisition of information regarding local institutions was a means of 'acquiring' control over the institutions themselves. Loomba has analysed the codification of ethnic groups by colonial authorities, particularly through photographs, as 'fixing' them in a particular social and temporal mode, with no room for change. The creation of official ethnographies reduced the population to a certain number of pages, their cultural contexts circumscribed within a prescribed textual limit.[68] The gathering of information relating to the temple by Groeme juxtaposed material resources as well as personnel into a common complex of 'resources', the networks of status and reciprocity connecting people and wealth being collapsed into a common framework for analysis by the authorities. Thus, myths, texts, rumours, opinions all fed into the construction of a particular view of the reality of the temple and the region. This view was perpetuated through official documentation and policy-formation, formulating a fixed category against which any transgression was regarded as deviation from the 'norm'.

Webb's report on temple 'disbursements' further encapsulated networks of reciprocity within an economistic framework, regarding the outflow of resources as 'expenses'. The detailed classification of such 'expenses' facilitated their penetration by bureaucratic ordering mechanisms, land revenue regulations and other administrative measures of control. In the case of the takeover of tanki lands discussed earlier, the report emphasized the extent of the lands to the minutest detail, as well as the amount of revenue that could be exacted from them. The notion of privilege attached to their ownership was merely mentioned in passing, as an unimportant fact. Thus, the process of classification of information was also a process of selection of material considered relevant to the interest of the administration.

The writing of official documents can also be viewed as representing specific ways of 'seeing' and projecting racial, social and cultural differences. Notions of 'protection' and 'conciliation' of local institutions presumes a polarization between them and the colonial government.[69] The rhetoric of benevolence and liberality on the part of the government serves to differentiate between temple and state by demarcating the direction of flow of government 'beneficence', from state to temple. A memo to the Board of Commissioners advocating the resumption of the pilgrim tax, illustrates this fact. 'There can be no objection to the British government of relieving itself from a heavy annual expense and of providing funds to answer the contingent charges of the religious institutions of the Hindoo faith maintained by the British government.'[70] The argument projected in the document depicts the formation of policy following careful negotiation between the evangelical protagonists and those who advocated a closer manipulation of the temple. However, it succeeds in alienating the temple from being an active agent in the process, while simultaneously designating it an object of the discourse. The penetrative 'gaze' of official reporting caused the temple to be viewed as a passive entity, circumscribed, decontextualised, but analysed, in colonial correspondence.

Forms of representation of local institutions in official texts depicted contradictory opinions and trends within the purview of administrative discourse. Perceptions of violence at the local level were overlaid by conflicting representations. In the next section, I have examined the ambivalence underlying colonial policy that reflected the tension between coercion at the local level and the overall coerciveness of the colonial state.

Ambivalence in Colonial Attitudes: Contradictory Representations in Official Texts

The policy of conciliation and 'protection' of local institutions articulated in Harcourt's despatch to Campbell, involved the enmeshing together of conflicting values and images of order. While Harcourt was to use all possible means '. . . to conciliate the inhabitants' of the town of Puri, this was qualified by the statement '. . . who shall not act against the British authority'. Pilgrims were to be 'protected'. The 'Bramins' were viewed as having derived much 'profit' from the temple, yet their 'rapacity' and 'religious prejudice' were to be left unchecked.

There has recently been an impetus, among scholars, to 'read against the grain' of colonial representation, implying that the images projected in official texts need to be deconstructed and re-examined. Lata Mani, in her analysis of eyewitness accounts of *sati* in the colonial period, observes that representations of the violence of widow burning must be viewed within the framework of the epistemic violence of colonialism. The policy of conciliation vis-à-vis the temple was a strategy of penetration and the acquisition of control. The takeover of the region was itself a military exercise, a factor that reinforced the dominance of the new regime. The rhetoric of 'protection' applied to pilgrims who would yield the tax revenue and subsequently the temple complex, also involved the establishment of apparatuses of control. The temple was engulfed within the sphere of colonial dominance, depicted as 'protection' by the administration.

The 'Bramins' were viewed as 'rapacious', extorting money from the pilgrims. Forms of incipient violence, such as the alleged extortion by the Brahmanas, were left un-confronted within the purview of the conciliatory policy. Yet the terminology used to describe the Brahmanas' actions was replete with violent epithets, 'rapacity' among them. The indirect projection of violence as part of local institutions was framed within the overall coercion exercised by the new regime. The texts hinted at the government's ability to 'check' the Brahmanas' 'rapacity' and 'religious prejudices', yet did not exercise the power. This notion of restrained authority is very much a part of the conciliatory ideal and the politics of ambivalence.

Issues of 'discipline' in the temple sphere which were highlighted in Groeme's report coalesced around the alleged 'embezzlement' of temple resources by the personnel. The imposition of criminal categories and a specific legal framework on the temple's status networks, alienated the institution from the networks within the administrative discourse. The functionaries' siphoning off of resources was contrary to the claims of the bureaucratic machinery created to exact revenue from the temple. Forms of localized control over resources was viewed as 'embezzlement', a transgressive exercise, while the assumption of control over the total wealth of the temple was rationalized by official discourse. This is also indicated in the manner in which Webb recommended the resumption of *tanki* lands, an exercise in coercion wherein traditional landholders lost their privileges. Colonial rhetoric rationalized its own actions to itself—as being 'liberal', 'anti-authoritarian', benevolent, etc. Yet, the entire discourse was within the closed circuit of the bureaucratic framework. The people were viewed as passive 'subjects', contributing little to the making of their own destiny. An overarching power structure, having appropriated the authority to control resources yet with no obligation of accountability, characterized the formation of the colonial state.

The bureaucratic discourse initiated by the entry of the British regime into the political and cultural realms of Orissa was an interlinked web of conflicting trends. The Company government's view of the temple as a socio-economic and political entity that was separate from the structures of state authority, characterized their initial policy towards its administration. Yet, there was an underlying awareness of the ritual link between the temple and the Gajapati regime, a link that they attempted to penetrate initially. The destruction of the traditional kingship through British military dominance did not result in the raja's removal from the scene, but involved the manipulation of his status vis-à-vis the temple, and the subordination of that status within the new discourse of power. Thus, power was not vested completely in any domain of the state, but constantly negotiated between the different structures of authority, the recontextualized Gajapati kingship and the new rulers.

The unfolding of the colonial discourse of power involved the penetration of traditional institutions by bureaucratic processes of documentation and classification, their objectification through representation. This did not divorce the new regime from the exercise of violent coercion, rather, it reinforced coercion through its sanitized representation within the parameters of textual material. The 'disciplining' of temple functioning through exhaustive categorization, the 'rationalization' of temple 'disbursements' through detailed accounting, all served to separate the categories of 'religion', justice' and 'administration'. Power, devoid of linkages of accountability, came to be vested in the vast bureaucratic structure of the colonial state, and in its continuous and plethoric representation, a reflection of itself.

NOTES

1. 'John Melville, Commissioner, Cuttack, to Governor General', in Eschmann et al., *Cult of Jagannatha*, p. 347.
2. Teltscher, *India Inscribed*, pp. 114-15.
3. Jemima Kindersley's account, ibid., p. 115.
4. Ibid., pp. 127-8.
5. Bernard S. Cohn, 'The Census and Objectification in South Asia', in B. Cohn, *An Anthropologist*, pp. 224-54.
6. Mani, 'Reading Eyewitness Accounts of Widow Burning', pp. 273-90.
7. 'Puri Sanad of Janoji Bhonsle', pp. 76-9.
8. Kalikinkar Dutta, 'Social, Economic and Political Effects of the Maratha Invasions between 1740 and 1765 on Bengal, Bihar and Orissa', *Proceedings of the Indian Oriental Conference*, 6th Session, Patna, 1930, pp. 189-98.
9. *Select Committee Proceedings*, serial no. 9, Fort William, 18 Feb. 1762.
10. 'From Chimna Sau, Subahdar, Cuttack to John Lowe, Resident at Cuttack,' *Foreign Secret Proceedings*, Fort William, 5 July 1764.
11. In Eschmann et al., p. 345.
12. Ibid.
13. Eschmann et al., p. 346.
14. *Bengal Secret and Political Consultations*, no. 46, 8 August 1803, Quoted in Mukherjee, *A Critical Study*.
15. N.B. Edmonstone, Secretary to Government to J. Melville, Commissioner for the Affairs of Cuttack and Lt. Col. Campbell, C.O., Northern Division of the Army under the Presidency of Fort St. George, 3 September 1803, *Bengal Secret Persian Correspondence*, India Office Records, no. 180.
16. F. Halliday, Secretary to Government of Bengal to Secretary, Government of India, 11 March 1844. Quoted in P. Mukherjee, *A Critical Study*.
17. It must be kept in mind that Halliday's report was written four decades after the initial negotiations with the Brahmanas at Puri, when the question of the pilgrim tax and the government's connection with the temple had once again assumed relevance. There was a large section of the bureaucracy that spoke for the continuation of the tax and of the government's role in temple affairs.
18. J. Melville to N.B. Edmonstone, 11 September 1803, *Bengal Secret and Political Consultations*, 1 March 1804, no. 13. Quoted in Mukherjee, *A Critical Study*.
19. Walter Ewer, 'Correspondence on the Settlement of Khoordah in

Pooree, 13 May 1818', in *OHRJ*, vol. 3, no. 1, p. 1 (hereafter *Ewer's Report*).

20. Kulke, 'Juggernaut', in Eschmann et al., p. 348.
21. Melville to Edmonstone, 19 September 1803, *Bengal Secret and Political Consultations* quoted in Mukherjee, *A Critical Study*, p. 27.
22. Ibid., pp. 27-8.
23. *Katakarajavamsavali*, Hermann Kulke and G.C. Tripathi, eds., pp. 113-15.
24. Raja's letter to Morar Pandit, in Mukherjee, *A Critical Study*, p. 28.
25. See Dirks, *Hollow Crown*, p. 126.
26. Fortescue to Morar Pandit, 11 September 1804, in Mukherjee, *A Critical Study*, p. 29.
27. Secretary, Board of Commissioners to J. Hunter, Acting Collector, Juggernath, 28 July 1804, Jagannatha Temple Correspondence, vol. I (hereafter JTC).
28. T. Fortescue to Charles Groeme, 15 December 1804, JTC, vol. 1.
29. Ajay Skaria, 'Being Jangli: The Politics of Wildness', *Studies in History*, 14, 2, 1998.
30. Mukherjee, *A Critical Study*, pp. 31-2.
31. Kulke, 'The Struggle', pp. 345-48.
32. Foucault, *Power/Knowledge*, pp. 5-45.
33. Harcourt to Shawe, 24 December 1804, in Mukherjee, *A Critical Study*, pp. 30-40.
34. Mukherjee, *A Critical Study*, p. 6.
35. Fortescue to Hunter, 19 September 1804, in Mukherjee, *A Critical Study*, p. 89.
36. Ibid.
37. Foucault, *Power/Knowledge*, pp. 78-108.
38. Mukherjee, *A Critical Study*, p. 91.
39. Ibid., p. 91.
40. Governor-General to Board of Revenue, 9 October 1806, ibid., p. 96.
41. Hunter to Robert Ker, Magistrate, Cuttack, 11 November 1806, JTC, vol. 1.
42. JTC, vol. 1, p. 145.
43. Dirks, *Hollow Crown*, p. 382.
44. Regulation IV of 1809, 28 April 1809, in Mukherjee, *A Critical Study*, p. 107.
45. Mukherjee, *A Critical Study*, p. 95.
46. Busby to Mitford, 15 May 1810, JTC, vol. 1.
47. Busby to Trower, 17 May 1810, JTC, vol. 1.
48. Richardson to Earl of Moira, 8 January 1814, in Mukherjee, *A Critical Study*, p. 102.

49. Loomba, *Colonialism/Postcolonialism*, pp. 91-5.
50. Mukherjee, *A Critical Study*, p. 1.
51. Charles Grant, Secretary, Government of India, 'Correspondence Relating to the Missionaries and Idolatry', in Mukherjee, *A Critical Study*, pp. 11-12.
52. 'Report of C. Groeme, Collector regarding the Establishment, Customs, etc., of the Temple of Jugunnath, submitted to the Commissioner for the Province of Cuttack', 10 June 1806, in Mukherjee, *A Critical Study*, p. 49.
53. Mukherjee, *A Critical Study*.
54. Ibid., p. 56.
55. Ibid., p. 63.
56. Ibid., p. 67.
57. Ibid., p. 59.
58. Daily Accounts.
59. Mukherjee, *A Critical Study*, pp. 63-4.
60. From George Webb, Collector, Zillah Cuttack to G.H. Barlow, President and Member of the Board of Revenue, Fort William, 19 December 1807, JTC.
61. Webb's Report, p. 3.
62. Mukherjee, *A Critical Study*, pp. 100-1.
63. Ibid., p. 99.
64. Parliamentary Papers, 1813, in Mukherjee, *A Critical Study*, pp. 102-3.
65. Loomba, *Colonialism/Postcolonialism*, pp. 99-100.
66. Secretary to Government to Board of Commissioners, 4 March 1805, Parliamentary Papers, in Mukherjee, *A Critical Study*.
67. Fortescue to Groeme, 11 March 1805, in Mukherjee, *A Critical Study*.
68. Loomba, *Colonialism/Postcolonialism*, pp. 95-100.
69. Ibid., pp. 32-3.
70. Secretary to Government to the Board of Commissioners, 4 March 1805, in Mukherjee, *A Critical Study*.

CHAPTER 5

Power and Property: The 'Profanization' of Temple Networks

> Oh Jagannatha . . . do not give me wealth, progeny, fortune . . . all I seek is a handful of the dust from your feet. . . .[1]

It is believed that the land of Puri is so infused with the divinity of Jagannatha, that a fistful of sand from the seashore is worth a lifetime's earnings. The correlation of material wealth with spirituality typifies the temple's cosmology and worldview, where property, power, ritual and privileges are linked and energized by a dynamic of sacredness. 'When the sacred manifests itself in any hierophany', writes Mircea Eliade, 'there is not only a break in the homogeneity of space; there is also revelation of absolute reality, opposed to the non-reality of the vast surrounding universe.'[2] The revelation of the sacred orients the surrounding space, imbuing it with a sense of order. On the contrary, 'profane' space is homogenous and relative, a conglomerate of 'neutral spaces' where man lives and moves, governed by the ever-changing needs of a 'secular' society.[3]

In this chapter, I have explored the colonization of the networks of temple property, and the rights and status accruing therefrom, in the first half of the nineteenth century. In the first section, I have examined the erosion of the territorial and ideological dominance of the raja through the exigencies of colonial policy. The subsequent section deals with disputes over access to temple property and services. Linking together the areas of conflict are certain common themes, particularly the ossification of relationships and boundaries through intensive definition and classification by colonial authorities. This period was marked by the large-scale imposition of new tenurial systems authorized by European law. The interaction between two disparate revenue and legal structures, the indigenous and the Western, led to peculiar situations of conflict. I have termed this entire process 'desacralization' or 'profanization', wherein the significant structures of privilege and dominance were decontextualized according to the requirements of colonial policy.

The profanization of temple resources and services involved the interaction between prevailing institutions of ritual and political authority and the Company administration, which sought to institute large-scale revenue and legal changes. Amidst arguments and counter-arguments at different levels of the bureaucracy and resistance from local interests, networks of rights and obligations and channels of material and ideological reciprocity were de-linked from their ritual context and placed within the purview of a colonial discourse. This is particularly true with respect to the appropriation of territory by the Company administration, wherein prevailing structures of access and control over property were re-configured through the working of colonial policy, and lost their legitimacy and authority.

Indigenous structures of adjudication that were common to much of Indian society by the eighteenth century, included local caste councils, village panchayats and the jurisdiction of dominant political groups, the zamindars and the raja.[4] In the realm of the Jagannatha temple at Puri, the *Mukti Mandapa Sabha* of Vedic (*sasana*) Brahmanas was an important authority on social disputes. The raja, even after the degeneration of his territorial influence, was the ultimate source of legitimacy and authority within the temple, which projected outwards through the pilgrim and landed networks.

The notion of property, as it had evolved in India until at least the eighteenth century, assumed multiple ownership, or at least 'coextensive rights' of several individuals to a single piece of property. Indigenous juristic literature, or what was collectively termed the '*sastras*', was primarily consulted by ritual experts on issues of rules of law, customary analogies of the laws, and 'general principles', through which custom was interpreted in the language of the *dharmasastras*.[5] A plethora of terms denoted the notion of ownership of property, subsuming all the nuances of the concept. Thus, *dhana*, *adhikara*, *bhoga*, *svamitva* and others implied 'ownership', 'right', 'mastery', 'enjoyment' and, by extension, came to apply to non-sanskritic local terms and concepts. The king's authority over all the land was often indicated, through his right to un-owned (*asvamika*) land, resumable tenures and heirless inheritances, rather than overtly defined through ownership.[6] The notion of 'trust', which came to apply to temple property in colonial times, was picturesquely termed *nivi*, literally the knot of a woman's lower garment. The analogy illustrated the private and secure nature of the transactions of such a fund, as well as the limits on the *adhikara* (rights) of the depositary as well as the beneficiary. Finally, the most distinctive feature of the indigenous notion of property, is the ability to share *svatva* (loosely, ownership) among several owners. There could be as many as five *svatvas* pertaining to a single piece of land: those of the raja, the ultimate *svami* and receiver of revenue, the *mula svami* or *bhaumika* (land-holder) the payer of revenue, the mortgagee and sub-mortgagee who collected the revenue and finally the cultivator.[7]

In this situation, administrative and legal changes implemented by the Company's government articulated peculiar contradictions. During the imposition of revenue and legal changes in India in the late eighteenth and nineteenth centuries, colonial policy oscillated between reformism and *laissez faire*. On one hand, we find explicit injunctions to leave intact local 'custom and usage' by colonial administrators, while simultaneously, there was a drive towards introducing 'uniformity and rationality' in indigenous revenue systems. [8] The result of this ambivalence was the importation of British legal principles, like 'equity, justice and good conscience', into Indian courts. Simultaneously, there was an effort to discover and codify Indian laws, 'a plan that was Roman in its aspirations and Benthamite in its inspiration', as Appadurai puts it.[9] The flood of litigation at the new courts, the nature and extent of the disputes and the 'corruption' of the litigants and their legal representatives (*vakeels*) mystified and disgusted the colonial officials. What emerged as a result of the interaction between British principles and the Indian reality was a unique and unexpected situation.

As we shall see in the following sections, control over temple resources was an issue at many levels. The pilgrim tax and the *Sataishazari* endowment for temple maintenance was argued and disputed amongst the entire bureaucratic hierarchy, from the local collector to the Court of Directors and the Governor-General. Although it was not acknowledged as such, the *Sataishazari* endowment was a matter between the colonial administration and the raja, the traditional head of the state and the temple. The pilgrim tax also involved the *pandas* and the *pratiharis* of the temple who petitioned for its continuation. These were, however, unheard voices in the mass of bureaucratic correspondence on the subject. What was debated with vigour, was the extent and the nature of the right to control property. Thus, efforts to control and manipulate resources and services led to regulation and bureaucratization on the part of the government, and disputes by the servitors.

THE SATAISHAZARI ENDOWMENT—DESACRALIZING THE TEMPLE–STATE LINK

The question of the government's 'withdrawal' from active participation in the temple's administration was a much debated one. A memo submitted to the Board of Revenue, Fort William, in 1839, expresses popular opinions in bureaucratic circles at the time. 'Much as we deprecate all personal interference with the ceremonies of a religion . . . of the most demoralizing and degrading character, it is yet . . . our bounden duty not only to tolerate that religion but to provide for its free exercise by our Hindoo subjects, to secure the due appropriation of the proceeds by which its endowments are supported, and lastly to maintain the public tranquillity in all places to which its votaries resort.'[10]

The colonial government had initially plunged into the temple realm with a view to acquiring social legitimacy and access to revenue. Two decades later, they found themselves submerged in cumbersome disputes regarding ritual matters beyond their comprehension. At a larger level, too, the shift away from direct administration marked the end of a phase in colonial policy, when straightforward revenue exaction gave way to a more indirect manipulation of temple affairs through subsidization and bureaucratization.[11] Thus, the process of 'withdrawal' was a multidimensional phenomenon, with different trends operating under varying pressures.

The contradictions between the rhetoric of 'withdrawal', as

repeatedly emphasized in official correspondence, and the setting up of apparatuses of control by the colonial state, finds focus in the prolonged transfer of the *Sataishazari* endowment to the raja for purposes of temple maintenance. In the following sections, I have analysed this process from different perspectives, as depicting friction between colonial officials and the raja, the conflicts of access and obligations within official discourse, official penetration of the temple realm through structuring and investigative mechanisms and the coercive elements underlying the official notion of 'protection'. The temple had by now become an arena for the enactment of a larger and more complex conflict than that between the Company administration and the Gajapati regime—there were now multiple foci of power and contention which were collectively subsumed in the articulation of the colonial discourse.

Control over Property: The Politics of Legislation

The notion of 'securing' the 'due proceeds' for the maintenance of the temple articulated in the above correspondence involved, first, the circumscription of the temple as a separate entity that was financially dependent on the state for support and second, the appropriation of the *Sataishazari* lands, already a part of temple networks, by colonial bureaucratic apparatuses and their realignment within those networks by the colonial government. The numerous Acts, settlements, and legislation in this regard served to reorganize the rights and relationships in the land and established the colonial administration's control over the resources.

Prior to Act X of 1840, the temple expenses, comprising approximately Rs. 53,000 were defrayed from the pilgrim tax collection by the government. Through the enactment of Act X, the pilgrim tax was abolished, ostensibly for the purpose of ending government support of idolatrous institutions. The amount for temple expenses, however, continued to be provided by the government. In 1843, the estate of *Sataishazari mahal*, assessed at an annual revenue of Rs. 17,420, was made over to the Khurda raja for the purpose of temple management. Consequently, the money payment was reduced to Rs. 35,738. Following an 'investigation' into temple expenses in 1845, it was found that Rs. 23,321 was the sum of certain endowments made by the Marathas and which had been resumed by the colonial government, and some former 'sayer duties' for which compensation was also due. Thus, the government reduced their obligation to Rs. 23,321, being simply the amount of the resumed endowments. In 1856, owing to the 'culpable neglect' of the Khurda raja, a police force was appointed for the 'protection' of the pilgrims at a cost of Rs. 6,804, to be defrayed from the state grant, reducing it further to Rs. 16,517. In 1858, the government decided to make no more cash payments to the temple, and instead transferred as endowment, certain lands yielding an equivalent of Rs. 16,517.[12] These lands were thereafter completely in the charge of the raja, as temple superintendent, with no enquiry to be made by state officials regarding crop conditions, floods, etc. These lands were to be 'held in trust' for the temple by the raja and his successors. The memo also declared that the government had no further connection with temple affairs, and that the raja was solely responsible for its administration. [13]

Presler has argued that the policy of 'withdrawal' of state support for temples by colonial authorities actually intensified their control through a shift in the details of regulation.[14] The process of making endowments to the temple actually gave them greater leverage in its landed relationships and redistributive networks. The shift from direct administrative control to a more indirect fiscal manipulation through the allocation of maintenance funds involved a realignment of the networks of access to resources within the temple realm. In the pre-colonial period, grants to the temple included rights of usage as well as the status accruing from the privilege of receiving the grant. The 'transfer' of the *Sataishazari* lands was, from the perspective of the Company administration, an official transaction, made to the raja in his capacity as an employee of the government. The difference between an 'act' legislated by the colonial administration and a pre-colonial *sanad*, both forms of authorization of land grants, lay in the discrepancy between alternate forms of authority—while the former alienated the land as well as the recipient from their contextual frameworks of rights and access and drew them together in an official discourse, the latter conferred status and obligation onto the recipient, thereby establishing three-way linkages of authority between the donor, the donee and the land.

The granting of the *Sataishazari* lands kept open channels for regulation and control over temple finances by the colonial administration, as is indicated by the numerous modifications of the grant. In an effort to minimize cash payments to the temple, the government's 'investigations' into the temple's fiscal history led to the realization that certain endowments made by the Marathas, which had been resumed by the Company government, could be utilized for the purpose of temple maintenance at this stage. It is ironical that lands, which had already been appropriated by the colonial government, were re-appropriated for the purposes of temple maintenance. We have discussed that the resumption of lands, particularly privileged tenures, by the colonial government, involved the restructuring of rights and linkages, and the breakdown of the hierarchy of landholders' status. This confusion was repeated twice over owing to the transfer of these lands to the temple.

The traditional obligation of a privileged landholder to ensure the well-being of the land as well as the people living in it, was inverted in the government's injunction to the raja to have complete charge of the lands which he 'held in trust'. The government would make no enquiry regarding floods, crop conditions, etc. The Western legal notion of 'holding in trust' alienated the raja from privileged links of reciprocity with the lands and the landholders, circumscribing his claim to his official position of temple superintendent, accorded by the government. Further, the demarcation of separate categories for the management of crops, floods, etc., that characterized colonial administration, involved the negation of the landholders' responsibility in these areas. Thus, colonial regulation of temple land involved realignment of the landholding hierarchy as well as the penetration of the existing rights and status vis-à-vis the land.

The *Sataishazari mahal*, as a separately demarcated estate for temple maintenance, was 'recreated' through such processes of colonial penetration. The endowment, so named because it may have once amounted to Rs. 27,000, was not originally a compact estate with well-defined boundaries and homogenous tenures. It was, however, an important ritual entity, and was managed by a special *pariccha*, the *Sataishazari pariccha*. According to an account by Baboo Madhubanunda Bose, a Deputy Collector at Puri in 1842, [15] the origin and details of the endowment are unknown, lost in '. . . a very remote period when the country was under the government of its own rajas. . . .' The endowment was made and presumably added to by the rajas, for the express purpose of covering temple expenses.

In reply to a question regarding the validity of the grant, Babu Bose replied that as there was no title for the holding, no '*sunnud* nor even *charohitti* (confirmation of former government), simply a customarily fixed amount for *jumma* (revenue) it was dificult [*sic*] to ascertain the extent and dimensions of the grant'. Since the endowment was a well-known temple fund, the question of validating its existence did not arise within pre-colonial temple-state relations. Rather, the rajas legitimized their own authority by endorsing the fund. Colonial processes of classification and 'systemization' required documentary evidence in order to confirm the validity of prevailing institutions within their own discourse. Thus, enquiries into the 'origins' of the grant, as well as its 'extent' and 'dimensions' were made. The production of such information was a form of power for the government, since it provided them with leverage for the manipulation of the supposed estate, the fixing of its boundaries and revenue.

According to Section 8, Reg. XII of 1805, those lands, the revenue of which are appropriated for the services of Jagannatha were not to be resumed and Groeme's report mentions the *Sataishazari* land being under the management of the *Sataishazari parichha* and other temple personnel.[16] Groeme also mentions other lands assigned to the temple, including those denominated under the *Kotha Khanja* (for the purpose of *bhoga*). Some of these were managed by *mathadharis*, but all disbursements were under the supervision of the *Parichhas*.[17] In that case it is curious that in the declaration of 1863, the *Sataishazari mahal* was referred to as the 'last remaining portion of the endowment of the Temple at the time of the acquisition of the province in 1803'. What became of the other lands?

The numerous investigations into temple property by the colonial government was a means of separating 'temple lands' from the rest of the region's property, primarily for the purpose of revenue maximization. The large-scale resumption of property ostensibly for 'resettlement', involved the breakdown of privileged tenures and the reorganization of land rights. 'Resettlement' also involved the realignment of tenures by the government in an effort to homogenize tenures. Despite the stipulations laid down by the Reg. XII of 1805 and notwithstanding the long-established custom of reserving the *Sataishazari mahal* for the temple, it was resumed in 1819. Its validity was questioned owing to the absence of a *sanad* legitimizing the grant, and also because its boundaries could not be ascertained. The *mahal* was said to include some *lakhiraj* tenures as well, which were resumed under Reg. XI of 1819. Other lands, whose tenures could not be ascertained, were included within the *mahals* as '*Tehsil alahida*'. These properties were resumed in order to place them under 'observation' for investigation. Once again, we observe the colonial obsession with classification and systematization. The object of the 'investigation' was the demarcation of the *Sataishazari mahal* as a separate estate, and the classification of unaccounted for lands in a separate category, as *Alahida*.

The proposal for handing over the estate to the raja in lieu of temple expenses assumed a resettlement of the lands, including the many diverse tenures that were a part of the endowment. These *lakhiraj* tenures, which were within, but still distinct from, the *Sataishazari mahal*, were to be 'enquired into, and confirmed or resumed according to their merits.' The larger 'merit' was, presumably, the uniform categorization of the properties and doing away with discrepancies in tenures. It has been mentioned that the *Sataishazari mahal* was a loose conglomerate of scattered properties. Different tenure holders had varying rights and status within the temple's redistributive system. Prior to the endowment of 1843, the scattered properties were resettled, and the revenue rates 'frozen', as it were. The raja could not independently negotiate the revenue rates directly with the landholders. In Taylor's settlement of Khurda, 1879, the question of the intermixed tenures came up, and it was debated whether the non-endowment *jagirs* should pay rent to the government or to the temple as part of the endowment. The notion of the lands being demarcated as a separate estate was, by now, so deeply ingrained, that the colonial officials decided to make the non-endowment *jagirs* over to the temple simply in order to preserve neat physical boundaries.

The transformation of a popular temple fund that was a part

of local custom and temple tradition into a circumscribed fiscal entity within the colonial parameters of an 'estate', depicts the manipulation of pre-existing institutions and their re-contextualization by the colonial regime. The penetration of traditional tenurial privileges by bureaucratic processes of documentation and categorization eventually led to their subordination, and the creation of a powerful official apparatus for controlling revenue structures. The numerous legislations and rules that were imposed upon existing linkages and relationships in the land, largely for systematic revenue exaction, also led to the 'fixing' of these relationships according to the requirements of the colonial regime.

The Raja and the Colonial Regime—Friction over Status and Resources

The Khurda raja occupied an ambiguous position vis-à-vis the colonial administration, as he was both a part of its framework as well as outside it, representing an alternate authority. These two domains of the raja's functions were at once simultaneous and discrete, and created considerable conflict between him and the administrative officials, which was articulated in the arena of the temple. The discrepancy between the raja's ritual and official status also created an imbalance in his relationships with other chieftains. Such conflicts, often expressed in terms of clashes of status within the temple sphere, were compounded by the presence of colonial officials, who sought to limit the raja's authority.

The transfer of the *Sataishazari* lands, we have seen, involved the refiguring of prevailing structures of access and authority and relationships of obligations and reciprocity. The negotiation of power between alternate domains, the colonial bureaucracy and traditional hierarchies of landed relationships, threw into relief the contradictions in the raja's role as recipient of the grant. It is ironical that the raja, traditionally the chief donor within his kingdom, was regarded as the receiver of a religious endowment. It is also interesting that the colonial state decided to take upon itself one of the primary roles of a traditional Hindu ruler, that of endowing a temple. Giving extensive donations to temples and *mathas* was a source of great status for a raja. The royal gift of land, in fact, displayed his authority over that land, and often brought disputed tracts within the purview of his influence, amicably (see Chapter 1). In the case of the *Sataishazari* endowment, the raja was given the management of the land, not as an honour, which is how a *sebayet* would have received a grant from the raja previously. It was simply a duty he was to perform owing to his position as an employee of the colonial government. Here, we see a most interesting travesty of the traditional process of *dana,* wherein the British government, as a part of their scheme of 'withdrawal' from temple affairs, 'made over' the *Sataishazari mahal* to the raja. The latter received no honour from the endowment, but was merely to perform his duty to the government. The endowment itself was not a 'gift': it was simply 'maintenance'. Thus traditional patterns of reciprocity wherein material and symbolic exchanges were interlinked, were appropriated and subverted by the dominant official discourse.

Often, we see that attempts by colonial officials to extend their sphere of control were resisted by the raja, whose 'domain' was threatened as a consequence. In 1857, the Khurda raja submitted a memorial to the Governor-General in Council, in which he protested that a police force had been appointed in the temple by the Magistrate of Puri and the Commissioner of Cuttack, without his knowledge. The force, ostensibly for the 'maintenance of peace', prevention of accidents and for the protection of the pilgrims, was to cost a sum of Rs. 6,804 and this was to be defrayed from the annual government grant of Rs. 23,321. The raja vociferously protested the reduction of the grant and suggested that he could arrange for a comparable establishment using the revenue from the pilgrims' offerings. He objected to the 'misuse' of the grant by government officials, claiming that the grant was originally a compensation for the temple's funds that had been appropriated by the government. The petition also stated that the presence of such a force would hinder the duties of the *pandas* and *pratiharis*, who were traditionally responsible for the welfare of the pilgrims, and was an embarrassment for the raja himself, in whom the management of the temple had been vested by the government. [18]

The Company government had impinged upon two important areas of the raja's sphere of authority, viz., protection of his subjects and arbitration of conflicts. These formed a significant part of his role as temple superintendent. The appointment of the force was a direct encroachment upon his jurisdiction, both as Gajapati as well as temple superintendent. The cost of appointing the force was unilaterally deducted from the government's maintenance amount. This served the twin purposes of reducing the amount as well as extending official control within the temple realm, a desirable end for the attending officials. It is interesting to observe that the raja objected to the 'misuse' of the grant by the officials. This was a challenge to the colonial bureaucracy on its own terms, since the 'misuse' and 'misappropriation' of funds was a common complaint voiced by many officials against the raja. This indicates that colonial categorization of resources was sufficiently well-entrenched for the raja to use it in his own defence: indigenous institutions had been appropriated by the colonial discourse and were articulated in its terminology.

The temple realm provided an ideological space for the raja to renegotiate his status and authority with respect to other chiefs, particularly within the context of an altered political scenario. A unique dimension was provided by the presence of British officials, who attempted to penetrate the raja's domain and establish their own apparatuses of control with respect to the temple sphere. In Chapter 4, I had discussed the manner in which the raja of Parlakhimedi was prevented from performing *darsana* and obtaining *mahaprasada* by the Khurda raja. According to the Collector, Samuel Busby, the 'ungrateful and atrocious behaviour of the Rajah of Khoordah' who had 'great ascendancy' over the temple personnel, amounted to the most 'refined chicanery'.[19] Colonial officials entered the realm of the temple's ritual functioning and infused the situation with their own concerns and prejudices. Conflicts of status between chieftains involving the transgression and reassertion of ritual boundaries and socio-political protocol were appropriated and expressed through the rhetoric of colonial dominance.

Such ongoing conflict depicts deep-rooted shifts in structures of power in the region, changing ritual norms in the context of the imposition of alternate economic and political relations. In 1814, Richardson, the Settlement Commissioner, wrote to Trower, Collector of Cuttack, complaining that the Khurda raja had debarred the raja of Khandpara from entering the temple along with his ceremonial emblems (see Chapter 4). Richardson went so far as to write to the Governor General supporting the Khandpara raja's right and complaining about 'the unwarranted interference' of the Khurda raja. In 1842, there was fresh conflict over the question of the raja of Dhenkanal having arrived in Puri with his royal umbrella (*chhatri*) unfurled, and blowing his conch (*kahali*).[20] The Khurda raja had declared his royal insignia to be invalid and inappropriate to his status, and had not agreed to the special privileges that the visiting raja had demanded.

Emblems, honours, insignia of rank and their accompanying privileges were symbols of status, which were relevant only when acknowledged. The expression of status was thus a process with its own protocol.[21] Padmanabha Narayanadeva, the raja of Parlakhimedi, had not requested the Khurda raja for permission to enter the temple, as had been the traditional practice with visiting chiefs. Instead, he had paid tax to the British government and had received their sanction for *darsana*, thereby acknowledging their authority over the Khurda raja. While this was politically correct at one level, the Company government being the new overlords of the region, it did not conform to the existing pattern of traditional usage in the temple. The Gajapati was still the *adya sebaka* of Jagannatha, a link that accorded him the highest position in temple affairs. In this respect, the Khandpara chief's action in carrying his royal insignia into the temple precincts was a challenge to the Khurda raja's authority over that realm, as only he had the privilege of performing worship while accompanied by his entire regalia. The Dhenkanal raja's demand that he be allowed the privilege of '*poora shood*',[22] along with his family, was another transgression of protocol according to the Gajapati, who agreed to sanction only the *darsana* for him.

The conflict over the symbols of status was actually a conflict over status itself. The visiting chiefs wished to exalt their position vis-à-vis the temple, their annual pilgrimage being an event of great political and ideological significance. They simultaneously denigrated the ritual authority of the Khurda raja, acknowledging the territorial supremacy of the British government instead. This would accord them an increased ritual status without threatening the colonial government, which was outside the temple's ideological networks. The Khurda raja, whose territorial power was diminished, however, did not tolerate the challenge to his ritual authority. Bound together with the other Gadajata chiefs in a network of material and ideological reciprocity, the push and pull of those links were extremely significant for him. The bestowal of temple honours was a subjective issue, based on the nature of relationships between the chiefs. The raja asserted his authority when he felt it challenged.

In the case of the Parlakhimedi raja, the *suaras* (cooks) too, had refused to prepare *mahaprasada* for several days, and thousands of pilgrims, who lived on the sacred food, had nearly starved in consequence. Busby suspected that the Khurda raja had incited them to neglect their task, and commented on the extraordinary power that he wielded over the temple personnel. We have observed that the Khurda rajas had begun to intensify their ritual role in the temple since the eighteenth century when their territorial status began to diminish. Through his authority over the temple *sebas* and the issuing of *chhamu chitau*, royal orders, the raja regulated the functions of all the *sebayets,* the *mathadharis* and other temple transactions and relationships with other chiefs as well. A *chhamu chitau* of the early eighteenth century, typically recording a royal visit to the temple, ran as follows: 'On the 22nd day (of the month) of *Karkata*, in the 5th *anka* of Maharaja Harekrsna, Chatrasinghadeva, the Raja of Sambalpur came on the back of the elephant accompanied by his *divan*. He got down from the elephant at the Lion Gate of the temple and removed his crown (*paga*) from the head but wearing upper cloth (*dopati duppati*) on his body and had *darsana* of the Lord.'[23]

There is a discernible pattern to this process, the conspicuous advent of the chief with his regalia and the prominent discarding of that regalia prior to temple entry. There is an account of a pilgrimage by the Khandpara raja in 1772, during the reign of Gajapati Virakesarideva, describing the honours that were conferred on him. A letter issued by the Khurda raja proclaimed his advent into Puri, and ordered that he be allowed the exclusive *darsana*. His family, however, entered the temple accompanied by the Bakshi of Khurda (Commander-in-Chief of the Paiks, the royal militia) and the head of the *chhatisa nijoga* (*Chhatisa Nijoga Nayaka)* and performed *darsana* in their presence. The royal guests were given a variety of sacred cloths, (*sadi*) cotton and silk, including a piece from the temple flag. The extension of ritual courtesies on both sides was a part of the protocol between the kings. When in 1814, the Khandpara raja demanded the privilege of '*poora shood*' for his family, it was not particularly significant for colonial officials. But to the Khurda raja, it was a breach of protocol as well as an affront to his authority: the Khandpara raja was attempting to improve his own ritual status at his expense.

The conflict with Padmanabha Narayanadeva must be viewed in the context of the rivalry that had existed between the Bhois of Khurda and the Parlakhimedi 'Gajapatis' since the accession of Ramacandradeva I to the Puri title in 1590. There is an incident described in a *chhamu chitau* of 1753, when Jagannatha Narayanadeva, then the raja of Parlakhimedi, had forcibly tried to perform the royal rituals (*raja upacara)* during the car festival. He had mounted the *ratha* of Jagannatha, Nandighosa, and performed *darsana* while wearing his turban, an honour reserved for the Puri Gajapati. The situation was diplomatically defused by the temple priests while the Khurda raja tactfully kept his distance, as he could not have hoped to withstand a military showdown with the Parlakhimedi chief (see Chapter 2). It may also be recalled that Virakesarideva of Khurda had allied with the Marathas to repulse an attack by the Parlakhimedi raja in 1759. In the process of repaying his military debt to the Marathas, he had ceded to them the four crucial *parganas* of Limbai, Rahang, Serain and Chabiskud.

Within temple conflicts, we see the working of multiplex relationships, a situation that the Company officials found difficult to comprehend. All through their ongoing friction with the raja, they called attention to his 'official' role as representative of the Company administration in the temple. They did not investigate, or perhaps, preferred to debunk his ritual status vis-à-vis the temple and among the other rajas of the region. In some accounts, they actually appeared to resent this status, and trivialized it as an impediment to their 'constructive' approach to temple management. Such an approach regarded the 'efficient' management of the temple, the maintenance of 'law and order' and peaceful interaction between pilgrims and personnel, as a means to maximize revenue exaction. Conflicts over status and authority, the exchange of material and symbolic resources, the significance of obligation rather than duty in the performance of temple functions, were elements that characterized the temple's links with the institutions of the region.

Issues of Access and Control within Bureaucratic Discourse—'Protection' as a Form of Coercion

We have observed the manner in which the official rhetoric of 'withdrawal' from temple administration masked a more insidious penetration of ritual and economic networks by colonial apparatuses of control. Bureaucratic discourse, however, also consisted of multiple voices that expressed divergent pressures, from the friction between local administrative officials and temple personnel to the Evangelical outcry against a 'Christian' government's support for an idolatrous institution. In their attempt to regulate yet separate themselves from prevailing social and political institutions in order to mediate between these discrepancies, the colonial government imposed categories of control that were overlaid by the rhetoric of 'protection' and 'conciliation'. In this section, I have attempted to examine the conflicting trends that went into making a complex discourse that appropriated many of the traditional functions of the state and recontextualized them in order to rationalize its own mechanisms of coercion.

During the ongoing negotiation for the transfer of the *Sataishazari* lands to the raja for temple maintenance, the Puri Magistrate and the Commissioner had appointed a police force to be stationed within the temple, ostensibly for the 'maintenance of peace', prevention of accidents and protection of the pilgrims. There were two major implications of this development: first, the amount spent on the force's maintenance was to be defrayed from the government's annual grant to the temple, and second, it represented the penetration of government control into an area that was previously out of bounds for them. The raja protested on both counts, claiming in his petition to the Governor-General that the appointment of the force was a 'misuse' of the government's grant. He claimed that he could have arranged for a comparable establishment using the funds from the pilgrims' offerings, and also that the force would hinder the duties of the *pandas* and *pratiharis*.[24] The primary issue underlying the appointment of the force by the colonial officials was the acquisition of control over temple functions. In doing so, they had appropriated an important segment of the raja's domain, the primarily royal obligations of protection and arbitration. The raja's protest that he could have arranged for such a force voices precisely this concern. His authority over the maintenance of order in the temple was undermined by the government's action. The significance of the appointment was not the police itself, but the power and control that it accorded to the colonial officials.[25]

Furthermore, the notion of 'order' was reinterpreted in official terms, no longer implying the resolution of conflict, as it had done previously under the raja. The force was a mechanism for the prevention of conflict, the maintenance of 'law and order', another ubiquitous official maxim. Its implications were manifold—a physical threat inciting obedience in all temple personnel, the display of a higher authority than that of the raja with respect to the pilgrims and the penetration of the temple by apparatuses of official control. The official categories of 'law and order' and the maintenance of 'peace and tranquillity' provided the government with enormous coercive potential to manipulate temple functions. Such coercion was also reflected in the policy of 'conciliation' that had characterized the Company administration's relations with the temple since their advent in 1803, resulting in the realignment of rights and linkages in land, the demarcation of categories of temple functions and status relationships that were focused on the temple. The official rhetoric of 'conciliation' and 'protection' with respect to the temple was initially dominated by the objective of revenue maximization. Following the abolition of the pilgrim tax in 1840, revenue from the tax was no longer an incentive to mediate with the raja and temple functionaries. Thus, the penetration of the temple sphere by official categories of 'law and order' assumed its own momentum and became an area for a contest of power between the bureaucracy and the raja.

There was direct conflict between local officials and the raja over issues of access to temple property and functions. This was primarily due to the ambiguous status that the raja occupied in the temple sphere, as both a representative of the government and that of the traditional state that had been destroyed by that government. The raja had been given an official status owing to his appointment as temple superintendent, and placed within the bureaucratic hierarchy of the colonial government. It was through this link that the officials sought to establish their dominance over him, since they tended to regard his official position as being subordinate to theirs. There were numerous protests about the raja's 'misbehaviour' and 'misuse' of his position and petitions requesting his removal from that position. An urgent memo submitted to the Secretary, Government of Bengal by the Commissioner, Cuttack requested the repeal of the Act X of 1840 and to 'authoritatively deprive the Rajah of Khoordah . . . of the charge of the Temple . . . to which he has a sort of presumptuous right. . . . Since the promulgation of the Act X of 1840, he has been entirely uncontrolled and has been led to regard the temple as a right of private property. . . .'[26] The Commissioner's protest was framed in the terminology of colonial categories of official status, the raja's position being defined according to the limitations of his role as temple superintendent which was conferred upon him by the Company administration. The raja's link with the temple as a descendent of the Gajapatis of Puri was thus viewed as 'a presumptuous right', the articulation of his royal status was viewed as an 'uncontrolled' exercise of authority. The higher authorities at Calcutta, however, disregarded the Commissioner's recommendation and allowed the raja to continue as temple superintendent.

The Company administration was under pressure to separate itself from the temple by a strong utilitarian–evangelical lobby in England. The pilgrim tax was viewed as support provided by a 'Christian' government for idolatrous institutions. The evangelical outcry over the government's support of idolatry dates back to 1806 when Claudius Buchanan, the Company's Chaplain at Fort William witnessed the *ratha jatra* at Puri and initiated a barrage of correspondence against 'the gigantic outrage upon all that is dear to God and man'.[27] Initially the Court of Directors attempted to restrain the missionaries' diatribe against Jagannatha. The latter, however, gained the sympathy of Charles Grant, the President of the Board of Control for the affairs of India. Grant pressed for the abolition of the pilgrim tax, which was seen as the vital link that kept alive the government's support for the temple.[28] He succeeded in passing an order on behalf of the Court of Directors that demanded the abolition of the tax.

The Revenue Despatch, dated 20 February 1833, did not insist on immediate implementation of the order and the process was delayed for another seven years. This was because of a strong pro-tax trend within the government. 'For the abolition of the Pilgrim tax, there is no reason of any kind, but that of saving you and me from the clatter of nonsense with which we are assailed (by the Missionaries). You may as well abolish the gin tax to make men sober. . . .'[29]

At one level the strongest argument for the continuation of the tax was the cost incurred by the government for the temples' maintenance. Moving to a different plane, support for the temple was considered to be in keeping with the British governments' character of 'liberality' and 'tolerance' and protection of the interests of their 'subjects'. Thus, the discourse articulating the Company government's 'progressive' attitude towards local institutions mediated between the missionaries' agenda for a 'civilized' Christian government, financial pressures incurred through maintaining the temple and the contest over power and structures of authority between local officials and temple functionaries, predominantly the raja.

Contradictory pressures underlay the evolution of the colonial discourse of power in this period. The representation of official policies as providing 'tranquillity' and the 'freedom' to exercise their religion for the 'Hindoo' subjects, also involved the simultaneous penetration of ritual structures by official apparatuses of control, and the coercion of resource networks by bureaucratic dominance. Categories defining the 'official' and the 'personal', 'right' and 'duty' were imposed upon prevailing linkages of obligation and reciprocity, thus causing the reconfiguration of power structures in the region. In the next section, we shall observe the manner in which temple *sebas* were reorganized within the context of colonial and legal changes.

THE DESACRALIZATION OF TEMPLE SERVICES

In the previous section, we observed the material and ideological conflict that arose as a result of colonial pressures acting on the traditional status of the raja. Inherent to the colonial discourse was a fragmented perspective of the raja's role vis-à-vis the temple and the region, there being a contradiction between his official role as temple superintendent and his traditional status as Gajapati. We shall now observe the discrepancies created between status and office, duty and service, rights and obligations as a result of the imposition of colonial legal and administrative structures upon prevailing social and economic networks. I view such a de-linking of existing institutions, temple sebas in particular, from their ritual and political contexts and their reconfiguration according to the requirements of colonial policy as their desacralization—the removal of sacredness, the ritual significance of the service by colonial legal and bureaucratic mechanisms.

The temple sphere was a complex of material and symbolic resources, wherein access to those resources was contingent upon status and privilege. Central to this ordered state was the notion of *seba,* a loaded term encompassing a range of meanings, from service to duty to ritual to honour. In the Jagannatha temple, the Gajapati was the *adya sebaka* of the deity, and presided over the distribution of *sebas.* The privilege of performing seba, or even a fraction of a *seba*, was co-ordinated by the raja as part of his temple duties, perhaps especially so during the colonial regime.[30]

The distribution of the *sebas* was conducted in a context where land, cash, sacred cloths and ritual services were legitimately exchangeable. The notions of property and exclusivity of ownership as defined by modern European law was not in evidence here, even after a century of colonial administration. An examination of cases of conflict over property related to the temple that were judged in colonial courts reveals the discrepancy between perceptions of 'ownership' and control over resources, colonial and indigenous. The significance of temple lands as providing *bhoga*, literally food for the deity, formed the crux of the linkages between the landed hierarchy and the temple, a ritual network that was subverted by the penetration of colonial laws and tenurial policies.

TEMPLE LANDS AND LITIGATION—CONFLICT OVER ISSUES OF ACCESS AND CONTROL

The Company government took over the administration of Orissa in 1803 with the establishment of a Board of Revenue at Cuttack. Over the next two decades they were intensively involved in the resumption and resettlement of those lands that were not under the purview of the Gadajata states. As a result of this massive effort at classification and 'systemization' of territory, a new perspective of property, as an alienable commodity, with fixed boundaries and ownership, crept into indigenous society. The European legal system with its establishment of courts and legal personnel and its inherent contradiction between the 'shaster' and British laws, crystallized only by mid-ninteenth century. The imposition of tenurial changes under the colonial regime was supported and legitimized by the legal system. It is interesting to observe that these processes were frequently resisted and modified by local concerns, which challenged their dominance.

A case in point is the establishment of the *Sataishazari mahal*, a conglomerate of scattered endowments, encompassing diverse tenures and interspersed with independent holdings. Prior to their being made over to the temple in 1843, the *mahal* was resettled and revenue rates 'frozen' as it were. The raja could not negotiate the rates directly with the cultivators (*ryots).* In Taylor's settlement of Khurda, 1879, the *Sataishazari* lands were uniformly assessed as a single estate, so that a precisely demarcated property could be recorded. This attitude of objectification and circumscription of temple property was largely instrumental in de-linking of resources from their context.[31]

In this way colonial policies altered the existing structure of landed relationships through tenurial changes authored by law. As a result, a flood of disputes were reported with respect to temple properties, particularly over issues of succession to offices. One such case describes the conflict between two *mahants*, Narain Das and Bindrabun Das, over succession to the superintendence of a 'religious edifice' (*matha*) in 'Pursootum Chutter' (Puri).[32] The position included the management of lands yielding an annual produce of Rs. 55,000. Narain Das claimed that the previous superintendent, Mouji Ram Das, had appointed him to officiate during his own lifetime and he had continued to do so for over a year after his guru's death. His claim was endorsed by the fact of his being the disciple of Mouji Ram Das's spiritual heir, Rughoonath Das (who was absent). Hence he viewed himself as being part of a line of succession to the title. He was dispossessed by Bindrabun Das, who produced a *hibbanama* (deed of gift) as well as letters from Mouji Ram Das, requesting him to assume the title. The Court's judgement was aided by a committee of ten 'mohunts', each claimant having chosen five, and ultimately went in favour of Bindrabun Das. Narain Das appealed in the provincial court of Calcutta where his appeal was dismissed.

At one level, this appears to be a conflict between two forms of succession, Narain Das claiming the title by descent whereas Bindrabun Das's claim was elective. The committee of 'mohunts' declared that succession by descent was not a 'normal' occurrence, and that the person nominated by the head was always given preference. Narain Das, pleading that as he had managed the institution for some time, he had already been accorded many of the privileges commensurate with the position. His dismissal was, in effect, a form of dispossession, and his petition questioned the fairness of depriving him of what was already his, a fact that was not accounted for in the judgement. Moreover, despite the appointment of the 'committee of mohunts' to incorporate local juridical practices, the British legal system was preoccupied with the notion of precedent in providing validity to the judgement. Hence, the emphasis on the 'normal' form of succession. The fact that Narain Das's claim represented an alternative to what the 'mohunts' described as 'normal', was the primary factor that disqualified it.

If we place the dispute within the context of the larger legal and economic changes occurring in the early colonial period, a number of important factors are highlighted. Commenting on the socio-economic changes wrought by the imposition of the Permanent Settlement in Bengal, Cohn argues that under the revenue changes brought about in 1793: '. . . it was assumed that stabilising landed relations, providing security for property, making people's rights explicit through the publication of the laws and providing an impartial judge making decisions on the basis of evidence and arguments in open court, the happiness and security of the Indian populace would be secured. In fact, this did not occur'.[33]

There were several fundamental issues where European law was in direct conflict with customary belief and practice. Chief among these was the notion of the equality of the individual before the law. The majority of Indian society operated on the reverse principle, that people were unequal on account of the station that they were born into, occupying different social niches. Another point of difference was between the indigenous notion of status, encompassing a multiplexity of relationships and the unidimensional link of the legal contract. In this context, the focus of European law was the decision and the notion of either winning or losing a dispute. Contrary to this perspective was the indigenous objective of compromise, in fact the postponement of a decision as such. It is thus clear that the crux of the conflict between the two systems of adjudication was the European legal tendency of de-linking the dispute from its surrounding relationships. These very links were given prominence in local forms of arbitration.[34]

The 'flood' of disputes that greeted the early introduction of British courts hinged on these problems. 'The secret of the flood of Indian cases . . . lay in the immediacy and the violence of the remedies offered . . . the chances of losing a good case were high, but if one won, the prizes were larger than would be available under the native system.'[35] The colonial administration may have been prepared for corruption and prejudice on the part of Indian litigants, but did not realize that their own rules could be taken advantage of from within their jurisdiction. Caste roles could be reversed, existing social and economic hierarchies challenged with amazing immediacy and thoroughness. The 'native' legal system had no access to the new laws, leading to confusion and a lack of accountability to either form of justice.[36]

In the light of these issues, succession disputes such as the one enumerated above, acquired a greater complexity. The dominant themes that emerged as a result of the court's decision were less related to the control over fairly substantial resources (Superintendence over the *matha* amounted to controlling an annual sum of Rs. 55,000), than a conflict over the status accruing from degrees of access to them. Through the 'legalization' of this conflict, an existing pattern of succession had been challenged, while a validating structure (the committee of *mahants*) had been artificially constructed to perform a role in this process. Forms of succession and rights of office had been defined, in the precise and decontextualized language of law. Finally, the decision demonstrates the superiority of the written document in the eyes of the court. Bindrabun Das had produced the *hibbanama* that named him the successor. This was another point where Indian litigants took advantage of Western legal principles—colonial records are full of instances where documents were forged and evidence perjured.[37] The sanctity of the legal statement or document did not have the same moral validity in the succession to the *matha* hierarchy as it did in European law.

The confrontation between the separation of functions and relationships through legal definitions, and the multiplex relationships of indigenous society, is further illustrated. A case appeared before the *Sadr Diwani Adalat* in 1856, in which Mohunt Khakee Bullaram Das contested the mortgage of a village by its former 'owner', Chytun Das, who had earlier gifted it to him through deed of gift. Later, Chytun Das mortgaged the land to the father of the present defendant, Nursingh Khooteah, despite Bullaram Das's protests. Eventually the village was resumed by the government and Bullaram's claim was not considered. Bullaram's case rested on three premises, firstly, that he possessed a document, i.e. the deed of gift to support his claim to the land. Secondly, he alleged that Chytun Das was 'old and imbecile' at the time of the mortgage, and finally, that the land was 'Amrit Mundhee'—*amrita manohi*, or temple land. [38]

The weak link in his case was that the village had not been named in the deed of gift, but was implied by the use of the term '*wughaira*'.[39] Bullaram's case was dismissed on the grounds that since the deed of gift was never implemented, it must have been revoked. Further, the case was invalidated under the Statute of Limitation, the events having occurred many years before its presentation in court.

Mathas occupied a position in the temple's redistributive network where access to material resources merged with the ritual mobilization of services for the temple. Access to the management of *amrita manohi* lands conferred upon the candidate the prestige of temple service as well as control over considerable resources. We have seen that access, not exclusivity of ownership, was important for temple *sebas*. A single service could be performed by different people. The transfer of *sebas* from one individual to another had a contextual, not fixed, logic. Thus, it may have been perfectly logical for a *mathadhari* to mortgage land that had previously been 'gifted' to another person.

The exclusive nature of the gift, accompanied by the authority of the deed, existed in the British legal sense only. Ownership was not the issue, access was.

It was only when the land came up for resumption that the question of ownership arose. Only then did the owner's identity have any bearing on the issue of rights to use the land. The discrepancy between the period when the 'dispute' occurred and the time when the case was filed may perhaps indicate this factor. Ironically, the case was dismissed under the Statute of Limitation. The time factor, which had little relevance in the prevailing code of moral validity, was the basis for its dismissal under colonial law.

Thus, land was demarcated both in terms of time as well as space under colonial law. The common term denoting usage of land, prevalent since early medieval times, particularly in the case of land grants, was *bhoga*, literally, to feed. The land was placed in a particular relationship with the entire hierarchy of users, from the cultivators to the landlord, through the notion of feeding. This perception also denoted the pattern of usage of the temple lands, the *amrita manohi*, those that provided food, or *bhoga*. In the next section we shall examine the manner in which *amrita manohi* lands were reconfigured according to colonial tenurial changes.

The Dispute over Mohana Bhoga: Resumption and Reorganization of Sacred Lands

The large-scale resumption and reassessment of all land, including temple endowments, following the advent of the colonial government, largely contributed to the conflict over land rights. This was partly due to the confusion within colonial bureaucracy itself over the degree and extent of control over property. In the case of the withdrawal of the pilgrim tax and the *Sataishazari* endowment, we have seen that contradictory voices spoke for and against the process from within the government. This led to the decontextualization and desacralization of processes of temple funding, as well as the transformation of temple lands and land rights within the colonial bureaucratic framework. Resumption of temple grants led not only to the demarcation and ossification of the lands and patterns of usage, but also called for heavy subsidization of the temple. Thus, colonial officials discovered to their dismay, a host of endowments mixed with the resumed lands for which they had to compensate the temple or the related institutions. This led to increased efforts on the part of the officials to 'fix' the boundaries of the grant, and to verify the claims of the *mahants* and *sebayets*. The situation of conflict was marked by the protests of local officials, straining under the government's obligation to the temple, the tussle for status and resources between the temple functionaries and the local landed groups, all situated amidst the inherent contradictions between the indigenous and the colonial view of property.

The dispute over the estate of Kodhar, granted for the provision of *bhoga* to the temple, illustrates such conflicting claims. A letter from W. Wilkinson, Collector, Puri, to H. Ricketts, Commissioner, Cuttack, in 1837, enumerates the endowments to the Uttaraparsva and Jagannathaballaba *Mathas* for purposes of supplying *Mohana Bhoga* (a private *bhoga*) to the temple and for feeding destitute pilgrims. The grant for *Mohana Bhoga* was made through lands donated from the *pargana* of Kodhar in Cuttack by the mother of Raghuji Bhonsla. Cash payments had been fixed for both grants, at Rs. 3,466 for *Mohana Bhoga* and Rs. 2,666 to the *adhikari* at Jagannathaballaba *Matha*. Of these two, the Kodhar endowment was part of a dispute that lasted over two decades and called into question the government's right to resume temple lands.

A *mahant* of the Uttaraparsva *matha* of Puri, Joyram Das, laid claim to the entire *pargana* of Kodhar, consisting of ninety-four villages, as being granted for the purpose of providing *Mohana Bhoga* at the temple. Trower, the Collector, had demanded that Joyram Das produce the necessary documents to support his claim. The *mahant* delivered to him the original *sanad* granted to a previous *mahant*, Pran Krishan Das, in 1178 *umli* (approximately AD 1770). This *sanad* apparently defined the grant as the revenue from fifty-one assessed villages, the other forty-three being 'desolate' and 'consequently not included'.[40] Thus, according to Trower, the annual amount due to the *mahant* was Rs. 3,504, for the purpose of the *bhoga*. Trower emphasized that the revenue of the fifty-one villages was 'distinct' from the non-endowed lands.

Subsequently, Joyram Das, allegedly 'in collusion' with Gopal Pandit, the head of the *matha*, produced a document bearing the seal of the *subahdar*, claiming the remainder of the villages. Trower believed this document to be forged and concocted in order to force the *mahant's* claim on the entire *pargana*. Another document, a '*Tehkeek Namah*' (an inspection report) bearing the seal of Raghuji Bhonsla and addressed to the *subahdar*, registered Joyram Das's complaint against the *zamindars* of Kodhar who had denied him possession of the entire *pargana*. Subsequently, a *vakeel* representing the zamindars reiterated that Joyram had been granted lands worth 13,000 *khawuns* (Rs.3,504) annually. The *zamindars* also complained that from 1205 *umli* (AD 1798) onwards, Joyram Das had not used that amount for *Mohana Bhoga* at all, and had simultaneously filed a false claim to the entire *pargana*. Owing to the land being under dispute, the government resumed the entire property and made a fixed annual payment to Joyram Das.

We have seen that the context of traditional land rights was one of 'shared privileges'. Different forms of dominance over property and people could coexist. Hence the non-specific nature of the *sanad* regarding the extent of the endowment is not surprising. The zamindar's petition, too, had no date or year, a point noted by Trower as being 'customary'. The dispute over the boundaries of the grant occurred when all lands were being resumed and reassessed. This was the time when Joyram Das laid claim to a larger share than was allotted to him, and he did so by producing a document as proof, since the new rulers relied so heavily on documentary evidence. A subsequent petition from the *kanungo* of Kodhar reiterated that Joyram's claim was fraudulent, and that he had already collected revenue from the entire *pargana* that was not his due. The *kanungo* requested that he be fined the amount that he had 'unjustly misappropriated'. This, the letter claims, was the 'proper' course of action.[41]

Despite Trower's outrage at the 'fraudulent' misappropriation of the grant, the colonial government was itself in a moral dilemma over the issue. Wilkinson's account of the dispute two decades later quoted from Regulation XII of 1805, wherein it was expressly stated that 'the established donations for the support of the temple of Juggernath and the charitable donations to the offices of certain Hindoo temples called Anoochutree . . .' were not to be resumed. There was an inherent contradiction within colonial policy, as the land which was earlier demarcated and denoted 'temple property' in line with the policy of conciliation, was later resumed for revenue settlement. The justification for the resumption of these very lands hinged on the manipulation of the term 'established donations'. On one hand, declaring the endowment to be under dispute could enable the government to resume it for purposes of settling the conflict amicably. On the other, 'donations' could be taken to imply that cash grants could replace landed endowments, which were then resumed. Thus, a heavy moral obligation fell upon the colonial government to maintain the cash donation, an obligation that local officials chafed under. The appropriation of territory, whether it was for 'protection' or revenue exaction, was the focus of administrative policy. Its simultaneous rationalization in accordance with the image of justice, humaneness and 'civilization' that was projected through official representation, created such contradictory situations. Thus, the colonial discourse mediated between appropriation of property and its representation in a manner that redefined the networks of rights and privileges that linked the temple with the land.

The appropriation of temple-related resources as well as services by colonial apparatuses of control was a process marked by contradictions. The exercise of coercive power by the dominant regime was overlaid by a rhetoric of tolerance and conciliation, and conflict between local officials and the raja was often viewed with ambivalence by higher authorities. The penetration of the temple's territorial and redistributive networks by legislation and documentation, conflict over domains of authority between the raja and officials and the inherent contradiction between official position and ritual status personified in the raja, depicted the unique patterns of resistance and mediation that characterized the functioning of temple institutions under colonial domination.

NOTES

1. Bhajan by Banamali Das, a seventeenth century Oriya poet.
2. Mircea Eliade, *The Sacred and the Profane,* New York: Harcourt, Brace and World, Inc., 1959, p. 21.

3. Ibid., pp. 23-4.
4. Bernard S. Cohn, 'Some Notes on Law and Change in North India', in Cohn, *An Anthropologist*, pp. 554-74.
5. J.D.M. Derrett, 'The Development of the Concept of Property in India, *c.* AD 800-1800', in Derrett, *Essays in Classical and Modern Hindu Law*, vol. 2, Leiden: E.J. Brill, 1977, pp. 8-130 (hereafter 'Development of the Concept of Property').
6. Ibid., pp. 40-1.
7. Ibid., pp. 86-7.
8. Appadurai, *Worship and Conflict*, pp. 166-7.
9. Ibid.
10. No. 1304, dated 11 May 1839, JTC.
11. Appadurai, *Worship and Conflict*, pp. 139-41.
12. Deed for the Transfer of the *Sataishazari* lands for temple maintenance, 1838, JTC, vol. 3.
13. Signed Assistant Collector, Puri, 30 March 1863. Seal of Rani Suryamani Patamahadei, Guardian of minor Raja Dibyasinghdeo of Khurda, and assorted witnesses. Misc. Corresp. Regarding the Temple, JTC, vol. 3.
14. Franklin Presler, *A Religion under Bureaucracy: Policy and Administration for Hindu Temples in South India*, Cambridge: Cambridge University Press, pp. 16-20 (hereafter *Religion under Bureaucracy*).
15. O.W. Malet, Esq., Officiating Collector of Pooree, to The Commissioner for the 19th Division, Cuttack, no. 86, dated Pooree, 23 February 1842, JTC, vol. 3.
16. 'Groeme's Report', in Mukherjee, *A Critical Study*, p. 46.
17. Ibid., pp. 45-7.
18. 'The Humble Memorial of Moharaja Beerkishore Deb, Raja of Khurda and Superintendent of the Temple, Juggernath, Puri, in Cuttack', JTC, vol. 3.
19. Busby to Mitford, 15 May 1810, in Mukherjee, *A Critical Study*, pp. 115-17.
20. Mukherjee, *A Critical Study*, pp. 122-3.
21. It has been argued that 'elaboration' or ritualization of symbolic norms and behaviour was done in an effort to resolve the 'discrepancies between reality and abstractions of status systems'. See Murray Milner Jr., 'A Theory of Status Relationships: Key Elements', in Milner, *Status and Sacredness*. I prefer a less instrumental approach, and view the ritual expression of status itself as a kind of power.
22. '*Poora Shood*'—an exclusive *darsana* when the temple was cleared of all pilgrims and personnel. See Mukherjee, *A Critical Study*, p. 122.

23. *Chhamu Chitau*, Sambalpur, 23 July 1719.
24. 'The Humble Memorial of Moharaja Beerkishore Deb, Raja of Khurda and Superintendent of the Temple, Juggernath, Puri, in Cuttack', JTC, vol. 3.
25. Minute of Lord Auckland to the Court of Directors, in Mukherjee, *A Critical Study*, pp. 190-3.
26. Commissioner to Secretary, Government of Bengal, 1851, no. 1164 1/2, Miscellaneous Correspondence Regarding the Temple, JTC, vol. 3, pp. 583-4.
27. J. Peggs, 'India's Cries to British Humanity', quoted in Mukherjee, *A Critical Study*, p. 147.
28. 'The British Government enrich themselves by the tax they levy, before they permit the Hindoos to behold their idol. This is sinking the British name to the lowest pitch of degradation.' 'Friend of India', October 1825, in Mukherjee, *A Critical Study* p. 154.
29. Lord Auckland to Sir John Hobhouse, President of the Board of Control, 23 August 1838. Mukherjee, *A Critical Study*, p. 155.
30. Temple transactions recorded by the *Deula Karana* (temple scribe) in the first decade of the twentieth century describe the manner in which the various *sebas* were distributed. For instance:

    'One fourth of *Dwari seba* was purchased by Acyuta Mohanty from Sambhu Mohanty.'

    'On Mesa 28, Rambha *Mahari* will do two extra *sebas*: *Teradhara seba* and *Isani seba*. She will receive two *sadis*. Her daughter Mukuta *Mahari* will also get two *sadis*.'

    'A Paika named Banamali Muduli will perform half of *Nishi seba*. From this half, another half will be sold to Gangadhar Muduli.'

    'Property that was given to Yudhisthir by the temple in return for his *seba* is to be transferred to Srikara Patnaik as the former was without issue. Rs. 15 for the *Kotha Bhoga* was given by Srikara Patnaik in return for the honour.'

    'Two devotees will be allowed to build a house near Athara Nala bridge. They will also use the *Bhoga* land near Gudia Pakhari but cannot sell it. They are to be allowed to perform *chaamara seba* in the Jagamohana (of the Temple)'. 'Daily Accounts'.
31. W.C. Taylor, 'Selection from the Correspondence on the Settlement of the Government Estate of Khoordah in the District of Pooree', Calcutta: Bengal Secretarial Press, 1881, pp. 225-56.
32. 'Narain Das *v.* Bindrabun Das', Case no. 1815, *Sadr Diwani Adalat Records*, Bengal, pp. 505-8.
33. Cohn, 'From Indian Status to British Contract', in Cohn, *An Anthropologist*, p. 472.
34. Cohn, 'Some Notes on Law and Change in North India', ibid., pp. 569-71.

35. Derrett, 'The Administration of Hindu Law by the British', in Derrett, *Religion, Law and the State in India*, p. 279.
36. Ibid., p. 280.
37. Cohn, 'From Indian Status to British Contract', in Cohn, *An Anthropologist*, pp. 474-5.
38. *Sadr Diwani Adalat Records*, Sudder Dewanny Adawlut Reports, Bengal, vol. 3, II, 1856.
39. '*Wughaira*'—a Persian term literally meaning, 'etc.', which can be used ambiguously to denote a variety of meanings.
40. From W.M. Trower, Collector, Cuttack, to J.P. Ward, Acting Secretary to the Board of Revenue, Fort William, 26 October 1816, JTC, vol. 1, pp. 242-7.
41. 'Petition of Modoosoodan Maintee, Mohurir of the Sudder Canoongo of Kodhaur in Zillah Cuttack', JTC, p. 256.

Conclusion

This study of the temple–state relationship in Orissa began with a modern retelling of a popular uprising in the Khurda–Puri area, the play, *Bakshi Jagabandhu.* I will now return to that account in order to illustrate the politico-ritual linkages that bonded together and energized the temple–state complex, making it a reference point for the affirmation of regional and local identities, even in modern times.

MUKUNDA. I am aware that the Paiks believe me powerless. In the last battle [with the British] they did not wish to stand by me. But what can I do, tell me? In this prison in Balisahi . . . in this firangi-encircled jail . . . am I here of my own will? Eating foreign-contaminated rice, does it give me pleasure? I, who am descended from a line of invincible conquerors, Kapilendra, Purusottama, Prataparudra, I who have inherited their lineage. . . .[1]

The force of the tradition that brought forth a line of heroes is a nostalgic allusion for the beleaguered Gajapati here. Memories of past glories are infused with a sense of connectedness between the kings and their *Paiks*, bonds that depict the 'proper' functioning of the political, territorial and ritual order in the region. These linkages converged on the temple and the deity, as illustrated by the final cry of Jayikrushna Rajaguru, as he was being led away for execution by the British forces—'Jaya Jagannatha! Jaya Jagannatha! May Khurda be victorious!'[2] Jagannatha and his temple were a symbol of cultural continuities that validated past networks of privilege and dominance, and bonds of loyalty in a contemporary context. A meeting place of political, cultural and historical trends, it provided a point of recall for popular memory, and therein lay its power. [Incarcerated by the British forces in a prison in Balisahi, Puri, Gajapati Mukundadeva addresses Bakshi Jagabandhu, who stands before him.]

This study is about continuities as well as dichotomies in the ongoing 'tradition' of temple–state relations in Orissa. In the seventeenth and eighteenth centuries there were a number of shifts and changes in the balance of power in the region. The ritual kingship of the Gajapati state was reconfigured owing to the rise to power of a number of feudatory chiefdoms. The Khurda raja was required to reaffirm his legitimacy as the successor of a popular and illustrious lineage, a process that found expression, to a large extent, in the temple realm.

The temple sphere had previously been a space for the contestation as well as legitimation of royal authority, during the reign of the Gangas and Suryavamsi Gajapatis. As a microcosmic representation of the ordered state, it was a nuclear zone for the networks of material and ideological reciprocity that linked the people with the land and resources. In this respect, it was also an arena for the enactment of relationships of dominance and subordination, obligation and privilege that determined the hierarchies of status. It was through such relationships, involving contestation over issues of power and authority that the ordered state was constantly renegotiated as well as reaffirmed.

The penetration of these relationships by colonial structures of power in the early nineteenth century led to the negation of certain institutions while others were retained. The tenurial changes introduced by the Company administration with a view to revenue maximization led to large-scale reorganization of the landed hierarchies, and in many cases, to a demolition of the linkages of status that connected people with resources. The raja's status vis-à-vis the region and the populace was completely reconfigured owing to his appointment as temple superintendent by the Company government.

Such a remodelling of the political and cultural context for local institutions through colonial processes of authority, such as legislation and codification, led to the formation of a unique discourse of power, and was a major departure from the past. The raja was not simply defeated and executed—he was 'reincarnated', so to speak, as a representative of the very regime that removed him. The indirect penetration of the temple realm, particularly its landed networks, by colonial apparatuses of control led to its circumscription and a breakdown of the channels of reciprocity that had supported it materially and ideologically.

The colonial discourse of power evolved through the fixing

of separate zones of subordination and dominance by the new government, the schism between the 'local'/indigenous and the 'official' realm of bureaucratic control. This separation facilitated the appropriation of the 'indigenous' by the 'official', whether it was material resources, ritual processes or forms of knowledge. The separation and appropriation was maintained and intensified through bureaucratic surveillance and control, overlaid by the rhetoric of 'systematization' and 'classification'.

This study owes much to the work of Hermann Kulke, whose examination of the ritual kingship in Orissa was a pioneering effort at developing a model for understanding the unique political structures in that region. Kulke's model for vertical and horizontal integration centred on a politico-ritual core, was, for me, a window to further horizons. Developing on some of his themes, I have constructed a nuanced analysis of the evolving discourse of power and dominance in the region, as expressed through temple ritual and services, honours, material and ideological reciprocity and status relations. I have gone further to examine the manner in which this order was subverted through colonial penetration, and how these subversions took the form of a separate discourse of power. My study is less about structures and deals more with shifts, changes and the ways in which structures altered, interacted and were subverted.

The work of Nicholas Dirks has also been a significant influence for this study, more in terms of the sheer depth and scale of his analysis than thematic content. His sensitivity to the complex enmeshing of ritual/symbolic forms with mechanisms of the state opened my own explorations to a more 'totalized' perspective of power and its representations. However, Dirks' study of the Tondaiman rajas of Pudukottai depicted the disempowerment of a 'little kingdom' by colonial penetration. The situation that I have encountered with respect to the Gajapati kingship in Orissa was a unique one, in that the state was ritually interlinked with the cult of Jagannatha and the temple to such an extent that it was the focus of the political, economic and cultural scenario in the region. Colonial penetration, in many ways, intensified and concentrated these linkages, so much so that despite having no territorial sovereignty, the Gajapati Maharaja of Puri is, at many levels, the highest political authority in Orissa even today.

To conclude, I return once again to a metaphor from the performing arts in order to express the point of my study on temple–state relations. The notion of *rasa* is a unique motif in Indian classical dramaturgy. It is an indefinable emotion that arises from the interaction of a performer and his audience and encapsulates their collective involvement in a performance. It is this elusive and ephemeral quality, captured in the unique stance and manner of a *sebayet* while he performs his service in the temple, that I feel represents the interweaving of structures of power and their symbolic expression. To borrow a point from Geertz, ritual is not merely the illustration of some other type of power: it is power itself. This is what I have attempted to communicate in my study.

NOTES

1. Manoranjan Das, *Bakshi Jagabandhu*, Cuttack: Binodbehari, 1989, p. 97.
2. Ibid., p. 38.

Bibliography

GOVERNMENT RECORDS

Foreign Secret Proceedings, 1764, National Archives, Delhi.

Foreign and Political Department Records, 1781-3; 1756-80, National Archives, Delhi.

Government of Bengal (Judicial Department), Case no. P. 3-P/11–31-34, 22 August 1902.

Government of Bengal, Home Department, 'History of the Rise and Progress of the Operations for the Suppression of Human Sacrifice and Female Infanticide in the Hill Tracts of Orissa', Calcutta, 1854.

Government of Orissa (Law Department), 'The Orissa Tenancy Act 1913' (Bihar and Orissa Act of 1913).

Jagannatha Temple Correspondence (JTC), vols. 1, 2, 3, 1804-32, Orissa Research Project (ORP), Ms. 130, Orissa State Archives, Bhubaneswar and The Orissa Archive, South Asia Institute, Heidelberg.

Judicial Consultations, 4 February 1818; 9 March 1818; 20 October 1818, Orissa State Archives, Bhubaneswar.

Land Revenue Records, Home Department, Revenue Branch, 1838-59, National Archives, Delhi.

Miscellaneous Old Correspondence Regarding Jagannatha Temple (Puri Collectorate), ORP Mss. 133, 134, 138, The Orissa Archive, South Asia Institute, Heidelberg.

N.B. Edmonstone, Secretary to Government to J. Melville, Commissioner for the Affairs of Cuttack and Lt. Col. Campbell, C.O. Northern Division of the Army under the Presidency of Fort St. George, 3 September 1803, Bengal Secret and Political Correspondence, India Office Records, no. 180.

Orissa Endowment Act (OEA), Case no. 235/92, 19 September 1994.

Private Collections of Sri Nilakanta Sahoo, Jeypore, Koraput and Sri S. Mohanty, Stewart Patna, Cuttack, Orissa State Archives, Bhubaneswar.

Puri District Gazetteer, 1977.

Record of Rights of Sri Jagannath Temple, comp. Sri L. Panda, 4 vols., Cuttack: Govt Press, 1953.

Report of the Special Officer under the Puri Sri Jagannatha Temple Administration Act, 1952, Law Department Notification, 6 September 1954.

Report of George Webb, Collector, Puri, submitted to G.H. Barlow, President and Member, Board of Revenue, Fort William, 1808, ORP, Ms. 131.

Revenue Consultations, 20 July 1818; 25 January 1836; 11 March 1839; 25 November 1839, National Archives, Delhi.

Sadr Diwani Adalat Reports, Bengal, 1815, 1853.

Second appeal from the decision of Baboo Tarakant Bidyasagar, Principal Sudder Ameen of Cuttack, dated 17 January 1855, Case no. 613 of 1856, *The Indian Decision Series*, vol. XVI, *Sudder Dewanny Adawlut Reports*, Bengal, vol. 13, part II, pp. 953-65.

Select Committee Proceedings, 1762, serial no. 9, National Archives, Delhi.

NON-GOVERNMENT RECORDS

Bernier, Francois, *Travels in the Mughal Empire AD 1656-1668*, translated on the basis of Irving Brock's version and annotated by Archibald Constable, 2nd edn. revd. by V.A Smith, 1st Indian edition by Munshiram Manoharlal, New Delhi, 1983.

Beveridge, H. (trans.), *The Akbar Nama of Abul Fazl*, Calcutta: Asiatic Society.

Blochmann, H. (trans), *Ain-i-Akbari of Abul Fazl Allami*, vol. 1, Calcutta, 1873.

Chhamu Chitau (a collection of royal letters issued by the Khurda raja, *c.* mid-17th century onwards). Collected and transcribed from the palm-leaf manuscripts by the Orissa Research Project, South Asia Institute, Heidelberg.

'Daily Accounts' a collection of temple accounts maintained by the Deula Karana. Collected and transcribed from the palm-leaf manuscripts under the Orissa Research Project (uncatalogued), South Asia Institute, University of Heidelberg.

Hamilton, Walter, 'Extract from the Geographical, Statistical and Historical Description of Hindostan and the Adjacent Countries', vol. 1, Cuttack: Utkal Sahitya Press, 1820.

Hunter, W.W., 'Orissa or the Vicissitudes of and Indian Province under Native and British Rule', Calcutta, 1872.

Jagannatha Sthalavrttantam, trans. Dr. Satyanarayana Rajaguru, ORP Ms. 441, South Asia Institute, Heidelberg.

Laurie, William F.B., *Orissa, the Garden of Superstition and Idolatry*, London: Johnstone and Hunter, 1850.

Niti (rituals pertaining to the Jagannatha temple, formerly belonging to the Deula Karana of Puri), trans. Sri S.C. De, ORP Ms. 429, South Asia Institute, Heidelberg.

Peggs, J., *Pilgrim Tax in India, Facts and Observations relating to the Practice of taxing Pilgrims in some parts of India and paying a Premium to those who collect them for the worship of Juggernaut at the Great Temple in Orissa*, London, 1830.

Pratishtha Pradipokta (Ratha Pratishtha Vidhi), ORP Ms. 679, South Asia Institute, Heidelberg.

Rajyabhishekavidhi, ORP Ms. 917, South Asia Institute, Heidelberg.

Sasana Karanam (the procedure for establishing a *sasana*), translated from Sanskrit by Sri Upendranatha Dhal, ORP Ms. 689, South Asia Institute, Heidelberg.

Sri Jagabandhu Samantaroy Carccika Mahatmya, Cuttack, 1968, ORP Ms. 61, South Asia Institute, Heidelberg.

Stirling, Andrew, *Orissa: Its Geography, Statistics, History, Religion and Antiquities*, London: John Snow, 1846.

Sanads from Rani Suryamani Pattamahadei of Khurda to the *Mahant*, Papudia Matha, Puri for the performance of *Alata (camara) seba*, 1885, 1890 (manuscript).

ROYAL GENEALOGIES

'Account of *Male Savara*', transcribed from Local Records, vol. 6, pp. 154-71, GOMLM (R.C. no. 143/L/71).

'An Account of Gangavamsa of Odradesa', transcribed from Local Records, vol. 47, pp. 9-14, GOMLM, ORP Ms. 419 (copy in South Asia Institute, Heidelberg).

'Account of Gajapati Kings of Kimidi', copied from Mackenzie Collection, vol. 405, fol. 60A, Oriental and India Office Collections, British Library, London.

'Account of Ganjam', Local Records, vol. 9, pp. 372-458, and 'History of the Rulers of Kimidi', copied from Local Records, vol. 47, p. 150, GOMLM, ORP Ms. 416 (copy in South Asia Institute, Heidelberg).

Barabati Virakrsnadeva, translated from Local Records, vol. 6, pp. 1-41, GOMLM.

Caitanya Matam (The Cult of Caitanya introduced in Odra), copied from Mackenzie Collection, vol. 16, fol. 9A, ORP Ms. 446 (copy in South Asia Institute, Heidelberg).

Cayini Cakoda, *Cakoda Pothi o Cakoda Bhasana*, ed. S. Pattanaik, Cuttack, 1959.

'Genealogy of the Royal Family of Ranapur', ORP Ms. 866.

'Katakarajavamsavali', ed. Hermann Kulke and G.C. Tripathi, *Journal of Ganganatha Jha Kendriya Sanskrit Vidyapeeth*, no. 40, 1984, pp. 1-20.

'*Kaifiyat* of Gajapati Kings', copied from Local Records, vol. 6, pp. 42-105, GOMLM, ORP Ms. 469.

Khallikota Zamindar, Local Records, vol. 59, GOMLM, ORP Ms. 423.

'*Kaifiyat* of *Barabati Kings*', Local Records, vol. 6, GOMLM.

K. Misra, *Kendujhar*, trans. P.C. Misra, ORP Ms. 552.

Krsnadasa, *Puri Deula Tola* (construction of the Puri Temple), trans. M. Sarma, Biswas Prabhati Pustakalaya, Cuttack, ORP Ms. 663.

Languleswara Itihasa (Account of the *taluka* of Sanakhemundi), Local Records, vol. 37, GOMLM, ORP Ms. 459.

Mukhalinga Ksetra Mahatmyam, ORP Ms. 461.

Odradesarajavamsavali (genealogy of the kings of Odradesa), Local Records, vol. 60, pp. 303-57.

'Pandita Sri Jogendera Kavyabisarade *Manjusa Ranjabansanaucarita*', Puri: Jagannatha Press, 1915 (translated from Sanskrit by Smt Sureswari Misra).

Rajabhoga Itihasa (royal genealogy) of *Madala Panji*, ORP Ms. 49, South Asia Institute, Heidelberg.

Sabara Bansabali, manuscript belonging to Sri S.N. Rajaguru, trans. Sri. P.C. Misra, ORP Ms. 471.

Silpi Patha, ORP Ms. 151.

Sri S.B. Moharana, *Hindola Itihas*, trans. Sri. P.C. Misra, ORP Ms. 293.

'Tekkali Zamindar', Local Records, vol. 59, pp. 144-62, GOMLM.

OFFICIAL REPORTS

Babu Balmakund Kanungo, Settlement Officer, 'Final Report on the Survey and Settlement of the Dompara Wards Estate in the District of Cuttack 1905–1907', Board of Revenue, Cuttack.

Bose, Debendranath, 'Final Report of Survey and Settlement operations in Killa Aul, District Cuttack 1892–1901', Bengal Secretarial Press, Calcutta, 1904.

'The Completion Report on the Settlement of the Hindol Feudatory State, 1910–1914', Board of Revenue, Prakash Printers, Cuttack.

Ewer, Walter, 'Correspondence on the Settlement of Khoordah in Pooree, 13 May 1818', *Orissa Historical Research Journal* (*OHRJ*), vols. 3 and 5, pp. 1-34, 59-129.

'Final report on the settlement of the Dhenkanal feudatory state, 1923-24', Board of Revenue, Cuttack.

'Final report on the survey and settlement of the jagir mahals in the district of Puri, 1906-09', Board of Revenue, Cuttack.

'Final Report on the Settlement of the Pallahara State, 1932', Board of Revenue, Cuttack.

Ghosh, Chandranatha, 'Kujang Settlement Report, 1893', Board of Revenue, Cuttack.

Maddox, S.L. 'Final Report on the Survey and Settlement of the Province of Orissa 1890-1900', vols. 1-2, Board of Revenue, Cuttack.

The Superintendent, Tributary Mahals, 1814, 'Twenty-five questions addressed to the Rajahs of the Regulation and Tributary Mahals', Calcutta, 1861.

Taylor, W.C., 'Selections from the Correspondence on the Settlement of the Government Estate of Khoordah in the District of Pooree', vols. I and 2, Bengal Secretarial Press, Calcutta, 1881.

BOOKS

Aitchison, C.U., *A Collection of Treaties, Engagements and Sanads Relating to India and Neighbouring Countries,* vol. 1, Calcutta: Superintendent, Government Printing, 1909.

Amin, Shahid, *Event, Metaphor and Memory: Chauri Chaura 1922-1992*, New Delhi: Oxford University Press, 1995.

Appadurai, Arjun, *Worship and Conflict under Colonial Rule*, Cambridge: Cambridge University Press, 1981.

Ahmed, Aijaz, *Lineages of the Present*, New Delhi: Tulika Publishers, 1996.

Bailey, F.G., *Tribe, Caste and Nation: A Study of Political Activity and Political Change in Highland Orissa*, Manchester: Manchester University Press, 1960.

Bakhtin, Mikhail, *Rabelais and His World*, trans. Helen Iwolsky, Bloomington: Indiana University Press, 1984.

Barker, Francis, Peter Hulme and Margaret Iversen (eds), *Colonial Discourse/Postcolonial Theory,* Manchester and New York: Manchester University Press, 1994.

Bayly, C.A., *Indian Society and the Making of the British Empire, The New Cambridge History of India II: I*, Cambridge: Cambridge University Press, 1987.

Blackburn, Stuart H. and A.K. Ramanujan (eds), *Another Harmony: New Essays on the Folklore of India*, New Delhi: Oxford University Press, 1986.

Boon, James A., *Other Tribes Other Scribes*, Cambridge and New York: Cambridge University Press, 1982.

Bourdieu, Pierre, *The Logic of Practice,* Cambridge: Polity Press,1990.

Braudel, Fernand, *The Mediterranean and the Mediterranean World in the Age of Philip II,* vols. 1 and 2, London: William Collins Sons and Co. Ltd., 1972.

Breman, Jan, *Patronage and Exploitation*, New Delhi: Manohar, 1979.

Bruns, Gerard, *Hermeneutics Ancient and Modern*, London: Yale University Press, 1992.

Burke, Peter, *Popular Culture in Early Modern Europe*, London: Temple-Smith, 1978.

Cannadine, David and S. Price, *Rituals of Royalty: Power and Ceremonial in Traditional Societies,* Cambridge: Cambridge University Press, 1987.

Carnac-Temple, Sir Richard (ed.), *Thomas Bowrey: A Geographical Account of the Countries around the Bay of Bengal, 1669-1679*, Cambridge, 1905.

Cassels, Nancy G., *Religion and Pilgrim Tax under the British Raj*, New Delhi: Manohar, 1987.

Clifford, James and George Marcus (eds), *Writing Culture*, Berkeley and Los Angeles: University of California Press, 1986.

Cohn, Bernard S., *An Anthropologist among the Historians and Other Essays*, New Delhi: Oxford University Press, 1987.

———, *Colonialism and Its Forms of Knowledge: The British in India*, New Delhi: Oxford University Press, 1997.

Cousins, Mark and Athar Hussain, *Michel Foucault*, Hampshire and London: Macmillan, 1984.

Das, Manoranjan, *Bakshi Jagabandhu*, Cuttack: Binodbehari (7th edn), 1989.

De, S.C., *A Guide to Orissan Records*, vols. 3 and 4, Bhubaneswar: Orissa Sahitya Akademi, 1961.

———, *A Descriptive Catalogue of the Copper Plate Inscriptions of Orissa*, Bhubaneswar: Superintendent, Research and Museum, 1961.

Dentith, Simon, *Bakhtinian Thought: An Introductory Reader*, London: Routledge, 1995.

Derrett, J.D.M., *Introduction to Modern Hindu Law*, New Delhi: Oxford University Press, 1963.

———, *Religion, Law and the State in India*, London: Faber and Faber, 1968.

———, *Essays in Classical and Modern Hindu Law*, vol. 2, Leiden: E.J. Brill, 1977.

Dirks, Nicholas B., *The Hollow Crown*, Cambridge: Cambridge University Press, 1987.

Dreyfus, Hubert L. and Paul Rabinow (eds), *Michel Foucault: Beyond*

Structuration and Hermeneutics, Sussex: The Harvester Press, 1982.

Dumont, L., *Homo Hierarchicus*, London: George Wiedenfield and Nicholson Ltd., 1970.

Eschmann, Anncharlott, Hermann Kulke and G.C. Tripathi, *The Cult of Jagannatha and the Regional Tradition of Orissa*, New Delhi: Manohar, 1986.

Foucault, Michel, *Power/Knowledge: Selected Interviews and Other Writings*, ed. Colin Gordon, Sussex: The Harvester Press, 1980.

———, *The Order of Things*, London: Tavistock Publications, 1970.

Frykenberg, R.E. (ed.), *Land Control and Social Structure in Indian History*, Madison: University of Wisconsin Press, 1969.

Fuller, C.J., *Servants of the Goddess*, Cambridge: Cambridge University Press, 1984.

Geertz, Clifford, *The Interpretation of Cultures*, New York: Basic Books Inc., 1973.

Gopal, S., *British Policy in India*, Madras: Orient Longman, 1975.

Grewal, J.S. (ed.), *Studies in Local and Regional History*, Amritsar: Guru Nanak Dev University, 1974.

Guha, Ranajit, *A Rule of Property for Bengal*, Paris: Mouton and Co. La Haye, 1963.

———, *Elementary Aspects of Peasant Insurgency in Colonial India*, New Delhi: Oxford University Press, 1983.

Heesterman, J.C., *The Broken World of Sacrifice*, Chicago: University of Chicago Press, 1993.

Hill, Christopher, *Puritanism and Revolution*, Middlesex: Penguin Books, 1958.

Hirschkop, Ken and David Shepherd, *Bakhtin and Cultural Theory*, Manchester: Manchester University Press, 1989.

Hunter, W.W., A. Stirling and John Beames, *A History of Orissa*, vols. 1 and 2, ed. N.K. Sahu, Calcutta, 1956.

Hutchins, F.G., *The Illusion of Permanence: British Imperialism in India*, Princeton: Princeton University Press, 1967.

Islam, Riazul (ed.), *Bahar ul Asrar of Mahmud bin Amir Wali Balkhi*, Karachi: Institute of Central and West Asian Studies, University of Karachi, 1980.

Kulke, Hermann, *Kings and Cults: State Formation and Legitimation in India and Southeast Asia*, New Delhi: Manohar, 1993.

Kulke, Hermann and B. Schnepel (eds), *Jagannath Revisited: Society, Religion and the State in Orissa*, New Delhi: Manohar, 2001.

Loomba, Ania, *Gender, Race, Renaissance Drama*, Manchester: Manchester University Press, 1989.

———, *Colonialism/Postcolonialism*, London: Routledge, 1998.

Milner, Jr, Murray, *Status and Sacredness: A General Theory of Status Relations and an Analysis of Indian Culture*, New York: Oxford University Press, 1994.

Mishra, K.C., *The Cult of Jagannatha*, Calcutta: Firma KLM, 1971.

Mahapatra, S.C., *Car Festival of Lord Jagannatha Puri*, Puri: Sri Jagannatha Research Centre, 1994.

Mahapatra, Sitakant, *The Realm of the Sacred*, Calcutta: Oxford University Press, 1992.

Mohanty, A.B., *Madala Panji* (Prachi edn), Bhubaneswar: Utkal University, 1969.

Mohapatra, Gopinath, *Jagannatha in History and Religious Traditions of Orissa*, Calcutta: Punthi Pustak, 1982.

Mohapatra, R.P., *Temple Legends of Orissa*, Bhubaneswar: Orissa Sahitya Akademi, 1989.

Mukherjee, Prabhat, *History of the Jagannath Temple during the 19th Century*, Calcutta: Firma KLM, 1977.

———, *History of Orissa in the 19th Century*, Cuttack, 1964.

———, *The History of the Gajapati Kings of Orissa and their Successors* Calcutta: General Trading Co., 1953.

——— (ed.), *A Critical Study of all the Important Temple Records During British Rule* (a collection of papers), Bhubaneswar: Orissa State Archives, 1984.

O'Malley, L.S.S., *Bihar and Orissa District Gazetteers: Puri*, Patna: Government Printing, Bihar and Orissa, 1929.

Panda, S.K., *Medieval Orissa*, New Delhi: Mittal Publications, 1991.

Pannikar, K.N., *Culture, Ideology, Hegemony: Intellectuals and Social Consciousness in Colonial India*, New Delhi: Tulika Publishers, 1995.

Pati, Biswamoy, *Resisting Domination: Peasants, Tribals and the National Movement in Orissa*, New Delhi: Manohar, 1993.

Patra, K.M., *Orissa Under the East India Company*, New Delhi: Munshiram Manoharlal, 1971.

Patnaik, Nityananda, *Cultural Tradition in Puri: Structure and Organisation of a Pilgrim Centre*, Simla: Indian Institute of Advanced Study, 1977.

Pattanayak, A.K., *Religious Policy of the Imperial Gangas*, Delhi: Discovery Publishing House, 1988.

Pratt, Mary Louise, *Imperial Eyes: Travel Writing and Transculturation*, London and New York: Routledge and Kegan Paul, 1992.

Presler, Franklin A., *Religion Under Bureaucracy: Policy and Administration for Hindu Temples in South India*, Cambridge: Cambridge University Press, 1987.

Raheja, Gloria G., *The Poison in the Gift: Ritual, Prestation and the*

Dominant Caste in a North Indian Village, Chicago and London: University of Chicago Press, 1988.

Rajaguru, Satyanarayana, *Inscriptions of the Temple of Puri and the Origin of Sri Purusottama Jagannatha*, vol. 1, Puri: Sri Jagannatha Sanskrit Visvavidyalaya, 1992.

Sahlins, Marshall, *Islands of History*, London: Tavistock Publications Ltd., 1987.

Schomer, Karine, Joan L. Erdman, Deryck O. Lodrick and Lloyd Rudolph (eds), *The Idea of Rajasthan: Explorations in Regional Identity*, vol. 1, New Delhi: Manohar, 1994.

Sen, Surendranath (ed.), *Indian Travels of Thevenot and Carreri*, part II, New Delhi National Archives of India, 1949.

Shils, Edward, *Tradition*, Chicago: University of Chicago Press, 1981.

Stein, Burton, *Essays on South India*, New Delhi: Oxford University Press, 1977.

———, *All the Kings Mana: Papers on Medieval South Asian History*, Madras: New Era Publications, 1984.

Stokes, Eric J., *The Peasant and the Raj: Studies in Agrarian Society and Peasant Rebellion in Colonial India*, Cambridge: Cambridge University Press, 1978.

———, *The English Utilitarians and India*, New Delhi: Oxford University Press, 1959.

Teltscher, Kate, *India Inscribed*, New Delhi: Oxford University Press, 1995.

Thapar, Romila, *Cultural Transactions and Early India*, New Delhi: Oxford University Press, 1994.

———, *Clan, Caste and Origin Myths in Early India*, New Delhi: Manohar, 1992.

Thapar, Romila and Sabyasachi Bhattacharya (eds), *Situating Indian History*, New Delhi: Oxford University Press, 1986.

Tilley, Christopher (ed.), *Reading Material Culture*, Oxford and Cambridge, Mas.: Basil Blackwell Ltd., 1990.

Vansina, Jan, *Oral Tradition as History*, London: James Currey, 1985.

ARTICLES

Ahmed, Aijaz, 'Between Orientalism and Historicism: Anthropological Knowledge of India', *Studies in History*, 7, 1, pp. 135-63.

Anderson, Perry, 'The Antinomies of Antonio Gramsci', *New Left Review*, 100, 1976-7, pp. 5-80.

Appadurai, Arjun, 'Kings, Sects and Temples in South India', *The Indian Economic and Social History Review*, 14, 1.

Appadurai, Arjun and Carol Breckenridge, 'The South Indian Temple:

Authority, Honour and Redistribution', *Contributions to Indian Sociology*, vol. 10, no. 2, 1976, pp. 187-211.

Asad, Talal, 'The Concept of Cultural Translation in British Social Anthropology', in *Writing Culture*, ed. Clifford and Marcus, Berkeley and Los Angeles: University of California Press, 1986, pp. 141-64.

'Asanakhali Plates of Narasimhadeva, AD 1302', *Epigraphia Indica*, 21, pp. 109-28.

Beames, John, 'Notes on the History of Orissa under the Mahomedan, Maratha and British Rule', *Journal of the Asiatic Society of Bengal*, 52, 1883.

Bhattacharya, Neeladri, 'Colonial State and Agrarian Society', in *Situating Indian History*, ed. S. Bhattacharya and R. Thapar, New Delhi: Oxford University Press, 1986, pp. 106-45.

Bose, Nirmal Kumar (ed.), 'Data on Caste: Orissa', *Anthropological Survey of India*, Calcutta, Memoir no. 7, 1960.

Breckenridge, Carol, 'From Protector to Litigant: Changing Relations between Hindu Temples and the Raja of Ramnad', *Indian Economic and Social History Review*, 14, 1, pp. 75-106.

Cohn, Bernard S., 'History and Anthropology: The State of Play', *An Anthropologist amongst the Historians and Other Essays*, New Delhi: Oxford University Press, 1987.

———, 'From Indian Status to British Contract', *Journal of Economic History*, 21, 1961, pp. 613-28.

———, 'Anthropological Notes on Law and Disputes in India', *American Anthropologist*, 67, 6, 1965.

Crapanzano, Vincent, 'Hermes' Dilemma: The Masking of Subversion in Ethnographic Description', in *Writing Culture*, ed. Clifford and Marcus, Berkeley and Los Angeles: University of California Press, 1986, pp. 51-76.

Dash, G.N., 'The Evolution of Priestly Power', in Eschmann et al., *The Cult of Jagannath and the Regional Tradition of Orissa*, New Delhi: Manohar, 1986.

Dirks, Nicholas B., 'Political Authority and Structural Change in Early South Indian History', *Indian Economic and Social History Review*, vol. 13, no. 2, 1976, pp. 125-58.

———, 'From Little King to Landlord: Property, Law and the Gift under the Madras Permanent Settlement', *Comparative Studies in Society and History*, 28, 1986.

'Draksharama Inscription', *South Indian Inscriptions*, vol. IV, no. 1329.

Dutta, Kalikinkar, 'Social Economic and Political Effects of the Maratha Invasions between 1740 and 1765 on Bengal, Bihar and Orissa', *Proceedings of the Indian Oriental Conference*, 6th Session, Patna, 1930, pp. 189-97.

Jackson-Lears, T.J., 'The Concept of Cultural Hegemony: Problems and Possibilities', *American Historical Review*, 9, III, 1985, pp. 567-93.

Jha, D.N., 'Temples as Landed Magnates in Early Medieval South India (*c.* AD 700-1300)', in *Indian Society: Historical Probings in the Memory of D.D. Kosambi*, ed. R.S. Sharma, New Delhi: Peoples Publishing House, 1974.

Kerr, Ian J., 'The British and the Administration of the Golden Temple in 1859', *Panjab Past and Present,* 10, 2, pp. 306-21.

———, 'British Relationships with the Golden Temple', *Indian Economic and Social History Review*, 21, 1, 1984, pp. 139-52.

Kulke, Hermann, 'Kings without a Kingdom: The Rajas of Khurda and the Jagannatha Cult', *South Asia*, 4, 1974, pp. 60-77.

———, 'Kshatriyaization and Social Change: A Study in Orissa Setting' in *Aspects of Changing India: Studies in Honour of Prof. G.S. Ghurye*, ed. S.D. Pillai, Bombay, 1976, pp. 398-409.

———, 'Early Royal Patronage of the Jagannatha Cult', in Eschmann et al., *The Cult of Jagannatha and the Regional Tradition of Orissa*, New Delhi: Manohar, 1986.

———, 'Royal Temple Policy and the Structure of Medieval Hindu Kingdoms', in Eschmann et al., *The Cult of Jagannatha and the Regional Tradition of Orissa*, New Delhi: Manohar, 1986, pp. 125-37.

———, 'Rajas and Rathas: The Car Festival of Puri', in *Car Festival of Lord Jagannatha Puri*, ed. S.C. Mahapatra, Sri Jagannatha Research Centre, 1994.

———, 'The Chronicles and the Temple Records of the Madala Panji of Puri—A Reassessment of the Evidence', *The Indian Archives*, 36, 1, 1987, pp. 1-24.

Lerche, Jens, 'Dominant Castes, Rajas, Brahmins and Inter-Caste Exchange Relations in Coastal Orissa: Behind the Façade of the Jajmani System', *Contributions to Indian Sociology*, 27, 2, 1993.

Mani, Lata, 'The Female Subject, the Colonial Gaze: Reading Eyewitness Accounts of Widow Burning' in *Interrogating Modernity: Culture and Colonialism in India*, ed. Tejaswini Niranjana, P. Sudhir and Vivek Dhareshwar, Calcutta: Seagull Books, 1993, pp. 273-90.

Menon, Dilip M., 'The Moral Community of the *Teyyattam*: Popular Culture in Late Colonial Malabar', *Studies in History*, 9, 2, pp. 187-217.

Moore, Henrietta, 'Paul Ricoeur: Action, Meaning and Text', in *Reading Material Culture*, ed. Christopher Tilley, Oxford and Cambridge, Mas.: Basil Blackwell Ltd., 1990, pp. 85-118.

Mubayi, Yaaminey, 'The Paik Rebellion of 1817: Status and Conflict in Early Colonial Orissa', *Studies in History*, 15, 2, 1999, pp. 43-71.

Ortner, Sherry, 'Theory in Anthropology since the Sixties', *Comparative Studies in Society and History*, 1984.

Patra, K.M., 'Management of Jagannatha Temple during East India Company's Administration of Orissa', *Bengal Past and Present*, vol. 88, 1969, pp. 61-81.

Pati, Biswamoy, 'The "high"–"low" dialectic in Fakirmohana's Chhamana Athaguntha: Popular culture, literature and society in nineteenth-century Orissa', *Studies in History*, 12, 1, 1996, pp. 83-104.

———, 'The Murder of Banamali: Collective Action, Popular Culture and Social History', *Social Scientist*, 24, 4-6, 1996, pp. 82-108.

Patnaik, Nityananda, 'Administration of the Jagannatha Temple in 18th century', *Man in India*, 43, 3, 1963, pp. 214-17.

Pfeffer, G., 'Puri's Vedic Brahmins', in Eschmann et al., *The Cult of Jagannatha and the Regional Tradition of Orissa*, New Delhi: Manohar, 1986.

'Puri Sanad of Janoji Bhonsle', *Journal of the Andhra Historical Research Society*, 16, 1945.

Raheja, Gloria G., 'India: Caste, Kinship and Dominance Reconsidered', *Annual Review of Anthropology*, 17, 1988, pp. 497-522.

Ray, B.C., 'Mirza Saleh in Orissa', *Journal of the Andhra Historical Research Society*, 23, 1954-5, pp. 145-49.

———, 'Bhavani Pandit in Orissa', *Journal of the Andhra Historical Research Society*, 24, 1956-8, pp. 15-17.

———, 'Raja Mansingh's First Conquest of Orissa', *Proceedings of the Indian History Congress*, Varanasi, 1969, pp. 243-53.

———, 'Raja Mansingh and the Final Conquest of Orissa', *Proceedings of the Indian History Congress*, Nagpur, 1950.

Reddy, M. Atchi, 'Rich lands and poor lords: Temple lands and tenancy in Nellore district, 1860-1986', *The Indian Economic and Social History Review*, 24, 1, 1987, pp. 1-33.

Robinson, Ronald, 'Non-European Foundations of European Imperialism: A Sketch for the Theory of Collaboration', in *Studies in the Theory of Imperialism*, ed. R. Owen and B. Sutcliffe, London: Orient Longman Ltd, 1972.

Sarkar, Jadunath, 'The History of Orissa in the 17th Century Reconstructed from Persian Sources', *Journal of the Bihar and Orissa Research Society*, vol. II, 1916.

Sircar, D.C., 'Puri Inscription of Anangabhima III', *Epigraphia Indica*, 30, 5, 1954, pp. 197-203.

———, 'Kapilas Inscription of Narasimhadeva', *Epigraphia Indica*, 33, 1, 1959, pp. 41-5.

———, 'Bhubaneswar Inscription of Anangabhima III', *Epigraphia Indica*, 30, 1953, pp. 17-23.

———, 'Puri Inscriptions of Codaganga', *Epigraphia Indica*, 34, 4, 1959, pp. 181-5.

———, 'Bhubaneswar Inscriptions of Raghava', *Epigraphia Indica*, 30, 1953. pp. 158-61.

———, 'Bhubaneswar Inscriptions of Bhimadeva', *Epigraphia Indica*, 30, 1953, pp. 232-6.

———, 'Dasgoba Plates of Rajaraja III', *Epigraphia Indica*, 31, 1955-6. pp. 249-62.

Sircar, D.C. and K.G. Krishnan, 'Bhubaneswar Inscription of Ganga Narasimha', *Epigraphia Indica*, 32, 1957-8.

———, 'Two Lingaraja Temple Inscriptions', *Indian Culture*, 3, 1, 1939, pp. 71-6.

Skaria, Ajay, 'Being Jangli: The politics of wildness', *Studies in History*, 14, 2, 1998.

'Sri Sri Lakshminarayan Harichandan Jagadeb Vidyavachaspati Rajah Bahadur of Tekkali "Rock Inscription" near Atagada Fort', *Journal of the Bihar and Orissa Research Society*, 15, 1929, pp. 195-203.

Stein, Burton, 'The Economic Function of a Medieval South Indian Temple', *Journal of Asian Studies*, 19, 2, 1960, pp. 163-76.

Thapar, Romila, 'Society and Historical Consciousness: The Itihasa-Purana Tradition', in *Situating Indian History*, ed. Romila Thapar and S. Bhattacharya, New Delhi: Oxford University Press, 1986, pp. 353-86.

Tripathi, G.C., 'Navakalevara: The Unique Ceremony of the Birth and the Death of the Lord of the World', in Eschmann et al., *The Cult of Jagannatha and the Regional Tradition of Orissa*, New Delhi: Manohar, 1986.

Wills, Clair, 'Upsetting the Public: Carnival, Hysteria and Women's Texts', in *Bakhtin and Cultural Theory*, ed. Hirschkop and Shepherd, Manchester: Manchester University Press, 1989, pp. 130-51.

Index